IMAGES
of America

MERCER COUNTY

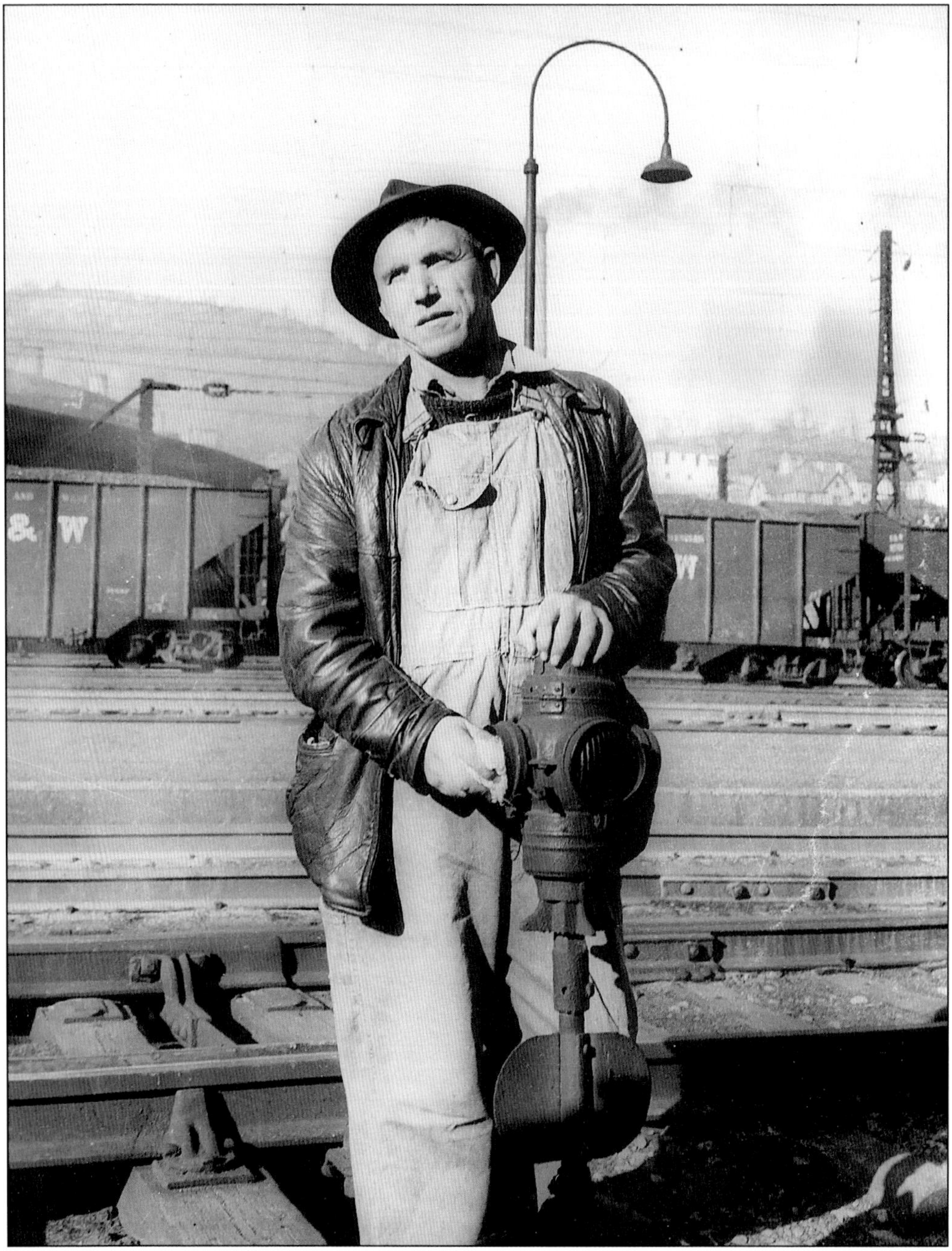

LAMPLIGHTER. Long before the days of advanced electrical service, Paul Malamisura had the singular job of walking through the (then) Norfolk & Western Bluefield yard each evening and lighting the railroad's complex system of signal lamps. Every morning, he would extinguish the lights and service each lamp. (Courtesy of Nick Buzzo.)

IMAGES
of America

MERCER COUNTY

William R. "Bill" Archer

ARCADIA
PUBLISHING

ISBN 978-0-7385-1351-5

Published by Arcadia Publishing
Charleston, South Carolina

Printed in the United States of America

Library of Congress Catalog Card Number: 2001088736

For all general information contact Arcadia Publishing at:
Telephone 843-853-2070
Fax 843-853-0044
E-mail sales@arcadiapublishing.com
For customer service and orders:
Toll-Free 1-888-313-2665

Visit us on the Internet at www.arcadiapublishing.com

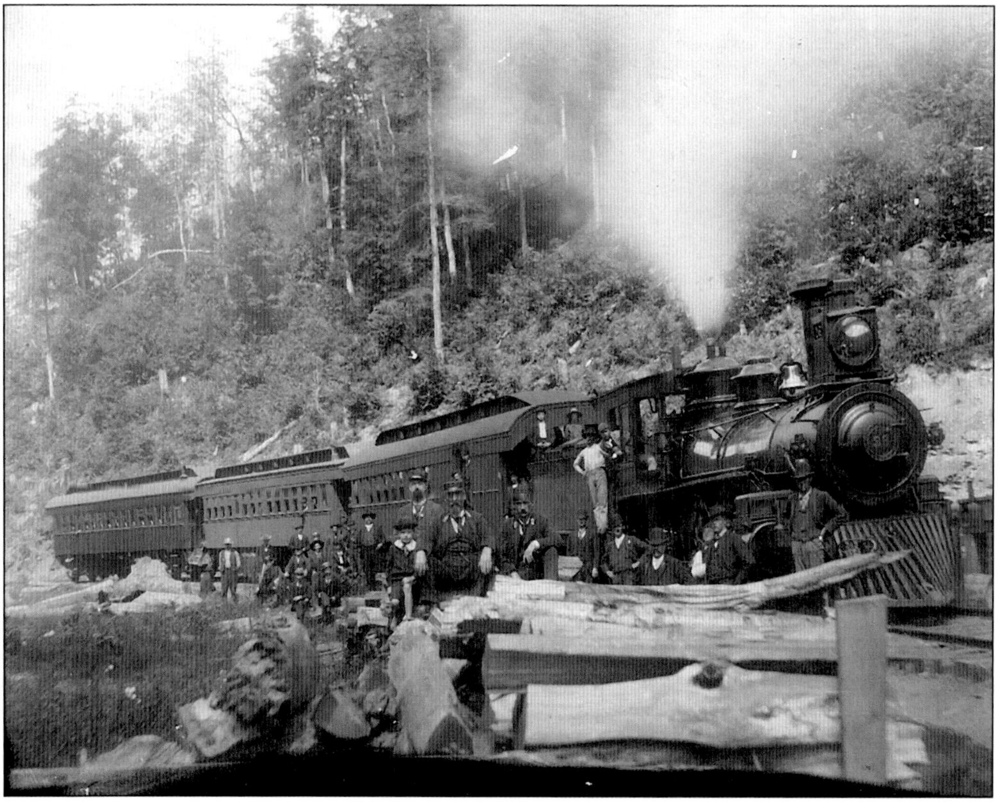

ON THE WESTWARD RUN. This unidentified Norfolk & Western train crew and the train's passengers paused somewhere in rural Mercer County to let off steam. The N&W Railway (now Norfolk Southern) pushed into Mercer County in 1882, and was instrumental in developing the region's vast coal and timber reserves. (Courtesy of Wayne Wright.)

CONTENTS

ACKNOWLEDGMENTS

This will mark my second book in the *Images of America* series for Arcadia Publishing. It has been a lot of fun getting the images for the book, and as in my previous effort, I owe a great debt of gratitude to many people who helped make this project possible.

First, I need to express my never-ending thanks to my wife, Evonda Archer, who chooses to stand on the sidelines, but who is every bit as responsible for any success I might experience as I am. Second, my true friend and colleague, Mel Grubb, whose collection of images, as well as his photographic expertise, made this work possible. Mel, you are an inspiration.

As in the previous work on Bluefield, I relied on friends including Heber Stafford, H. Edward "Eddie" Steele, Nick Buzzo, Eve Cooper Murphy, Betty Goins, Wayne Wright, the Mahood family, Doug Campbell, my colleague Samantha Perry, Dorothy Garrett and the late Elliott P. Garrett, Rob Radspinner, Mr. and Mrs. Arthur Charlton, Bruce Hansen, Joyce Coleman, Bill Luppold, Joe and Jackie Thorn, Max Kammer, Peery Mooney, Bud Coppinger, Rick and Jeanie Owens, George Santon, Bob Denver, Elizabeth (Jones) Greever, Clyde Bailey, Elhanier and Juanita Willis, Joe Davidson, Ron Crabtree, Dollie Lawrence, Charles Owens, John Nelson, Eric DiNovo, Fred Brown, and many others. I would also like to express my thanks to Gary Adkisson, publisher, and Tom Colley, executive editor of the *Bluefield Daily Telegraph*, for their support of this project as well as their commitment to providing a vehicle for service in the communities we all love and serve.

Finally, I'd like to thank my mom, Florence V. Archer. I appreciate everything you do for everyone. Thanks Mom. This book is for you.

INTRODUCTION

The story of Mercer County is as complex as the story of the United States itself. The county was formed in 1837, from pieces of Giles and Tazewell Counties in Virginia, and at that time, it was essentially a collection of a few farms primarily situated in what little bottomland there was available. Much of the land was acquired by purchase or through grants for soldiers who served in the Continental Army during the American Revolution.

Like the geography of the land itself, there is an unusual pride of diversity that flows through the history of Mercer County. People who grew up in the farming tradition probably have little in common with families who came for the jobs in the coal or timber industry. Mercer County is one of the most culturally diverse counties in West Virginia, and Bluefield, the county's largest city, has the highest African-American population of any city in the state. People from many cultures, creeds, and nations have combined in Mercer County's "melting pot" to make the county what it is today.

Because Mercer County has stood as a crossroads of two mighty railroads—the Norfolk & Western and The Virginian (now both Norfolk Southern)—it is easy to overlook the natural beauty the county has to offer. Pinnacle Rock remains as one of the most recognizable landmarks in Mercer County, but visitors from throughout the region, nation, and world continue to marvel at the beauty of Pipestem State Park. Camp Creek State Park contains unexpected beauty, and Brush Creek Falls remains raw and primal in an undeveloped state.

Even more compelling than the story of Mercer County's geography is the story of its people. The first European explorers to visit Mercer County, Thomas Batts and Robert Fallam called Mercer County "a pleasing tho' dreadful sight to see mountains and hills as if piled one upon another," in their 1671 exploration of the region. Early settlers like the Mitchell Clay family and the Andrew Davidson family found the Native Americans were not anxious to welcome European settlers. The Clay family settled in Clover Bottom (now Lake Shawnee) in 1775; eight years later (1783), a Shawnee raiding party killed three Clay children, and took a fourth, Ezekiel Clay, to an Indian town near present Chillocothe, Ohio, and burned him at the stake.

The Davidson family settled in Mercer County in 1780. In the spring of 1791, Mrs. Andrew (Rebecca Burke) Davidson and three of her children were abducted by Indians and taken to Ohio. The three Davidson children were executed as well as a baby Mrs. Davidson gave birth to along the way. She would ultimately be sold to a farm family in Canada. Her husband found her three years later—although now white-haired—and bought her freedom. They returned to Tazewell County, Virginia, where she resumed farming and raising a family.

Mercer County was created by an act of the Virginia General Assembly on March 17, 1837. At the time, the county's population was 2,233, a number that includes the 98 slaves at the time. While it has swelled and shrunk through the years, the 2000 census puts the county's population at 62,980.

Mercer County was named for Gen. Hugh Mercer, a native of Scotland and a Revolutionary War officer who was killed during the Battle of Princeton, New Jersey. Although there's no record of Mercer ever having visited the West Virginia county that bears his name, two Union Army officers who were destined to become presidents of the United States camped in Princeton in 1862. Lt. Col. Rutherford B. Hayes and his commissary sergeant Lt. William McKinley, were with the 23rd Ohio in the region.

A storied past that includes an alleged visit by the notorious bank robber Jessie James proved to be a prelude to events on the horizon. In 1882, the Norfolk & Western Railway pushed its mainline railway through Mercer County and tapped into the fabulous coal mineral wealth of southern West Virginia and southwestern Virginia. In 1909, the Virginian Railway emerged in Mercer County and ignited one of the great rail competitions in U.S. history.

Growth, wealth, power, and position exploded in Mercer County almost overnight. With the county's ample coal deposits and hearty timber stands as lures, thousands of people from almost every quarter of the world descended on the region to take advantage of a myriad of opportunities that awaited them.

For more than 50 years, the region's wealth grew as if there were no tomorrow. However, at mid-20th century, tomorrow arrived. Coalmines worked out. Diesel-powered locomotives replaced labor-intensive steam locomotives, and mine mechanization increased efficiency to a point where a single modern coal miner can produce about as much coal in a day as a coal miner of 100 years ago could mine in two months.

Throughout its history, Mercer County has stood as a crossroads of the Industrial Revolution. The county's fertile river bottomland could only support a few families during the agrarian pioneering times, but when industrialists began carving out fortunes from the region's coal and timber resources, where and how people lived took on a whole new meaning for the people of Mercer County. This is their story.

One

COAL

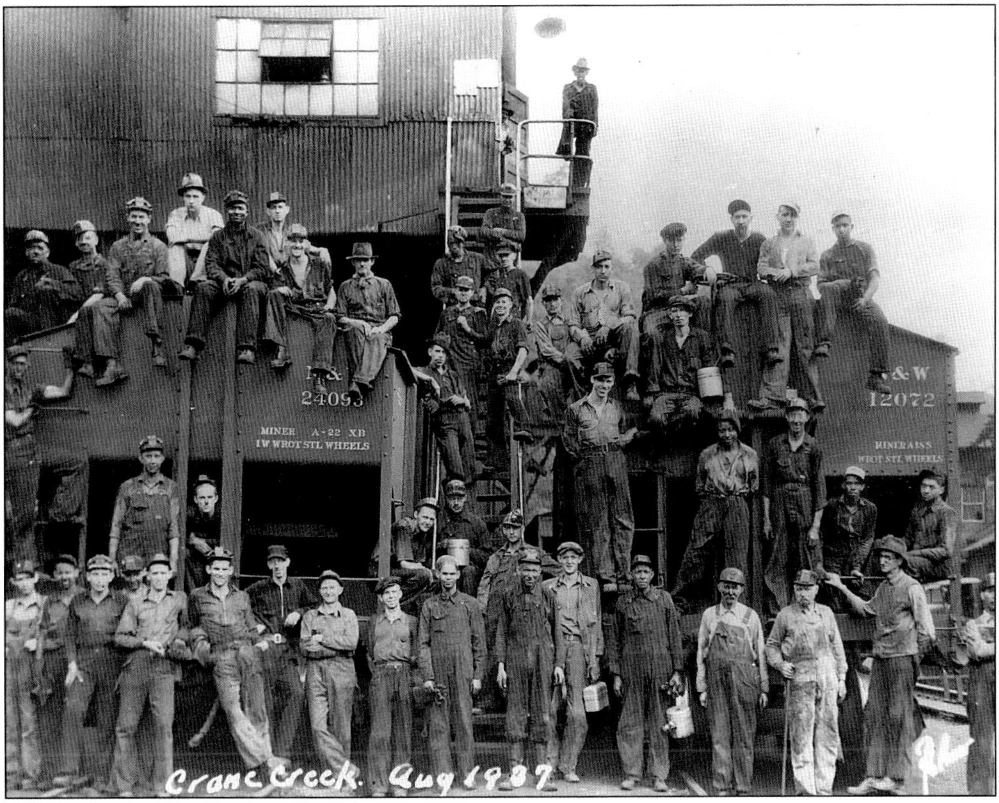

WORKING IN A COAL MINE. The men shown here were pictured before the beginning of a shift in 1937 at the American Coal Company Crane Creek Mine near McComas. Crane Creek was opened in 1902 and became part of the Pocahontas Fuel Company in 1955, one year before Poca Fuel was acquired by Consolidation (now CONSOL) Coal. (Courtesy of Grubb Photo Service.)

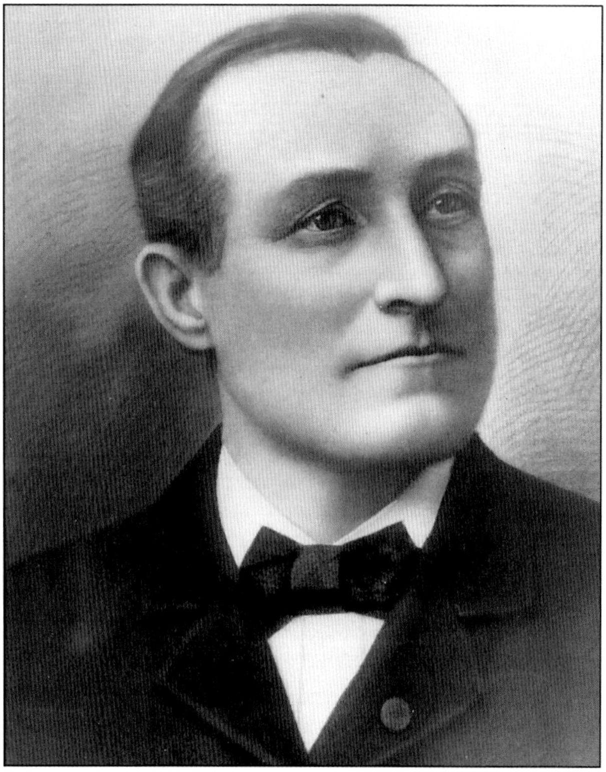

FATHER OF THE SOUTHERN WEST VIRGINIA COALFIELDS. In 1866, John Cooper, a native of Staffordshire, England, set sail with his bride, Maria, to establish a family in America. He worked in the coalfields of eastern Pennsylvania but, in 1884, came to Mercer County to open the Mill Creek Coal & Coke Company. (Courtesy of Eve Cooper Murphy.)

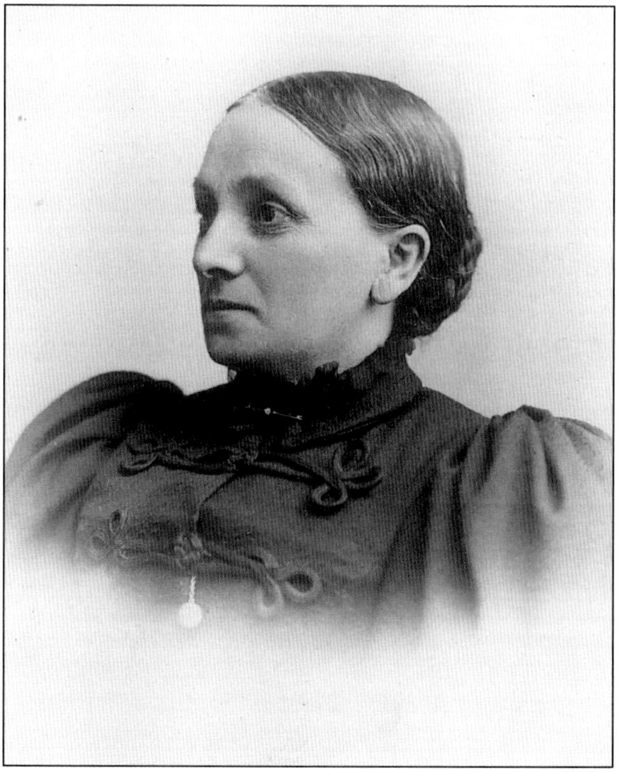

THEY CALL THE WIND MARIA. Maria Padbury married John Cooper on December 17, 1866, and they came to the New World shortly thereafter. Maria Cooper was a supportive and powerful woman who was a constant source of strength in her husband's efforts to establish a coal business. (Courtesy of Eve Cooper Murphy.)

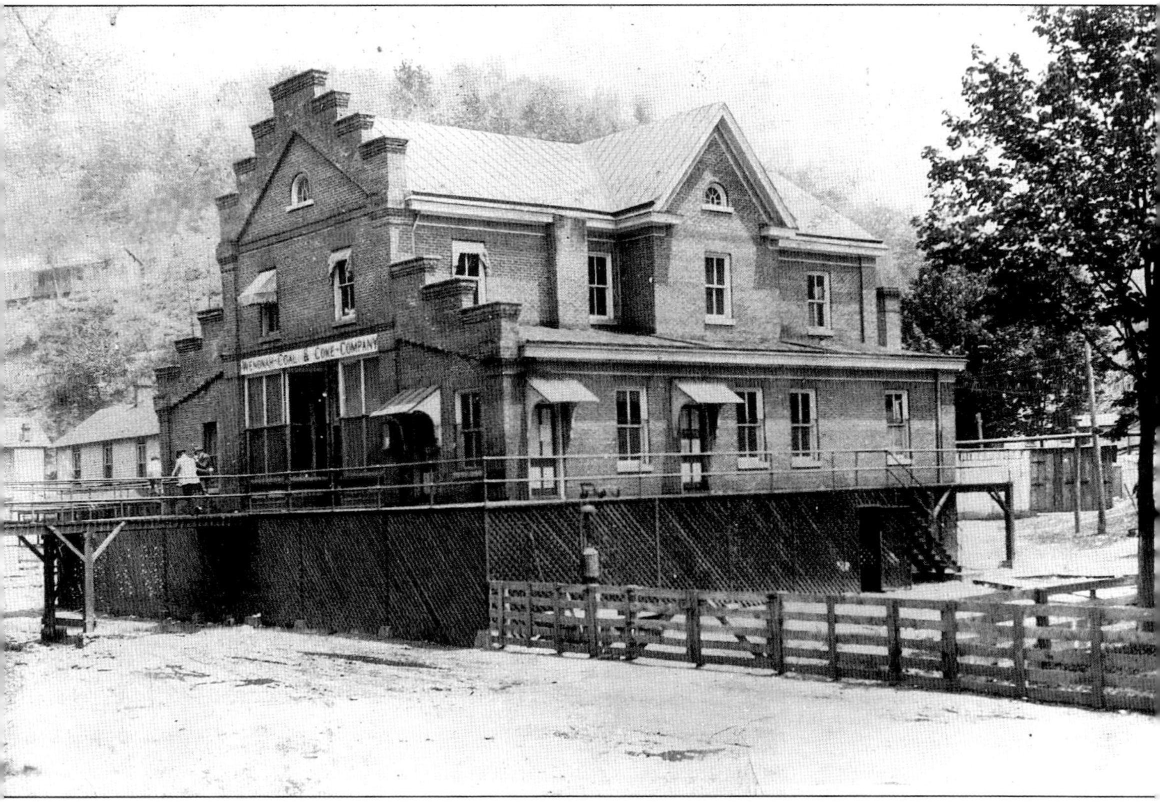

To the Company Store. Early coal operators came into southern West Virginia and had to essentially bring everything into the area with them. In order to provide housing, goods, and services for employees, coal mine operators created self-contained coal camp communities, with the central element being the company store like the one shown here. Weyanoke Coal & Coke Company was located in Arista and started operations in 1904. (Courtesy of Grubb Photo Service.)

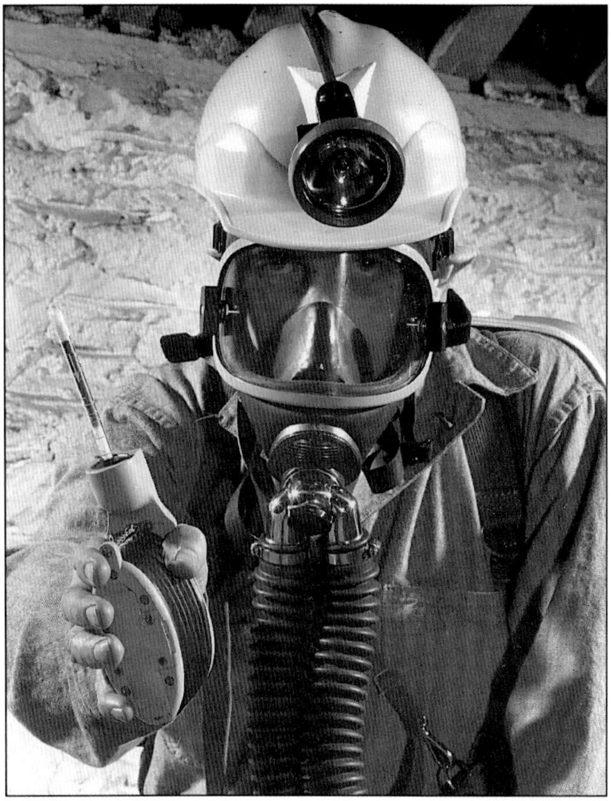

JOURNEY TO THE CENTER OF THE EARTH. A modern coal miner is shown here holding a device used to test for methane gas and wearing a self-rescuer breathing apparatus. The coal industry has taken a vigorous approach to safety throughout the 20th century, with the result being a much safer work environment. Nationwide, coal mine fatalities have gone from a high of 3,242 deaths in 1907, to 38 mine fatalities in 2000. (Courtesy of CONSOL.)

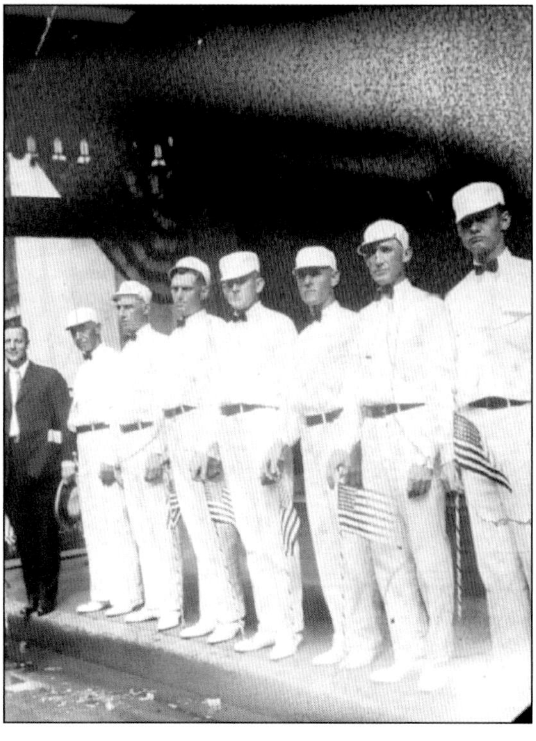

MINERS TO THE RESCUE. The mine rescue team shown here represented the Louisville Coal & Coke Company of Goodwill in the 1920 mine rescue contest held in San Francisco, California. (Courtesy of the Garrett family of Duhring.)

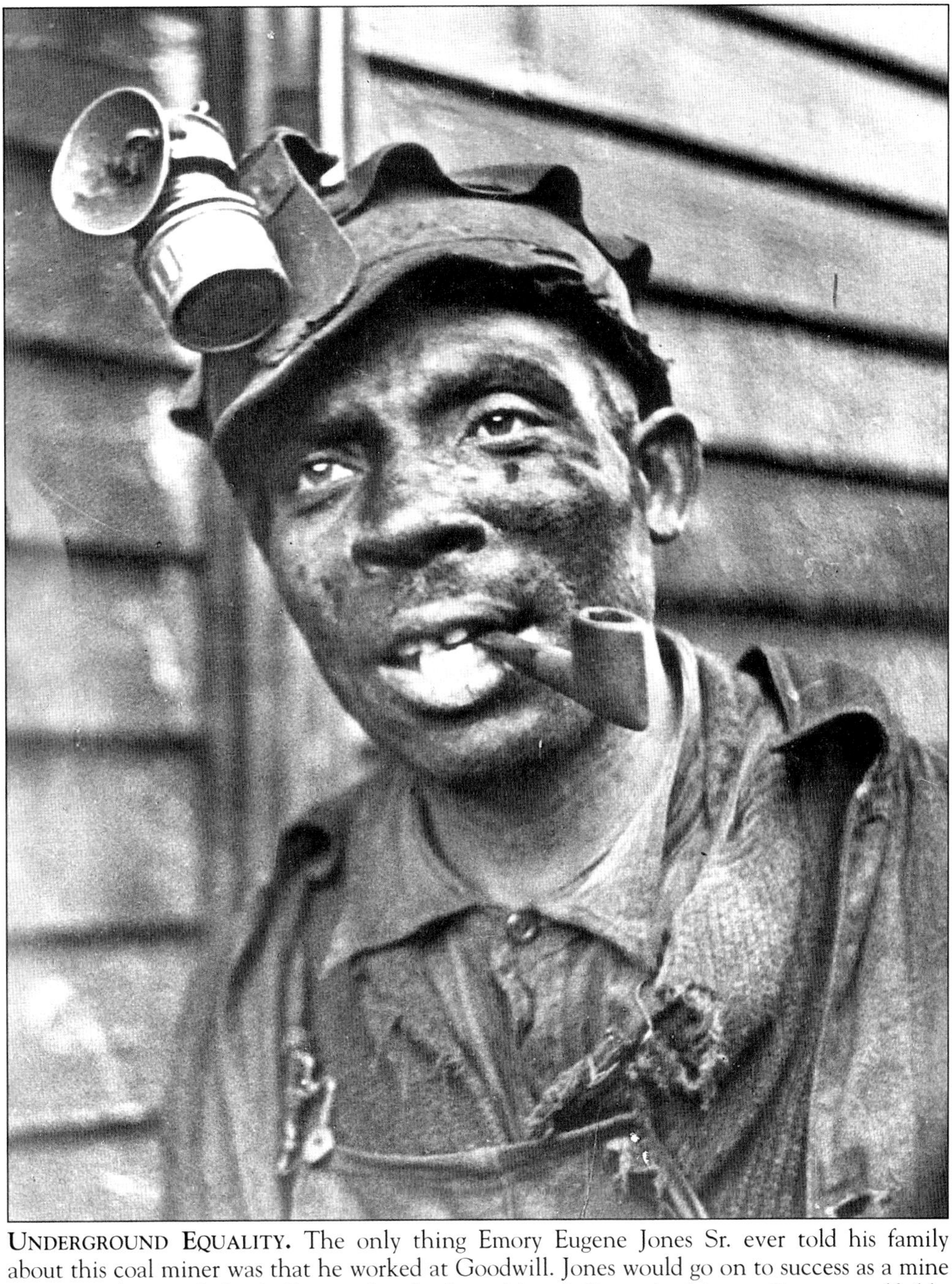

UNDERGROUND EQUALITY. The only thing Emory Eugene Jones Sr. ever told his family about this coal miner was that he worked at Goodwill. Jones would go on to success as a mine superintendent in Raleigh County, but he honed his skills in the Mercer County coalfields. This picture has been used extensively in coal publications but is rarely cited. Work in the coal mines was hard for everyone and the pay was short, but African-American coal miners received the same pay as their white counterparts. One coal miner of the era is alleged to have observed, "Everyone's black underground." (Courtesy of Elizabeth Jones Greever.)

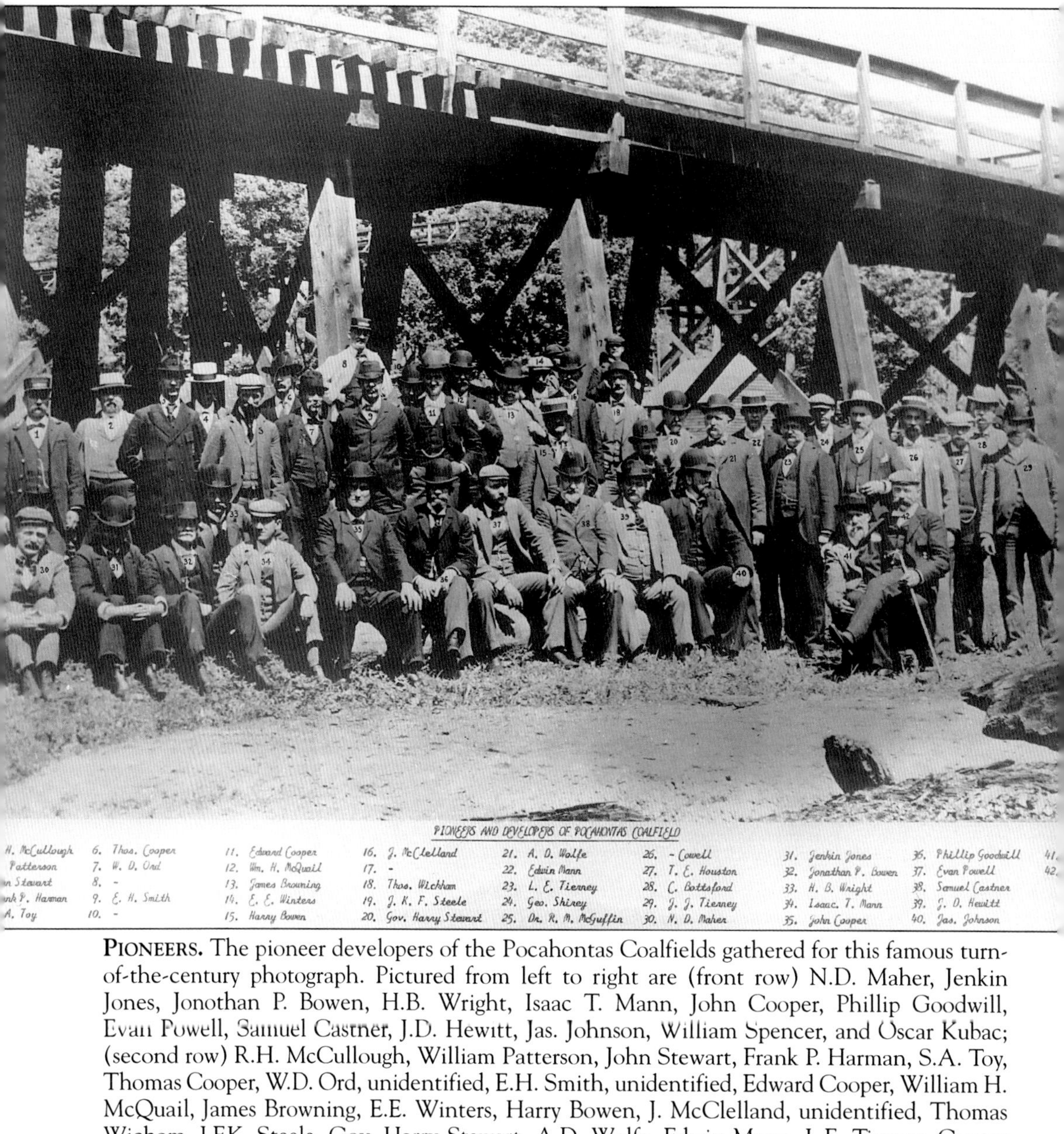

PIONEERS. The pioneer developers of the Pocahontas Coalfields gathered for this famous turn-of-the-century photograph. Pictured from left to right are (front row) N.D. Maher, Jenkin Jones, Jonothan P. Bowen, H.B. Wright, Isaac T. Mann, John Cooper, Phillip Goodwill, Evan Powell, Samuel Castner, J.D. Hewitt, Jas. Johnson, William Spencer, and Oscar Kubac; (second row) R.H. McCullough, William Patterson, John Stewart, Frank P. Harman, S.A. Toy, Thomas Cooper, W.D. Ord, unidentified, E.H. Smith, unidentified, Edward Cooper, William H. McQuail, James Browning, E.E. Winters, Harry Bowen, J. McClelland, unidentified, Thomas Wicham, J.F.K. Steele, Gov. Harry Stewart, A.D. Wolfe, Edwin Mann, L.E. Tierney, George Shirley, Dr. R.M. McGuffin, ? Cowell, T.E. Houston, C. Bottsford, and J.J. Tierney. (Courtesy of Grubb Photo Service.)

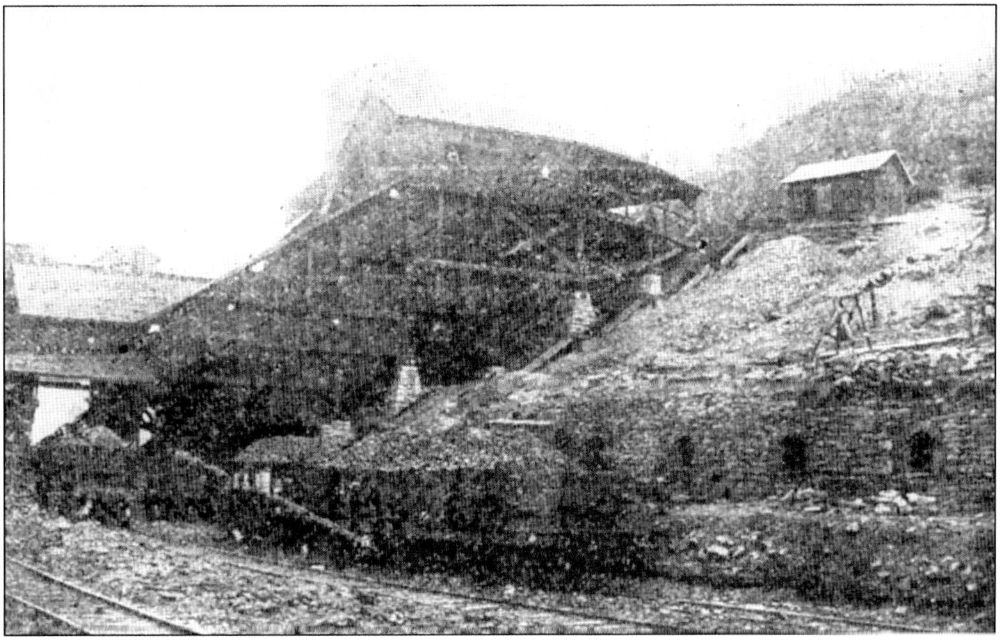

OLD COAL TIPPLE. The Buckeye Coal and Coke Company tipple shown here went into operation in 1886. The mine was located in Freeman, near Bramwell. (Courtesy of Grubb Photo Service.)

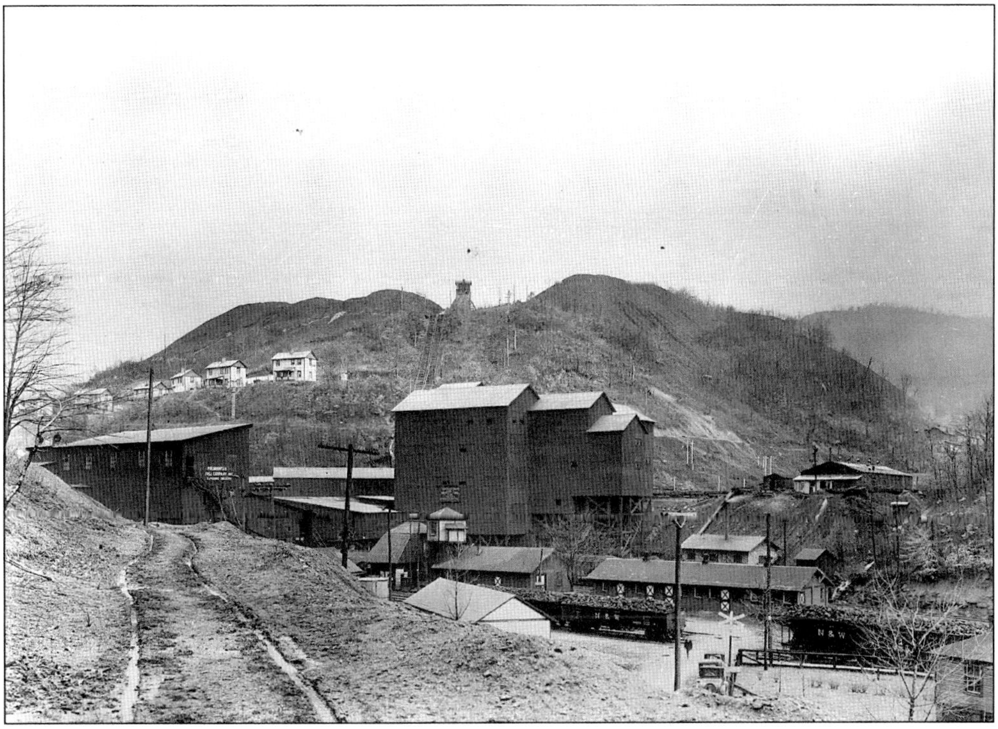

SAGAMORE. The old Sagamore Coal and Coke Company was a mainstay in the McComas area for more than half of the 20th century. The mine was opened in 1902. (Courtesy of Grubb Photo Service.)

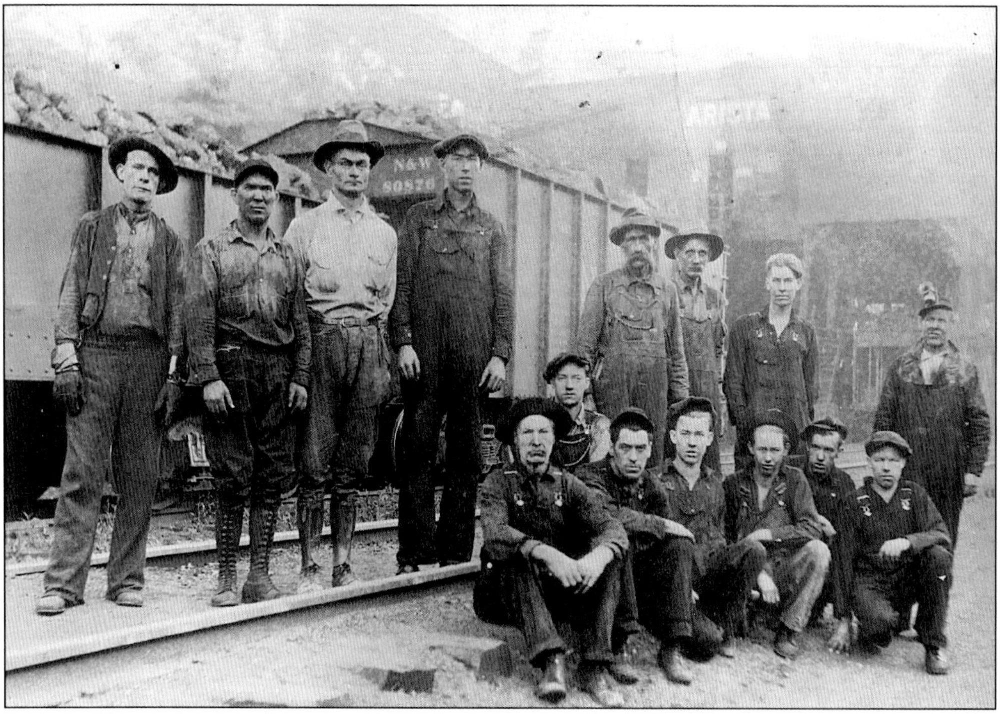

ARISTA TIPPLE CREW. The Arista Prep Plant crew posed for this 1930 photograph before going to work and are identified, from left to right, as follows: (seated) Jim Wharf, Kenneth Bailey, Josiah Thompson, Lyle Bailey, Roy Fagg, Raymond Gillespie, and Wilbur McKinney; (standing) Clarence Stoots, Dave Bland, George Mills, Ralph Groda, Manns Wingo, Clyde Bailey, and Harry Fagg. (Courtesy of Clyde Bailey.)

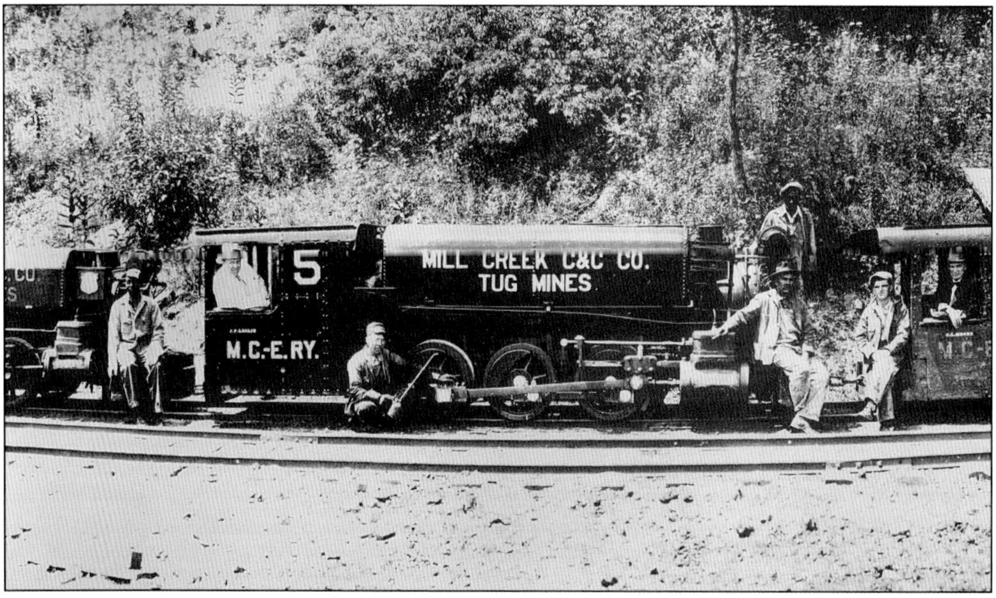

UNDERGROUND MOVEMENT. The locomotive crew of the Mill Creek Coal & Coke Company is shown here taking a break. Mill Creek went through Coaldale Mountain and emerged at the Tug Mines in McDowell County near Anawalt. (Courtesy of Grubb Photo Service.)

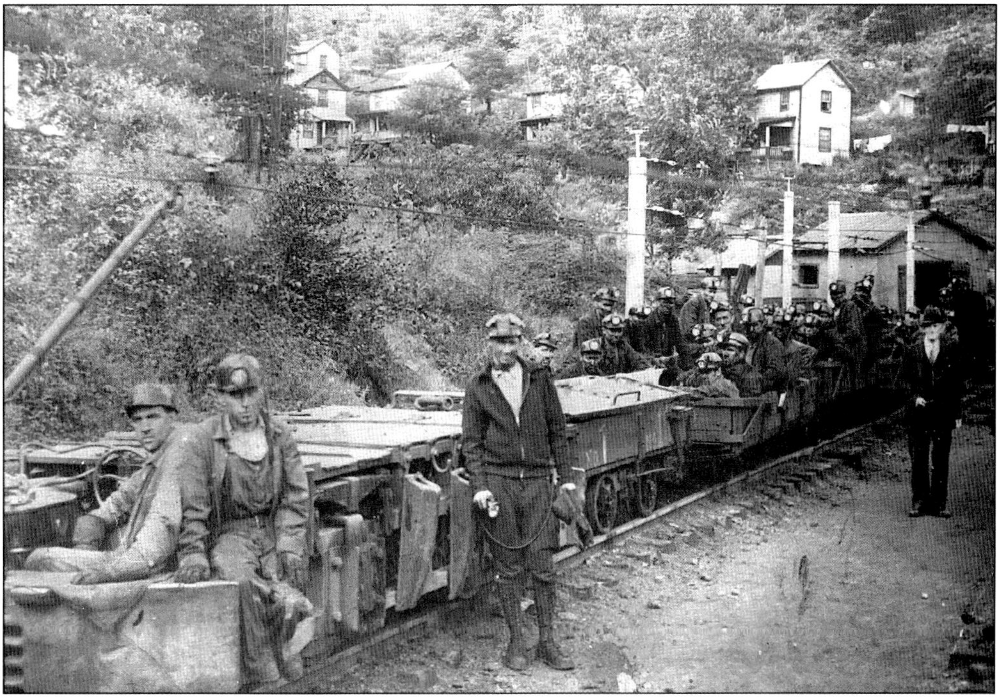

MOTORMAN. Shift change is shown above at the American Coal Company Crane Creek Mine near McComas. Note the proximity of homes to the mine opening. (Courtesy of Grubb Photo Service.)

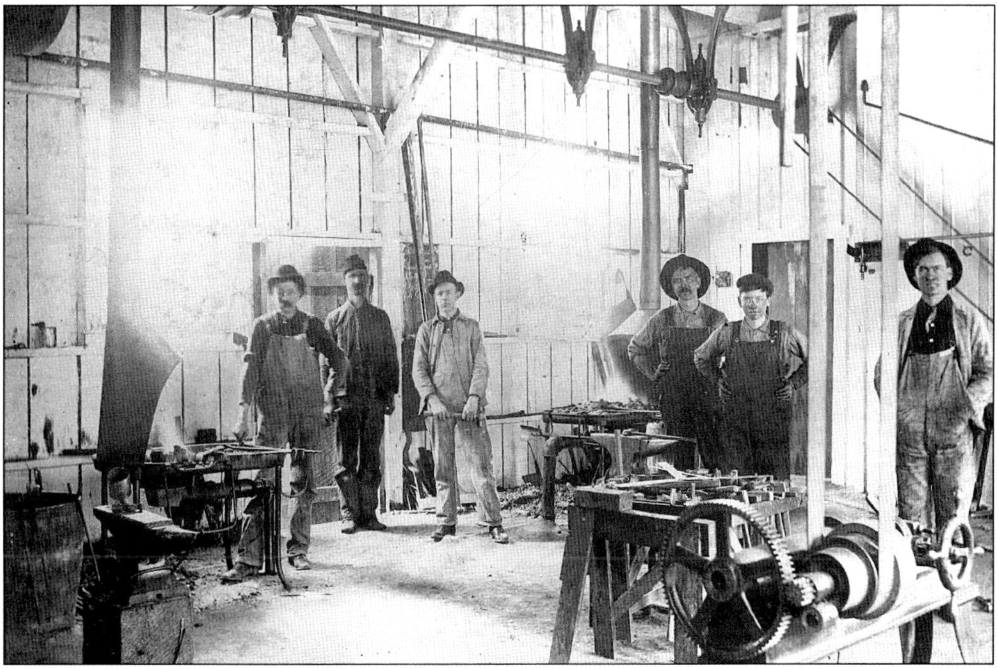

CLOCKWORK MACHINERY. Workers are shown here in the Crane Creek Mine repair shop. Most coal operations throughout the region were self-contained and self-sufficient. (Courtesy of Grubb Photo Service.)

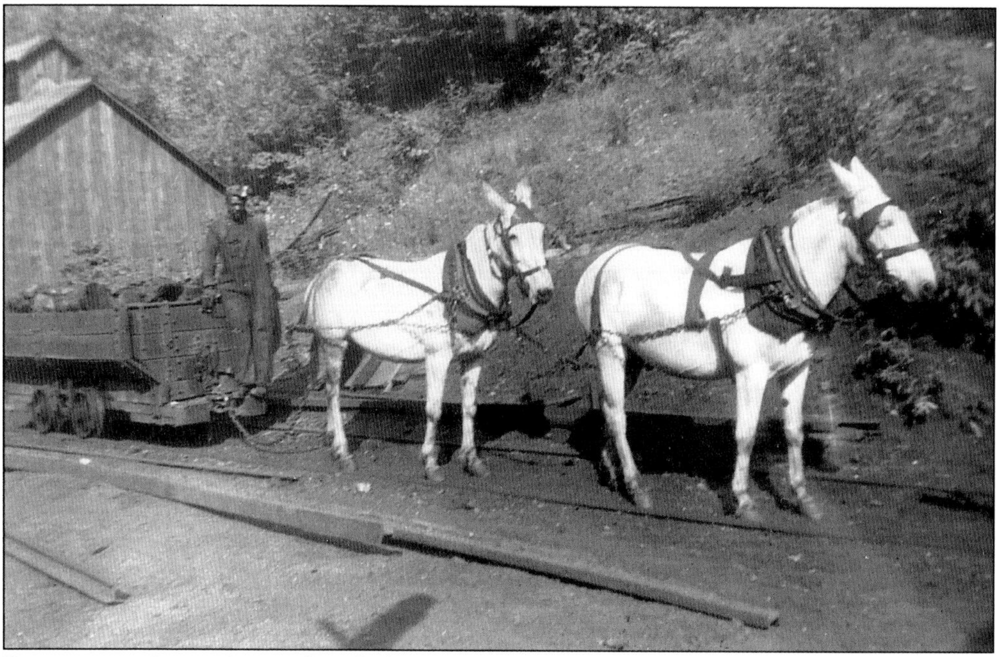

End of the Line. An unidentified coal miner is shown here bringing the last car of coal powered by mules out of the old Buckeye Mine near Freeman. Mules were kept in underground stables and were often said to be blind because they were born underground and remained underground through most of their lives. This long-held myth proved untrue. (Courtesy of Grubb Photo Service.)

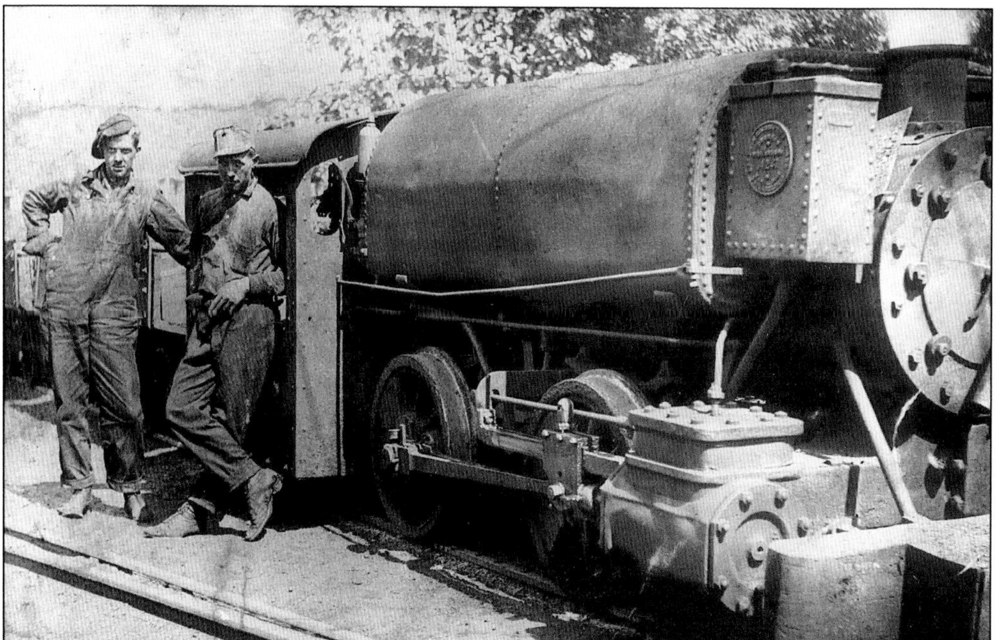

Waiting for a Train. Two unidentified coal miners are shown here near a locomotive at the Booth-Bowen Mine in Simmons near Bramwell. Early coal miners were faced with a wealth of challenges. (Courtesy of Grubb Photo Service.)

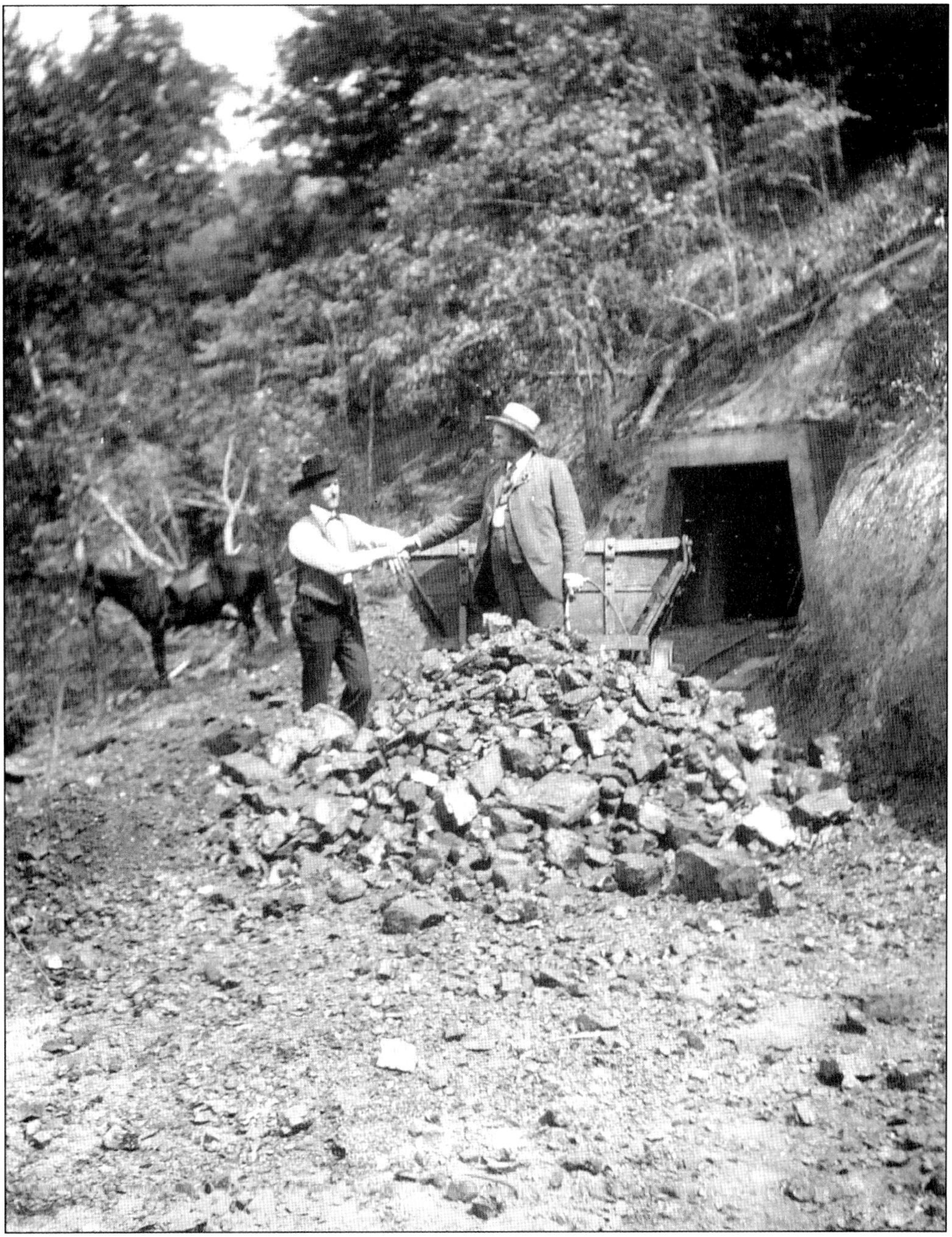

The Start of Something Big. Dr. R.M. McGuffin (left) is shown here shaking hands with Tom Cooper in this 1903 photograph that is most likely some kind of a symbolic recreation of the opening of the Mill Creek Mine near Coopers. Tom Cooper would have been about 34 years old at the time the picture was made. He was the first son of John and Maria Cooper and was listed as secretary of Mill Creek Coal & Coke when the company was established in 1884. (Courtesy of Eve Cooper Murphy.)

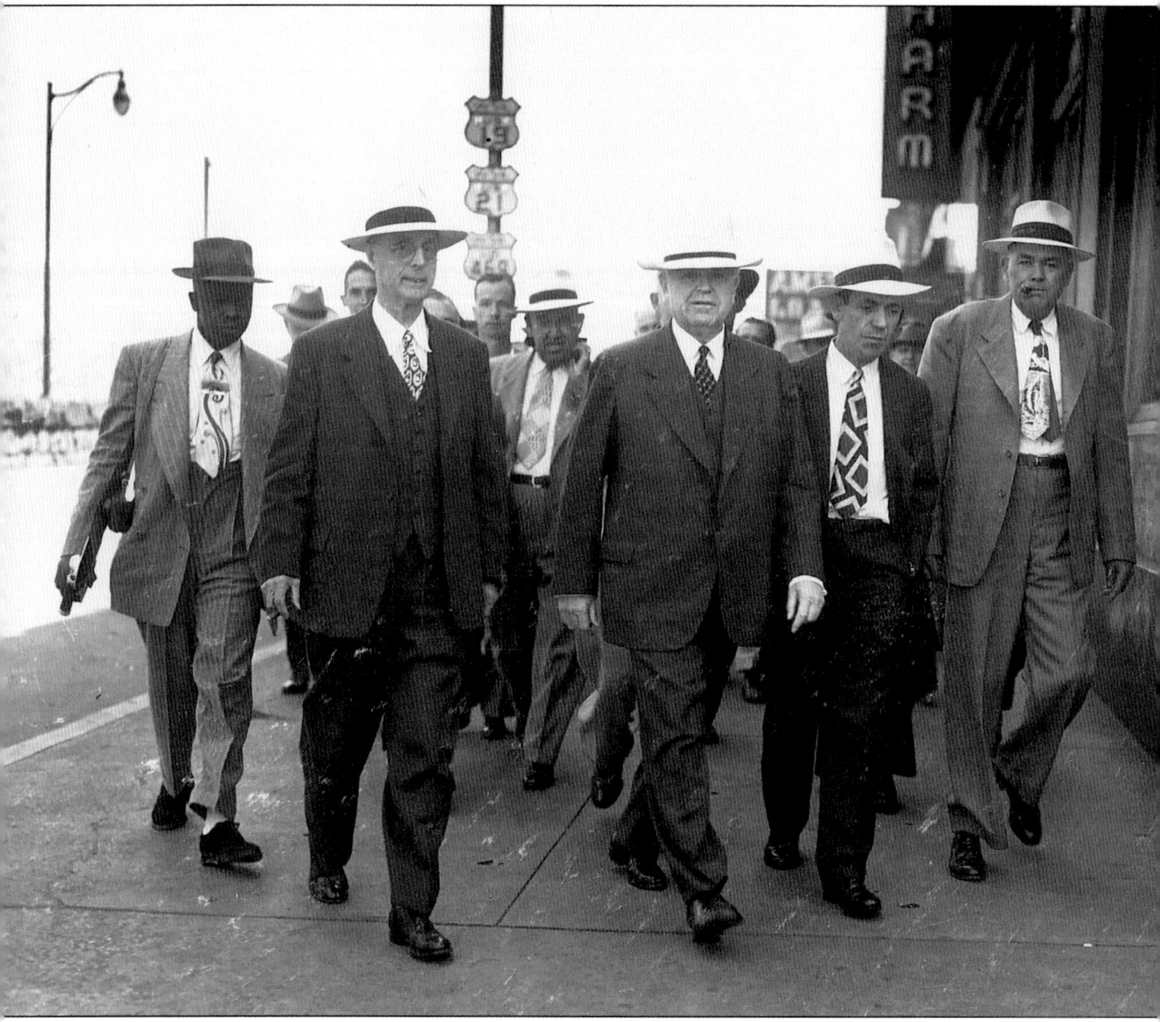

Dynamic Leadership. John L. Lewis (above, center) was the dynamic leader of the United Mine Workers of America from 1920 until he retired in 1960. For many years, Bluefield was considered to be under the control of the coal industry, and as a result, he did not make frequent public appearances in the city. However, on May 25, 1949, Lewis came to Bluefield for contract negotiations with the Bituminous Coal Operators' Association. It had been 30 years since Lewis had made a public appearance prior to his arrival at the Matz Hotel that day. (Photo by Mel Grubb.)

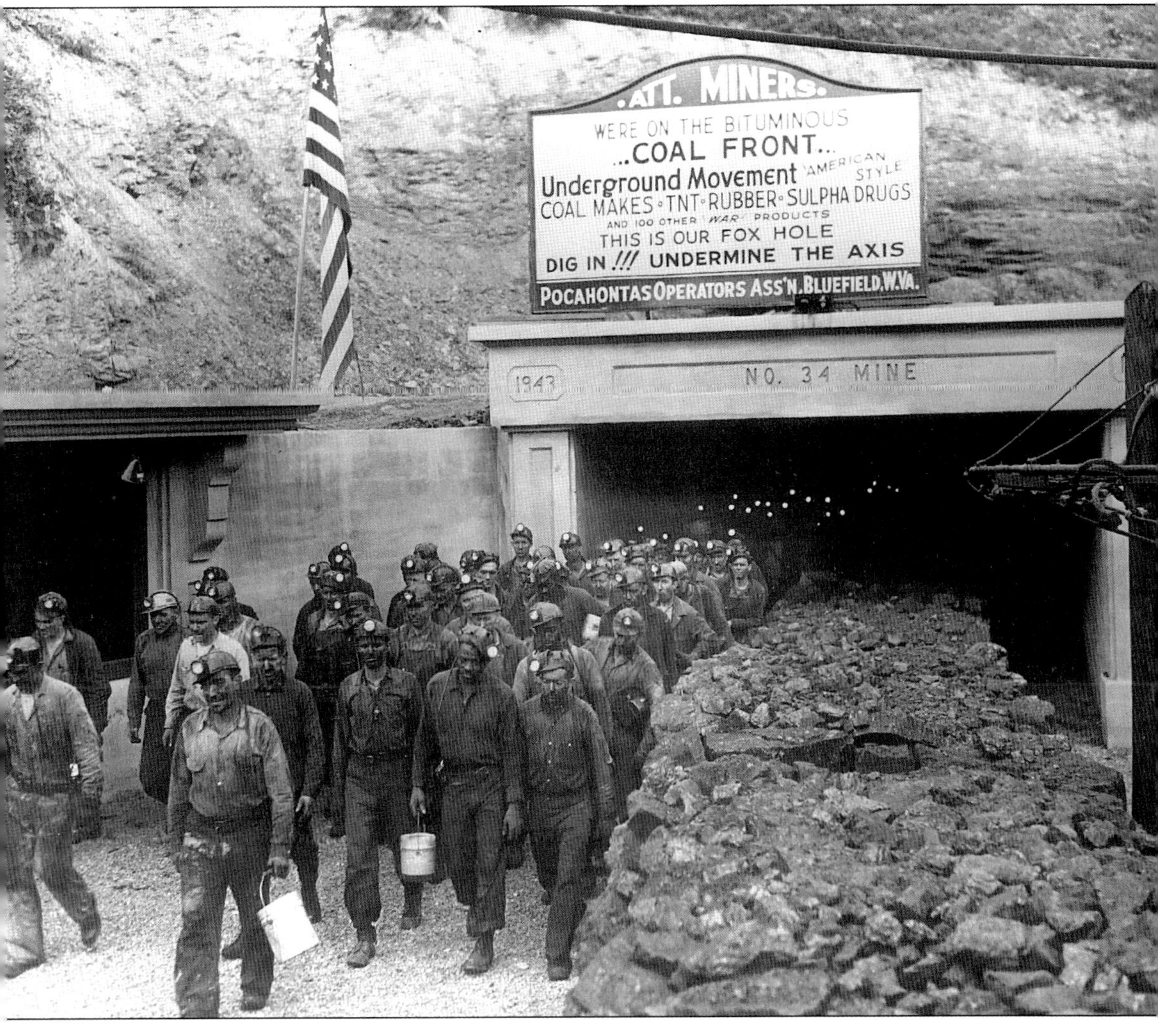

UNDERGROUND ARMY. Although this photograph is of underground coal miners finishing their shift at the No. 34 Mine in Bishop, McDowell County, the mine was a Pocahontas Fuel mine and a member of the Bluefield-based Pocahontas Operators Association. Coal miners were considered "essential" to the war effort, and were therefore, exempt from military service during World War II. (Courtesy of Grubb Photo Service.)

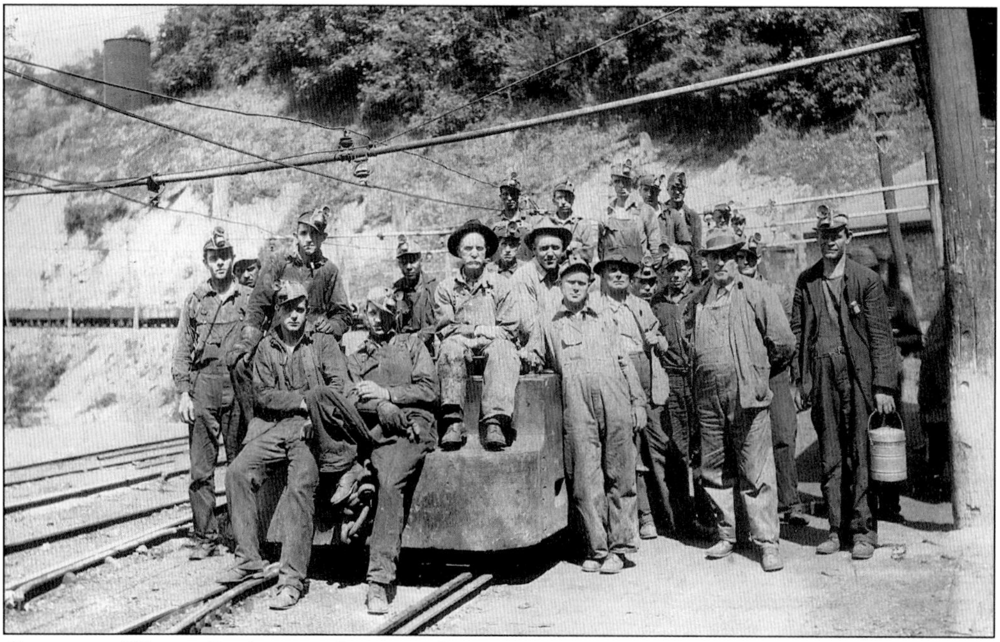

GOING TO WORK. Coal miners here are shown preparing to work their shift at the Mill Creek Coal & Coke Mine. The dinner bucket held by the coal miner at the right was designed to hold water in addition to food. (Courtesy of Grubb Photo Service.)

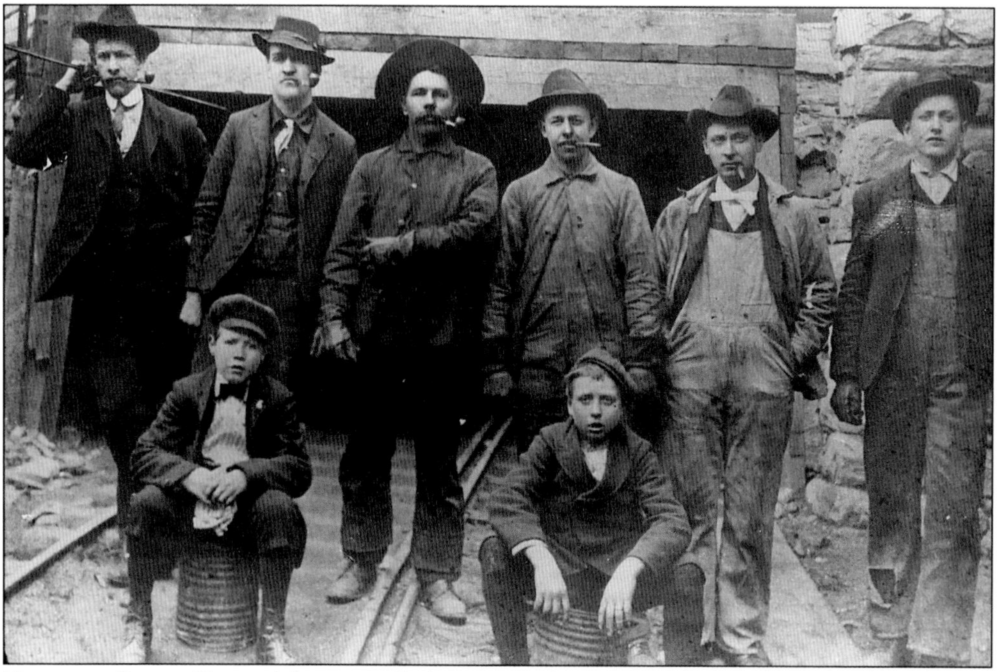

TRAPPER BOYS. Young laborers called "trapper boys," like the two shown in this old photograph, were called on to open and close trap doors in the mines for haulage as well as to open up trap doors on ventilation shafts because they could fit into tight places. Child labor laws eventually ended the practice of using trapper boys in underground coal mines. (Courtesy of Grubb Photo Service.)

Two

TIMBER

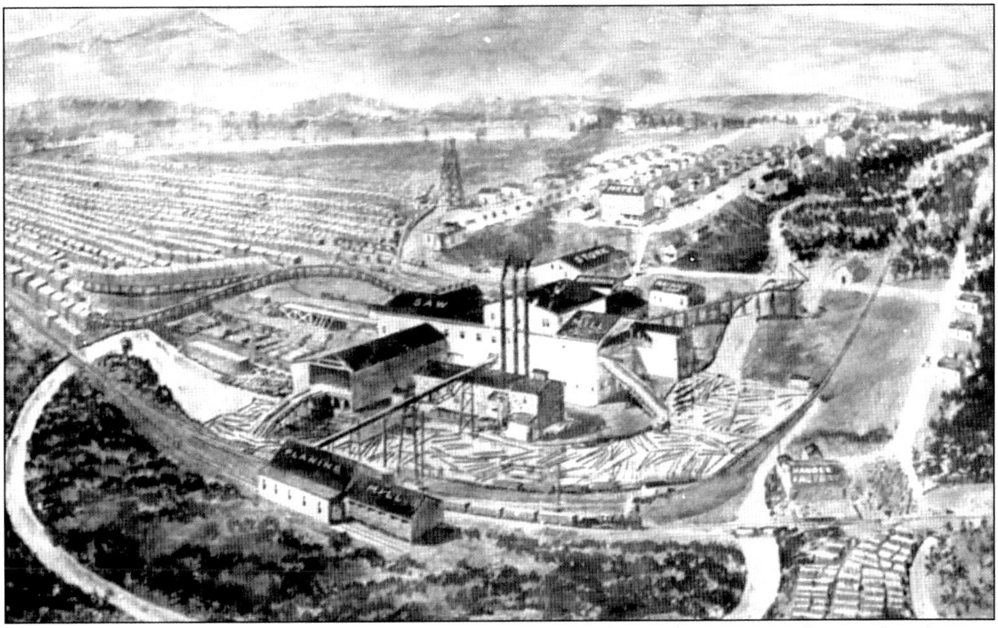

WE'RE LUMBER ONE! In the modern era, it is hard to believe that a sawmill complex the size of the Bluestone Land and Lumber mill at Gardener Road existed. Dr. William Luppold, one of the nation's leading forest economists, pointed out that while the stacks of timber to the left in the drawing above may be an artistic embellishment, the rest of the detail in the drawing is essentially accurate. (Courtesy of U.S. Forest Service.)

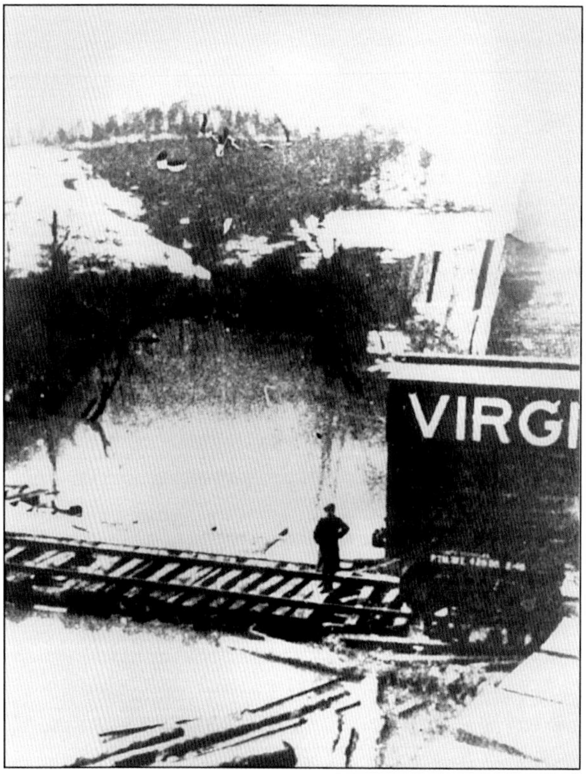

LOGS ON. This photo from a 1909 postcard shows a Bluestone Land and Lumber worker observing logs on the pond. The Virginian Railway arrived on the scene in 1908 to provide Bluestone a way to get finished products to market. (Courtesy of U.S. Forest Service.)

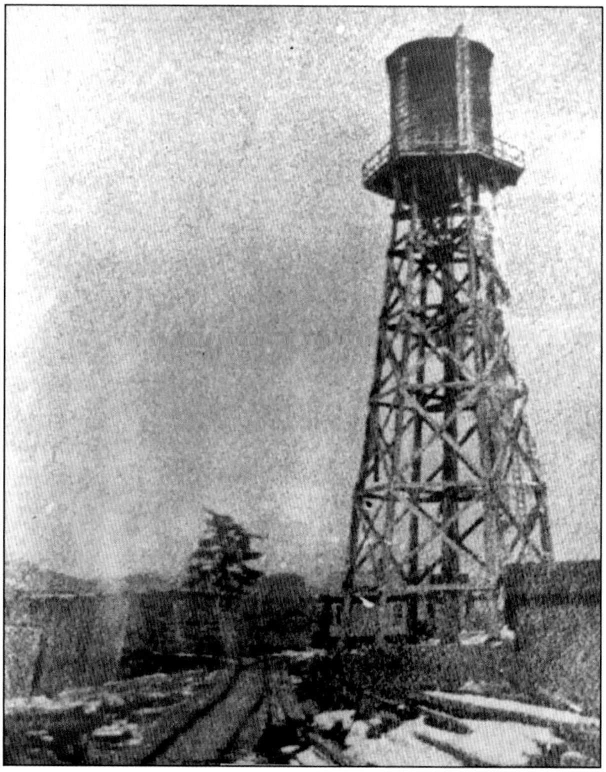

WATER EVERYWHERE. In another photo taken in 1909 at the Gardner complex, this 90-foot-tall water tower shows how industry had to bring its own infrastructure into a remote location. (Courtesy of U.S. Forest Service.)

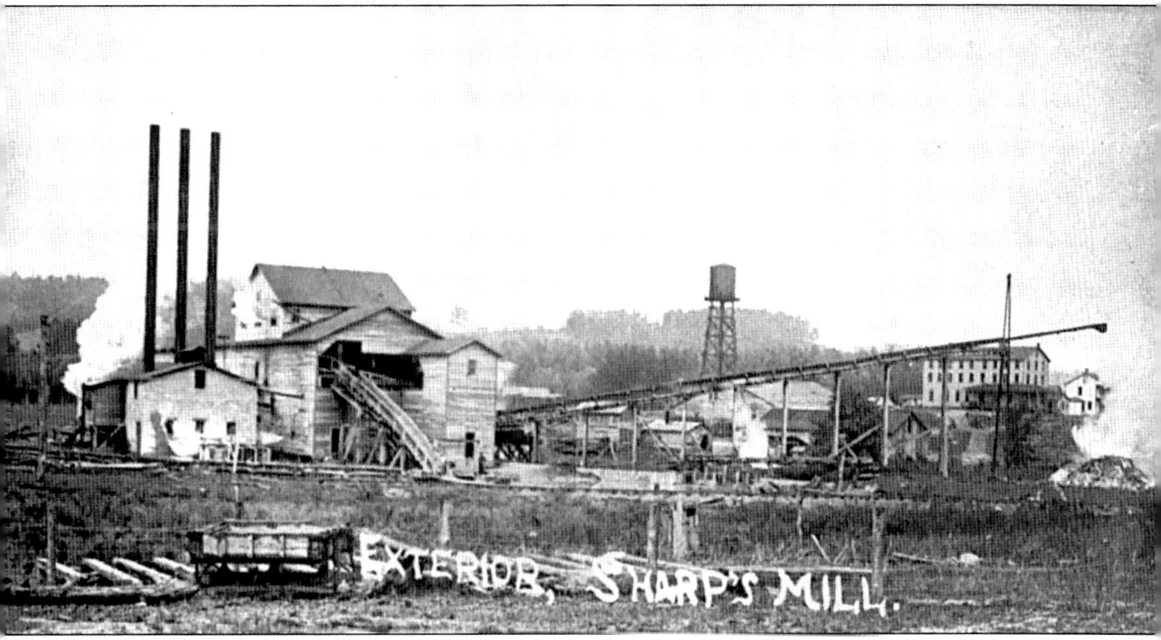

BUILDING BLOCKS. Sharp's Mill at Gardener was similar to the band mill located in Pocahontas County in the community now known as Cass. Both band saw operations featured an endless steel-toothed chain on pulleys and exhibited voracious appetites for large amounts of timber. Much of the region's timber was clear cut during the first two decades of the 20th century. Discarded limbs from logs created a forest fire hazard, and by the early 1920s, the region's landscape looked barren. The U.S. Forest Service, working in harmony with responsible timber companies, has restored the region's forest to a healthy condition. (Courtesy of U.S. Forest Service.)

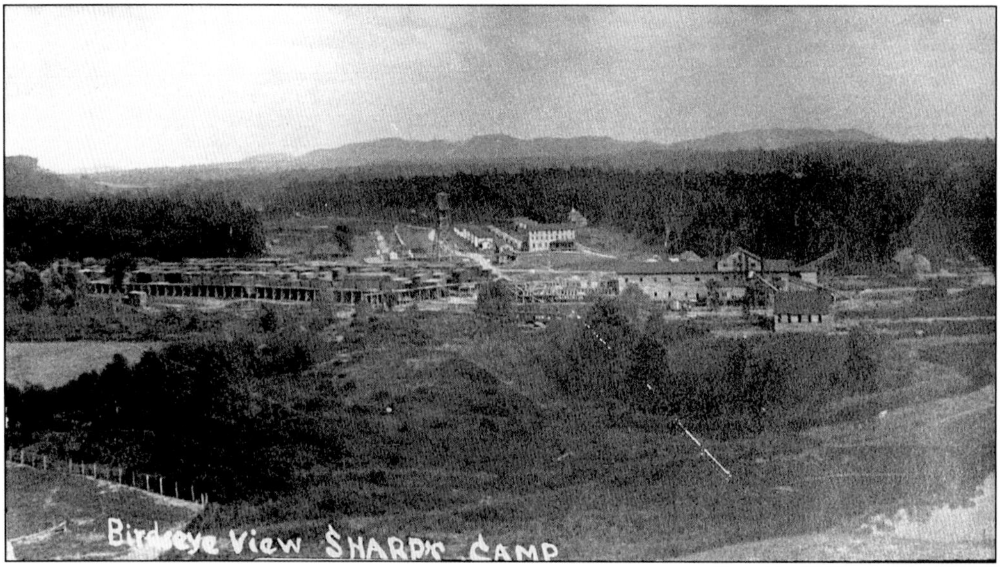

CITY BUILT OF WOOD. The Sharp's Camp at Gardner was located on about the same site as the West Virginia Department of Highways District 10 Headquarters now stands. Of course, the complex extended into the right-of-way of what is now I-77 near Pikeview High School. (Courtesy of U.S. Forest Service.)

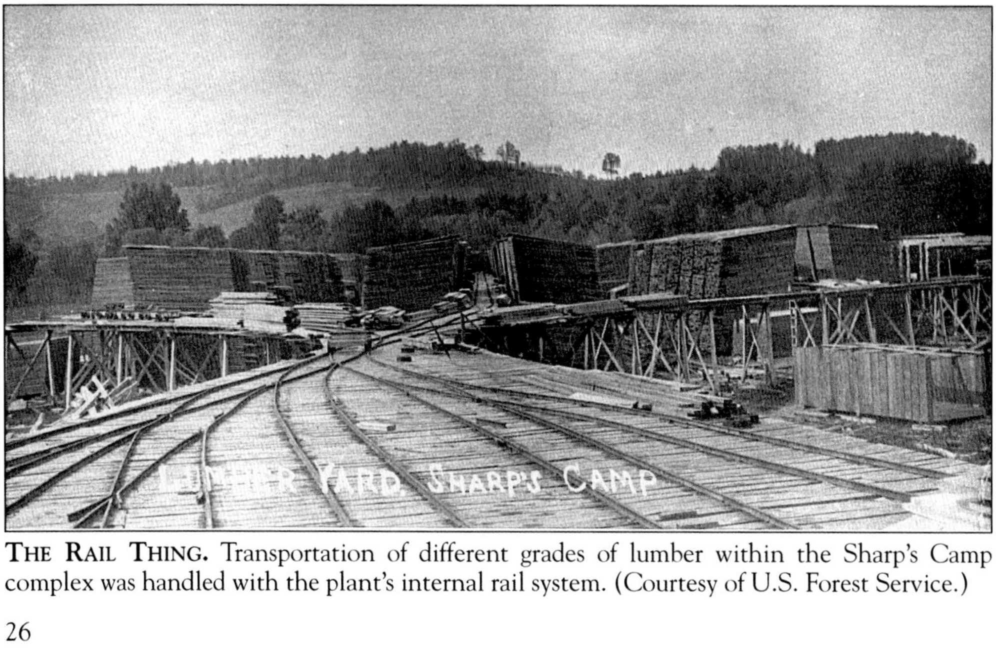

THE RAIL THING. Transportation of different grades of lumber within the Sharp's Camp complex was handled with the plant's internal rail system. (Courtesy of U.S. Forest Service.)

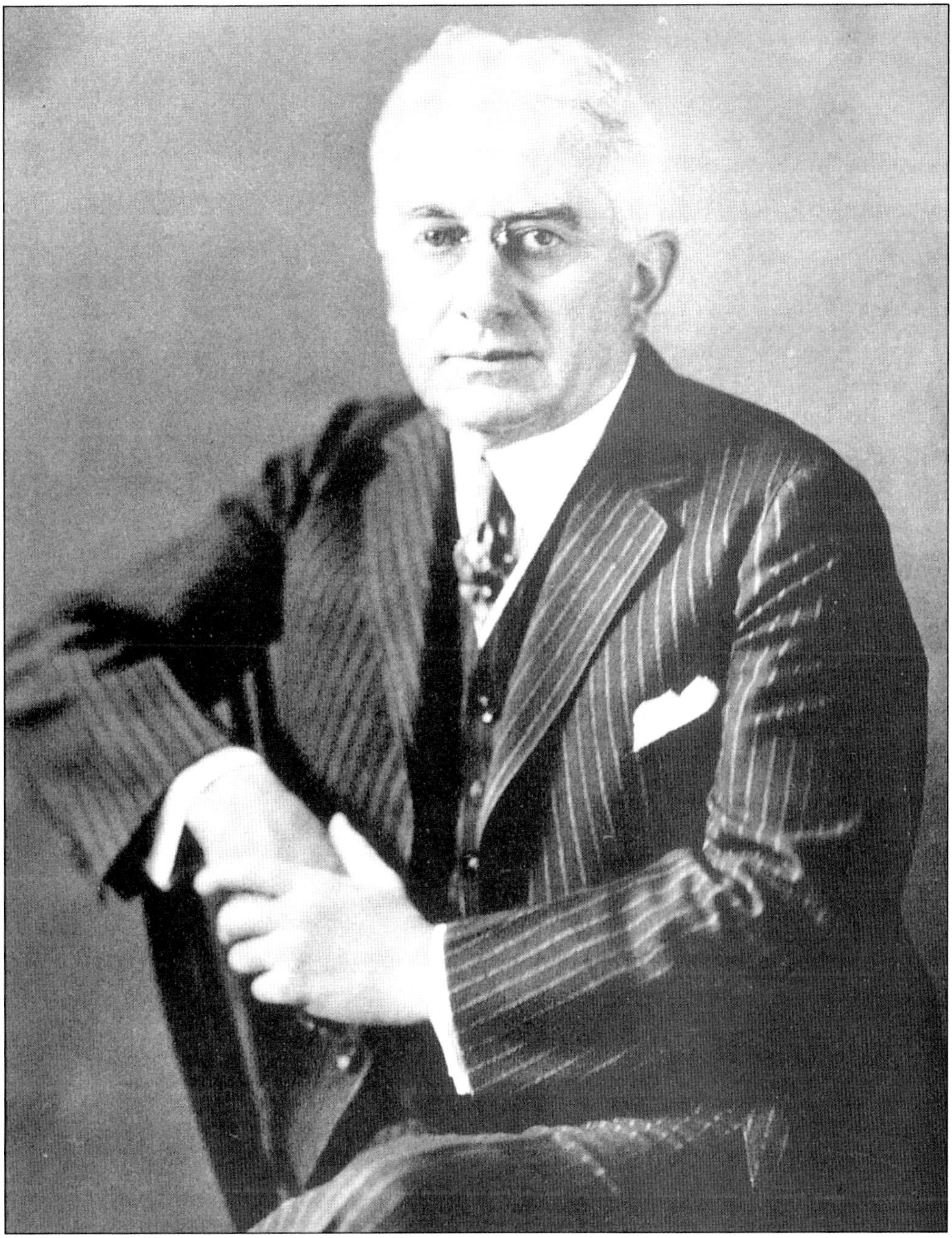

FROM TINY ACORNS, MIGHTY EMPIRES GROW. William M. Ritter, a Pennsylvania native, came to southern West Virginia in the 1890s, and built a great timber and coal company that would become part of the foundation of Georgia-Pacific, now The Timber Company. Although his operations extended throughout the eastern U.S., the first load of logs Ritter loaded out was from Oakvale, Mercer County in 1890. Ritter was the son of Elizabeth Morris Ritter, of the family of Robert Morris of Philadelphia, the "Financier of the American Revolution." Ironically, Robert Morris once held the deed to millions of acres in the region that W.M. Ritter would later make his fortune harvesting. (Courtesy of Bob Radspinner, The Timber Company.)

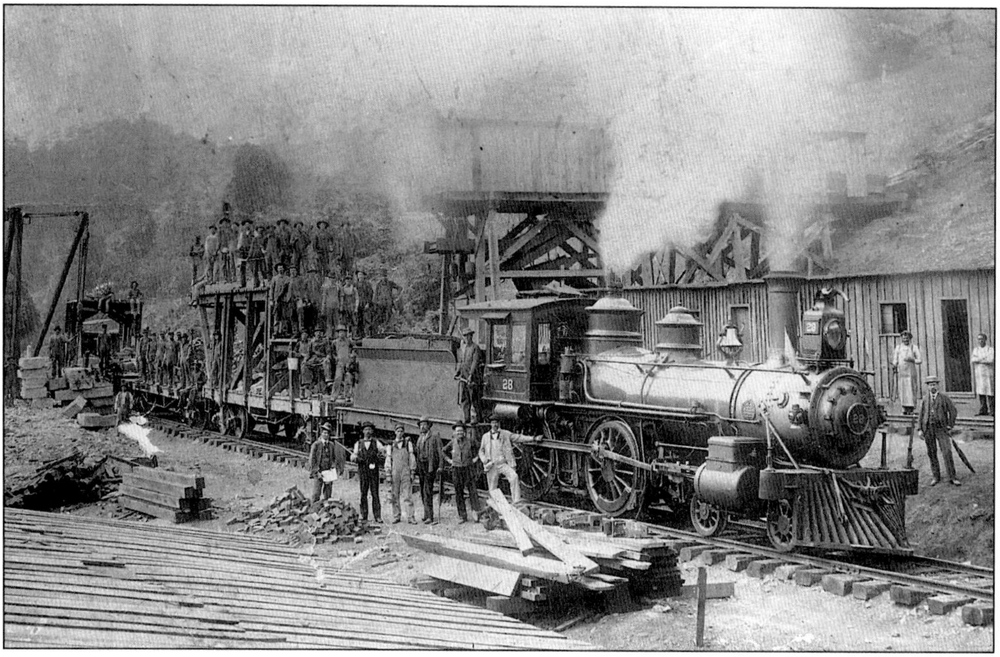

TIMBER BINDS NATION. Throughout their county's history, Americans have relied heavily on the North American continent's renewable resource—timber. From railroad crossties to mine roof supports and housing, timber formed a backbone of national growth. The timber business also provided many jobs as evidenced by the photo above at an unidentified mill operation. (Courtesy of Grubb Photo Service.)

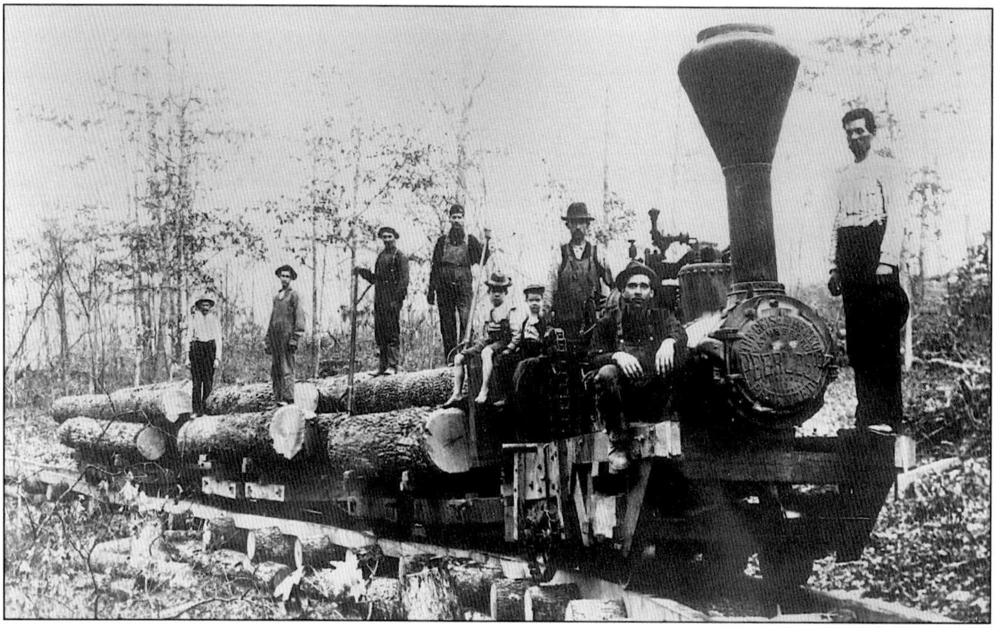

LUMBER JACKS. Timber roads and railroads were often unsophisticated operations like the makeshift rail operation shown above. The unidentified loggers shown here created a rail system with enough artistry to keep their "climax locomotive" on the track. (Courtesy of Grubb Photo Service.)

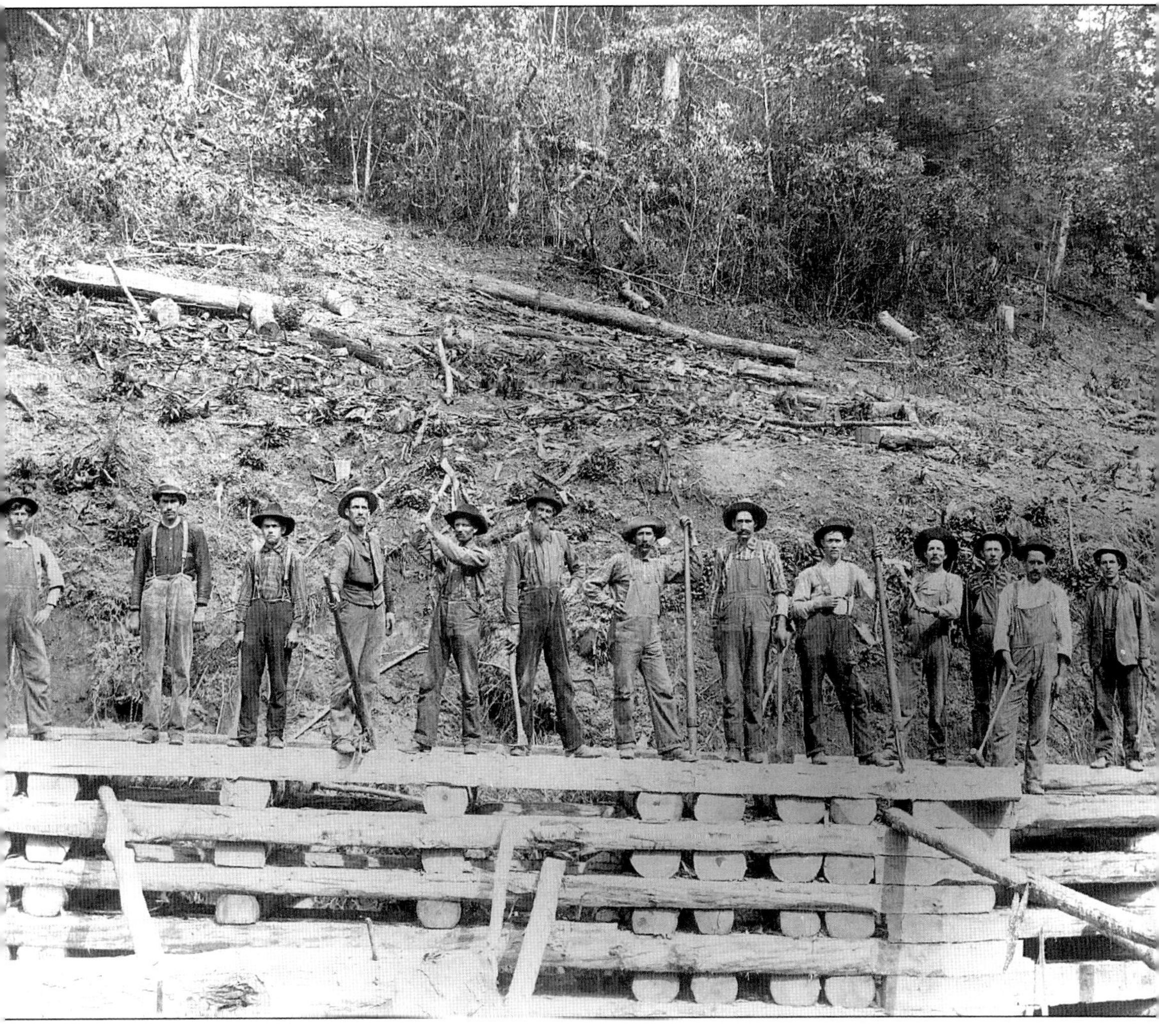

LUMBER LABOR. Strangely enough, the early coal operators did not see the opportunity to develop a coal and timber industry at the same time. Most coal operations like this *c.* 1905 unidentified crew at the Pawama Coal & Coke Company Mine near Matoaka, were focused on extracting the coal and primarily used the timber resource for rudimentary structures at the mine or to check erosion. The coal miners shown on the cover of this book are working the Pawama Mine, an operation that produced 1.8 million tons of coal between 1905 and 1927. (Courtesy of Grubb Photo Service.)

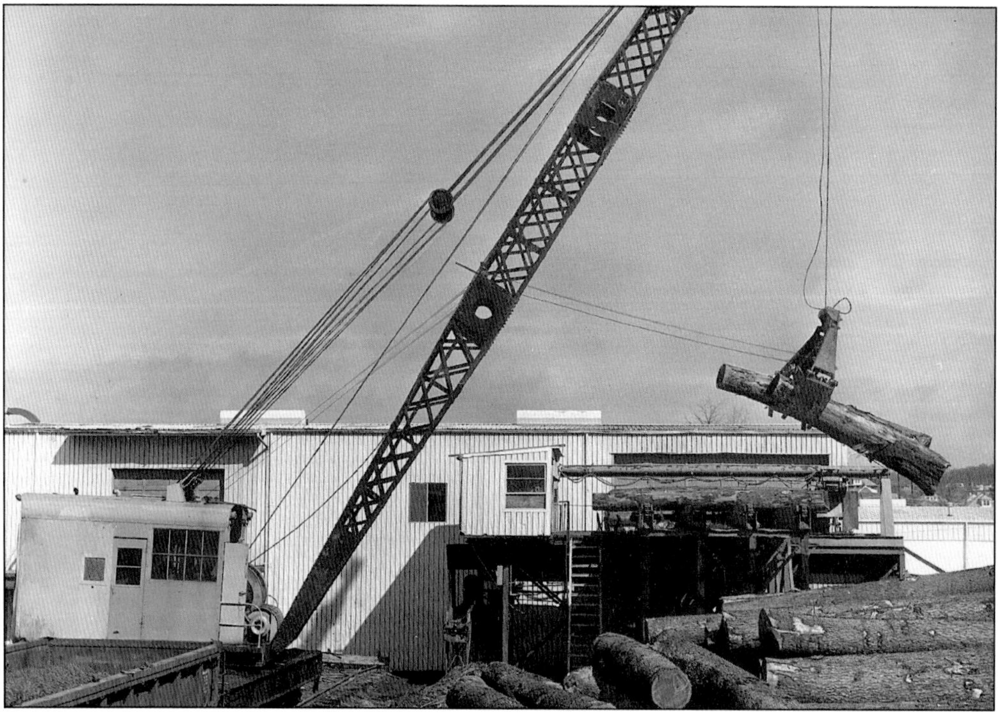

STILL THE ONE. Lumber still serves as a backbone of Mercer County's present economic base. An example of that is the Dean Company of Princeton shown above. The Dean Company continues to expand and supply products for customers worldwide. (Courtesy of Princeton/Mercer County Chamber of Commerce.)

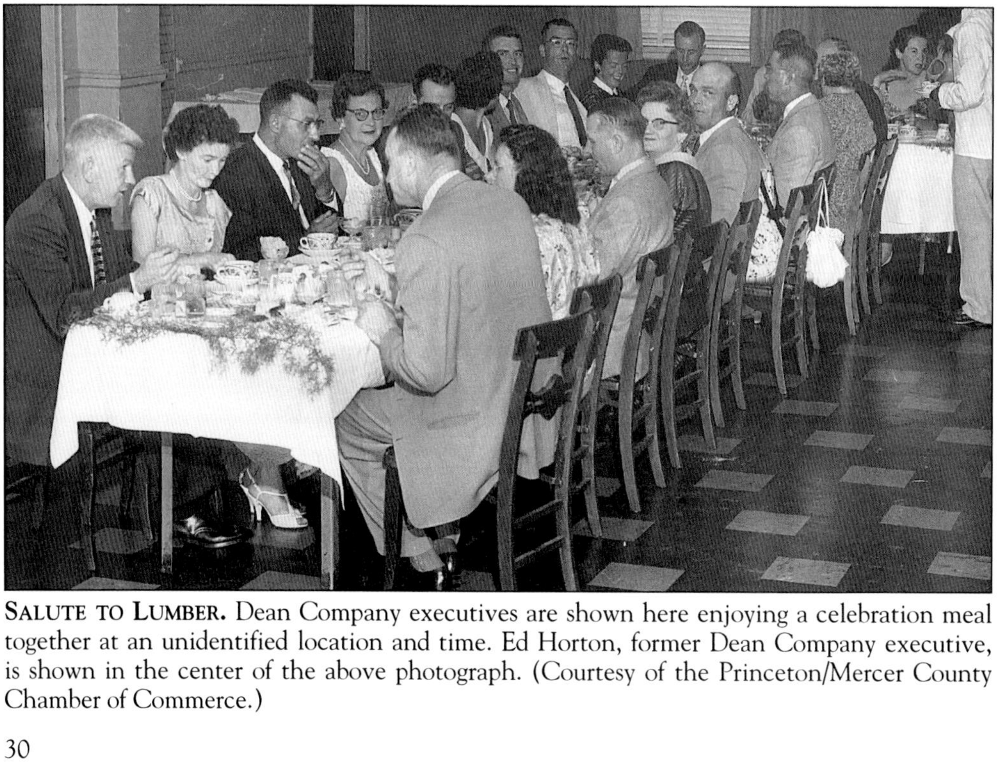

SALUTE TO LUMBER. Dean Company executives are shown here enjoying a celebration meal together at an unidentified location and time. Ed Horton, former Dean Company executive, is shown in the center of the above photograph. (Courtesy of the Princeton/Mercer County Chamber of Commerce.)

Three

PLACES

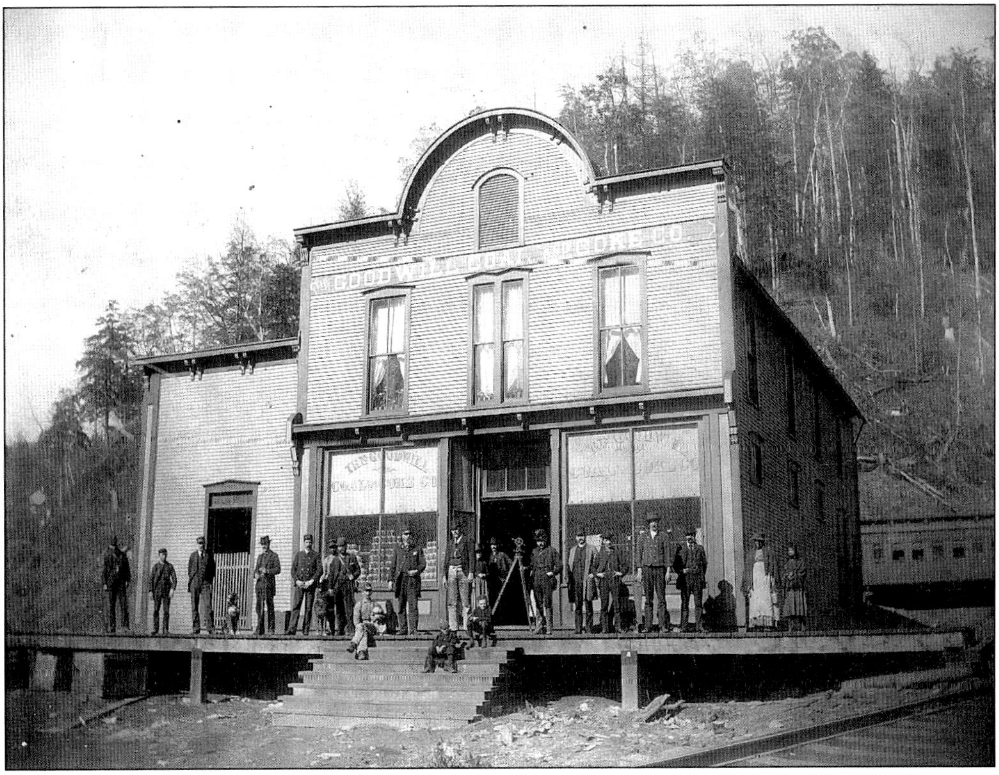

PLACE OF GOODWILL. The Goodwill Coal & Coke Company Store and office building was one of the first structures erected in that coal camp. Phillip Goodwill of Bramwell opened the mine in 1887. The company would soon be renamed the Louisville Coal & Coke Company, and operate into the 1950s. George Thomas is shown in the center of the photo here. Bob Brown, Pocahontas engineer, is shown to Thomas's left and Jessie Shell is shown to Brown's left. Brakeman Tommy Price, third from left, is the only other person identified in the photograph. (Courtesy of Wayne Wright.)

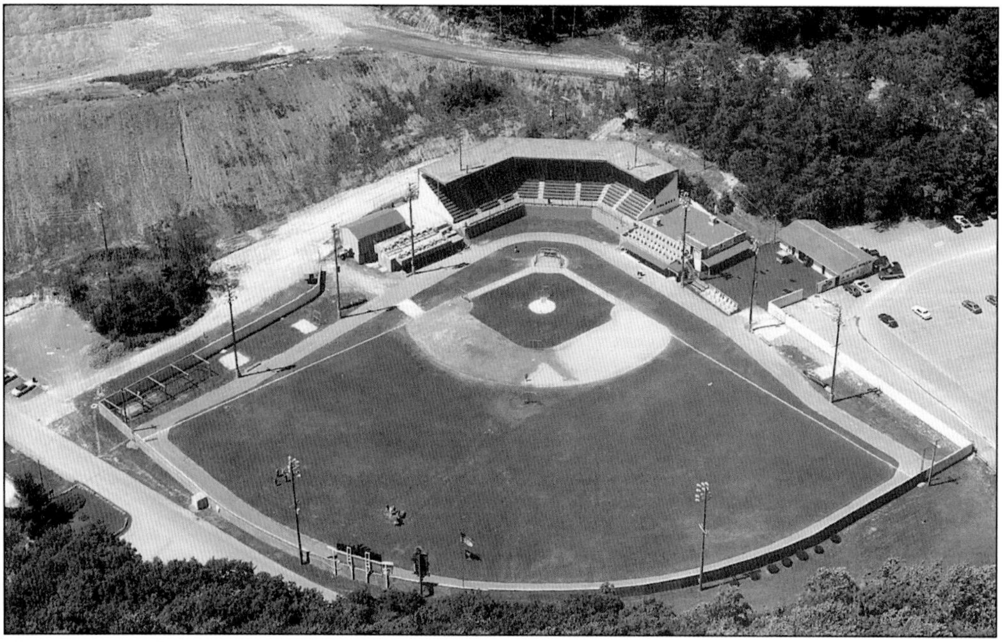

HOME OF THE BABY BIRDS. For almost 40 years, the Baltimore Orioles of Major League Baseball have maintained a Rookie League team, the "Baby Birds," at Bluefield's Bowen Field. It is the longest running affiliation between any Major League club and a city hosting a minor league club. (Photo by Mel Grubb.)

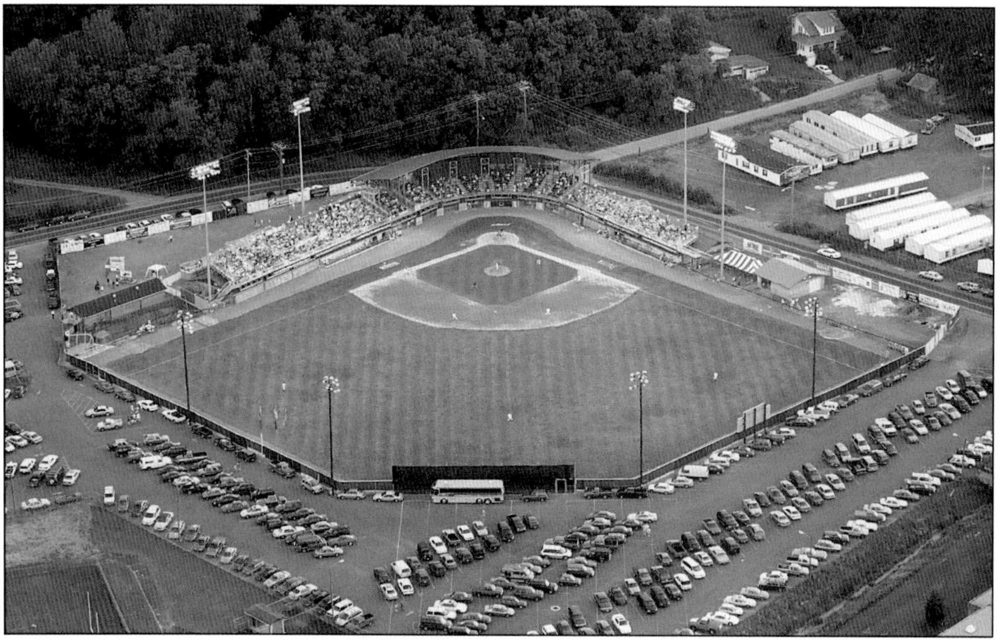

DEVIL IN THE DETAILS. Hunnicutt Stadium in Princeton is home to the Rookie League Tampa Devil Rays that perform (like Bluefield) in the Appalachian League. The Hunnicutt sports complex includes a football field that serves as home to the Princeton Senior High School Tigers football team. The photograph here was taken during the 2000 season when the new grandstand project was finished. (Photo by Mel Grubb.)

LIKE A TREE PLANTED BY THE WATER. This mighty maple tree that sits atop Crumpecker Hill on U.S. Route 460 in Green Valley was once featured in a publication of "Ripley's Believe It or Not." The tree appears to be growing out of solid rock, but local botanists speculate that its root structures penetrate into the soil through a crevice in the stone. Local reporter/editor Barbara Hawkins led the most recent fight to spare the botanical oddity from the woodsman's axe during a highway improvement project. (Photo by Eric DiNovo.)

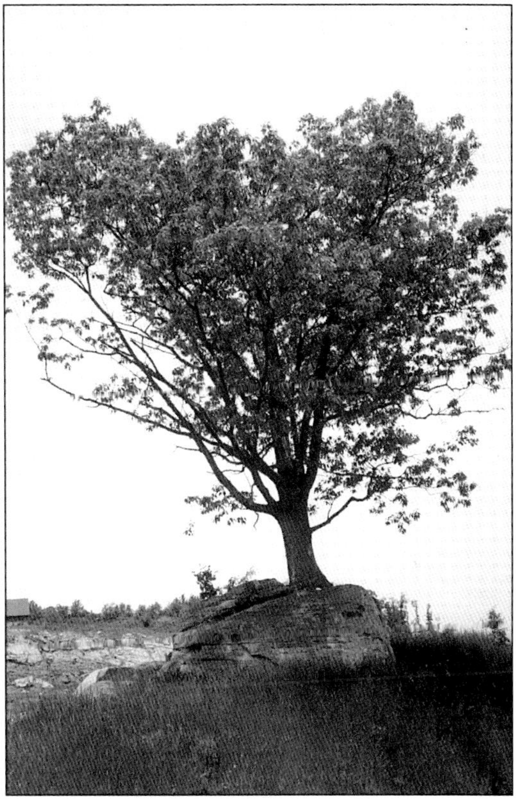

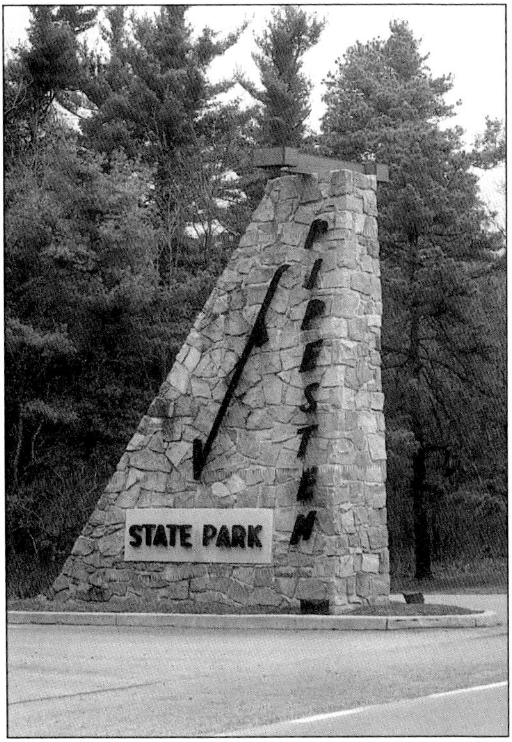

SHARED BY TWO COUNTIES. Beautiful Pipestem State Park is located on a 4,023-acre tract of land and is part of both Mercer and Summers Counties. Pipestem includes two lodges with a total of 143 rooms, two golf courses, a mountain tramway into the Bluestone River gorge, horseback riding, campsites, two swimming pools (indoor and out), and a wealth of outdoor activities. (Photo by the author.)

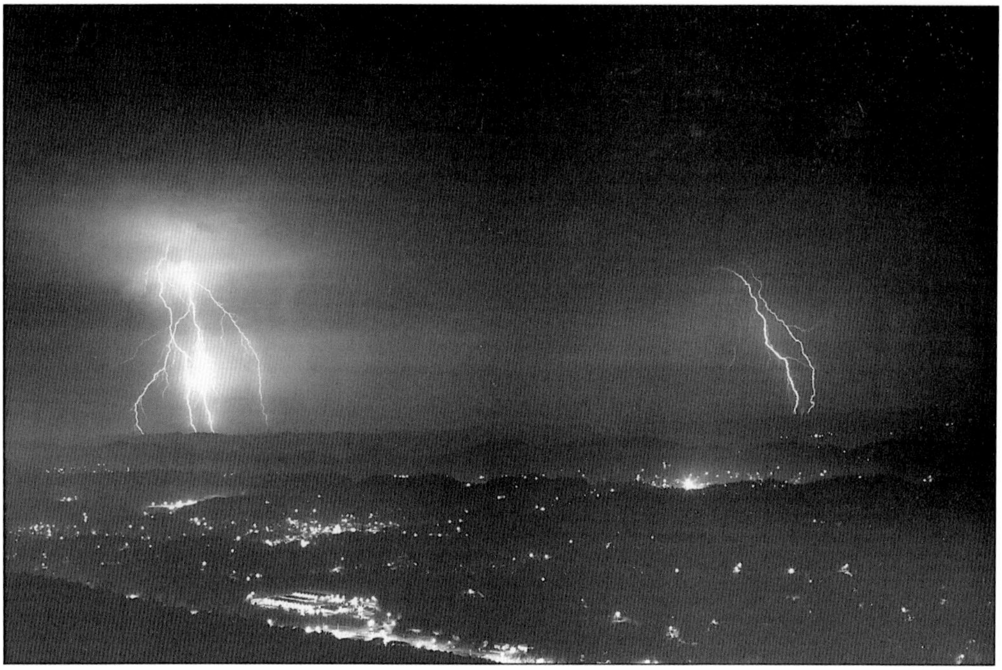

LIGHT SHOW. Famed regional photographer Mel Grubb captured this dramatic view of double lightening strikes from the East River Mountain Overlook above Bluefield. In recent years, the Greater Bluefield Chamber of Commerce spearheaded a drive to clean up the mountaintop and provide facilities for visitors. (Photo by Mel Grubb.)

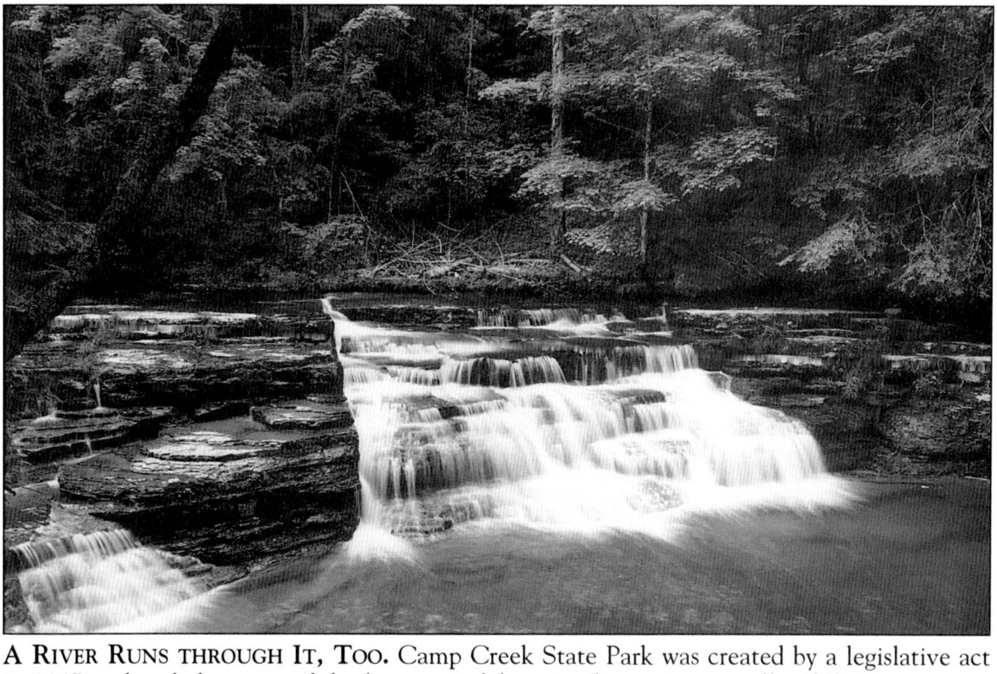

A RIVER RUNS THROUGH IT, TOO. Camp Creek State Park was created by a legislative act in 1987 and includes some of the best trout fishing in the region as well as hiking, camping, and hunting in season. The park includes 5,300 acres, although only 550 acres of that has been developed as part of the park. (Photo by Mel Grubb.)

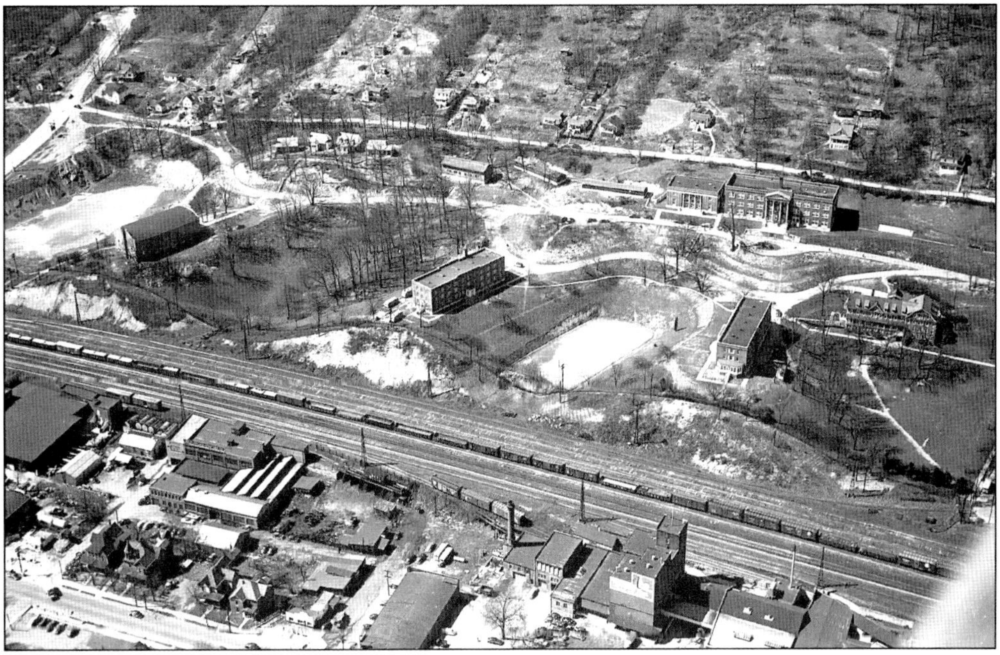

ON TERRACED HILLS. Bluefield State College, shown in this 1950s vintage photograph, was established on February 21, 1895, as a college to serve African-American students of the region. It grew through the years and became noted for both academic and athletic excellence, winning the National Colored Inter-Collegiate Athletic Association Football Championship in 1927 and 1928. (Photo by Mel Grubb.)

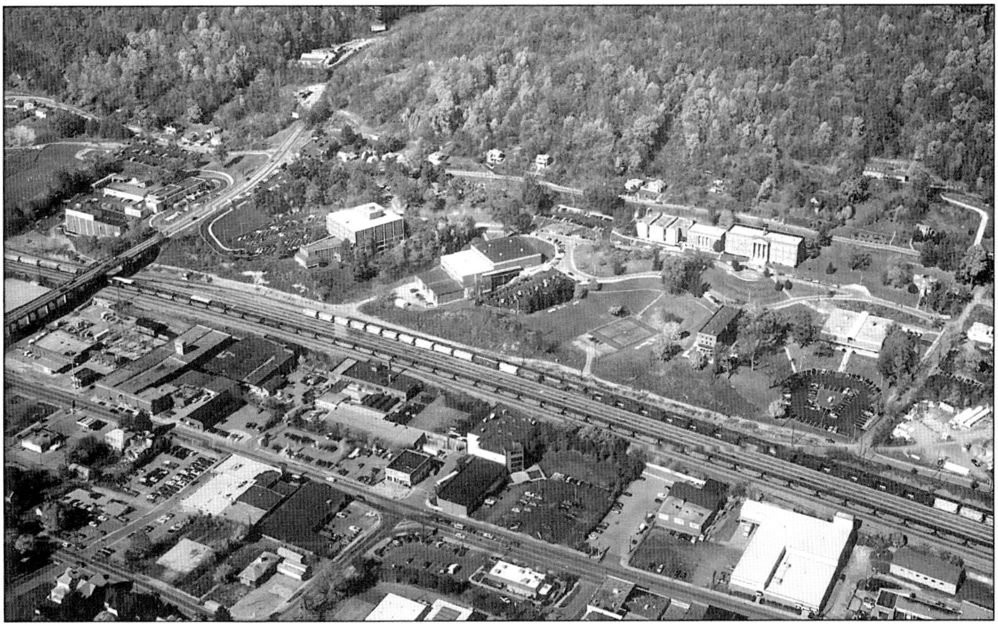

BSC TODAY. Along with integrating and making welcome students of all races, creeds, and nationalities, Bluefield State College has experienced dynamic growth in the past 40 years. Among additions through the years include Dickason Hall, west of U.S. Route 52; the Ned Shott Gymnasium; and the Othello Harris Jefferson Student Center. (Photo by Mel Grubb.)

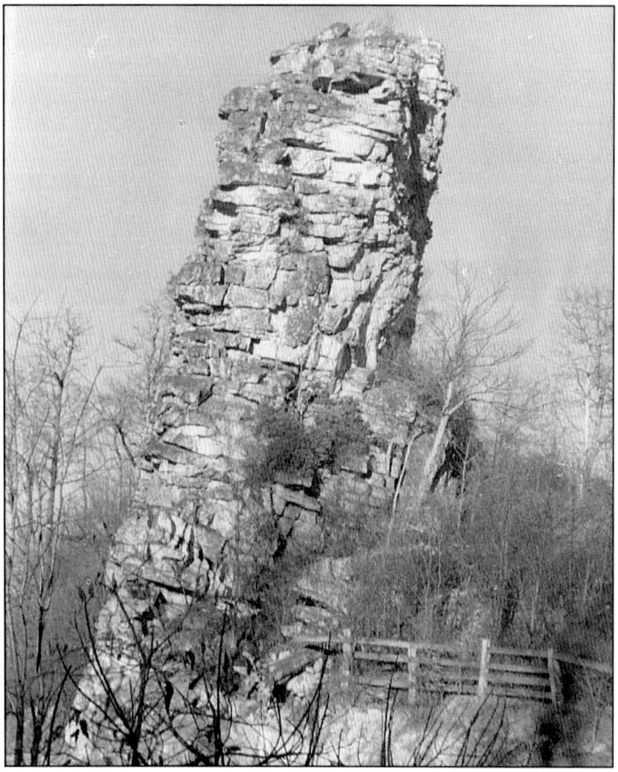

Piece of the Rock. Pinnacle Rock is one of Mercer County's most often-pictured geological formations. Created millions of years ago when the African plate slammed into North America, continental forces pushed the Upper Maxon sandstone level from horizontal to perpendicular. Pinnacle Rock is 2,700 feet above sea level. (Photo by Emory Eugene Jones Sr.; courtesy of Elizabeth Greever.)

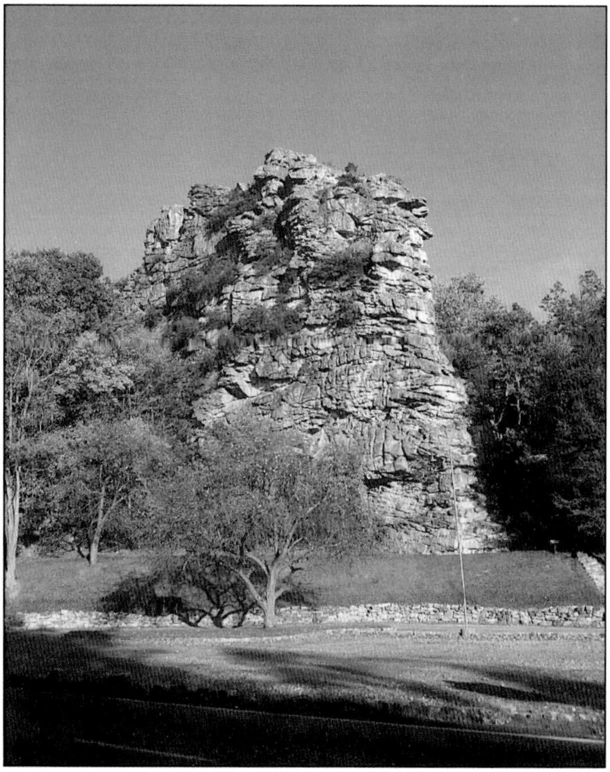

Rock and Roll. Pinnacle Rock is one of the state's smallest state parks, consisting of only 364 acres. The park offers campers picnicking and hiking for day use. (Photo by Mel Grubb.)

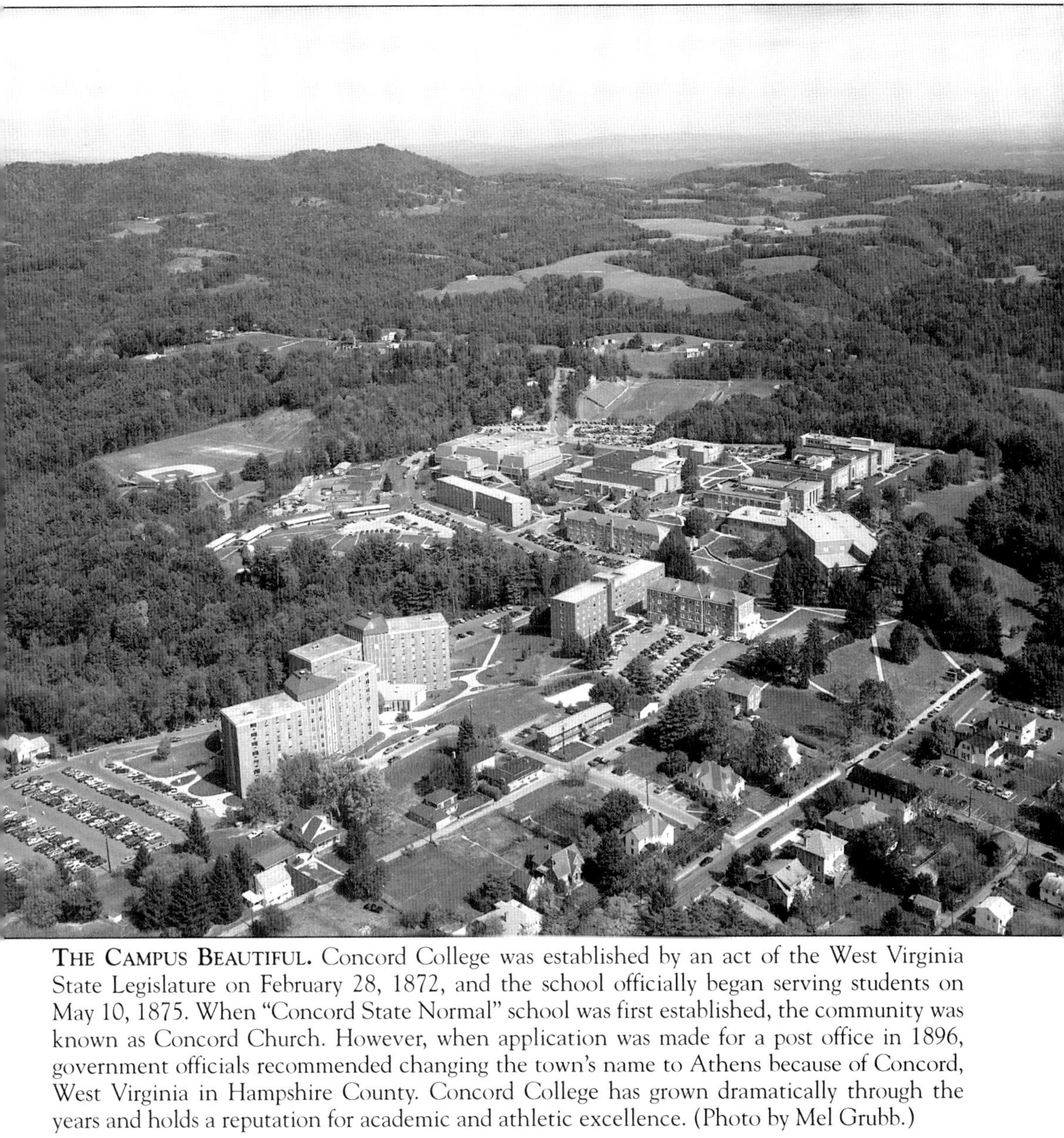

THE CAMPUS BEAUTIFUL. Concord College was established by an act of the West Virginia State Legislature on February 28, 1872, and the school officially began serving students on May 10, 1875. When "Concord State Normal" school was first established, the community was known as Concord Church. However, when application was made for a post office in 1896, government officials recommended changing the town's name to Athens because of Concord, West Virginia in Hampshire County. Concord College has grown dramatically through the years and holds a reputation for academic and athletic excellence. (Photo by Mel Grubb.)

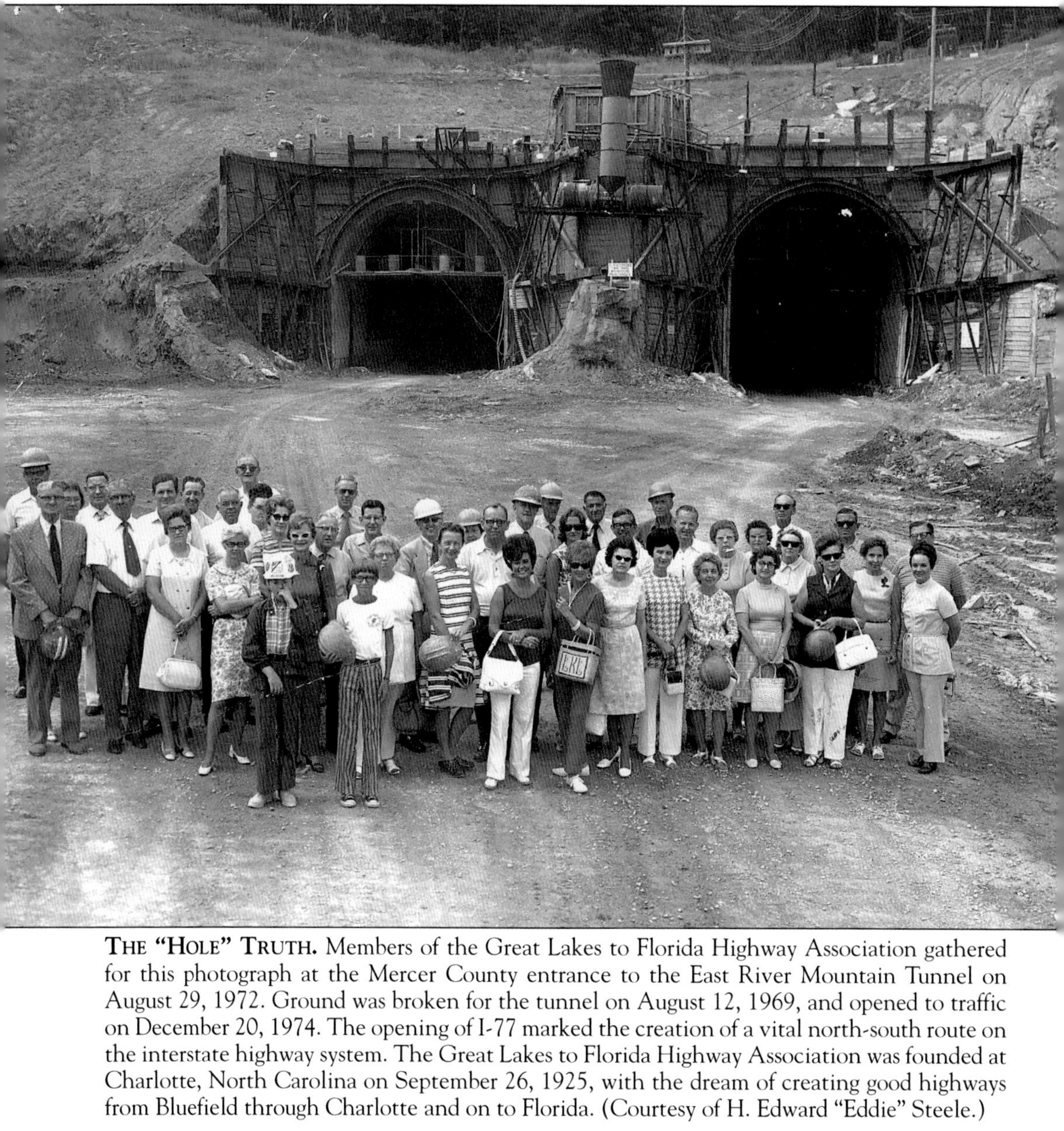

THE "HOLE" TRUTH. Members of the Great Lakes to Florida Highway Association gathered for this photograph at the Mercer County entrance to the East River Mountain Tunnel on August 29, 1972. Ground was broken for the tunnel on August 12, 1969, and opened to traffic on December 20, 1974. The opening of I-77 marked the creation of a vital north-south route on the interstate highway system. The Great Lakes to Florida Highway Association was founded at Charlotte, North Carolina on September 26, 1925, with the dream of creating good highways from Bluefield through Charlotte and on to Florida. (Courtesy of H. Edward "Eddie" Steele.)

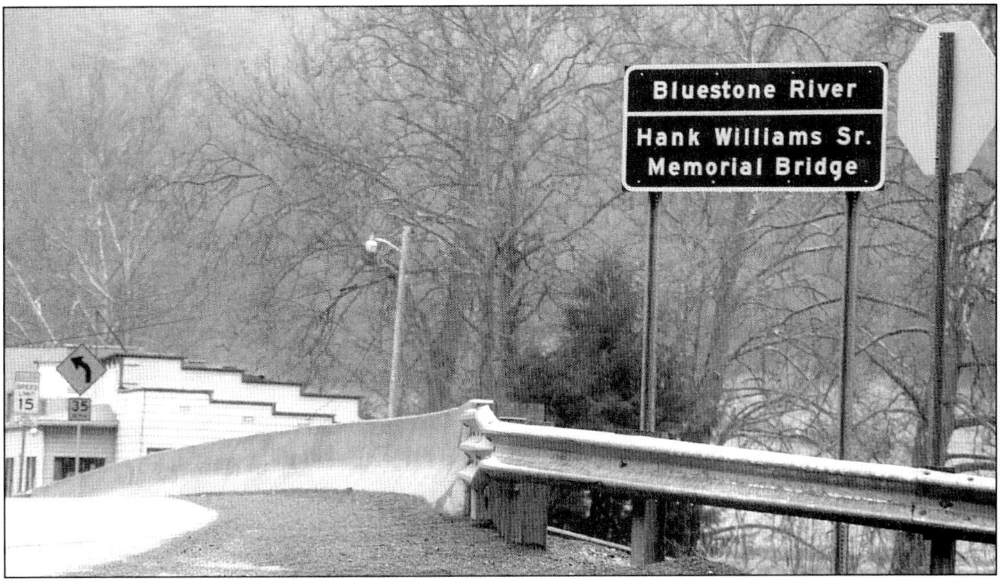

LONG, LONESOME HIGHWAY. Somewhere along this isolated stretch of U.S. Route 19 near Spanishburg, Hank Williams Sr. drew his final breath. The young, country music troubadour was discovered dead at Oak Hill, West Virginia on January 1, 1953. Williams's driver, Charles Carr, was driving the artist to a concert date in Canton, Ohio. Carr stopped at Bluefield's Dough Boy Lunch and hired Don Surface to travel with him. The bridge was dedicated in the 1990s. (Photo by the author.)

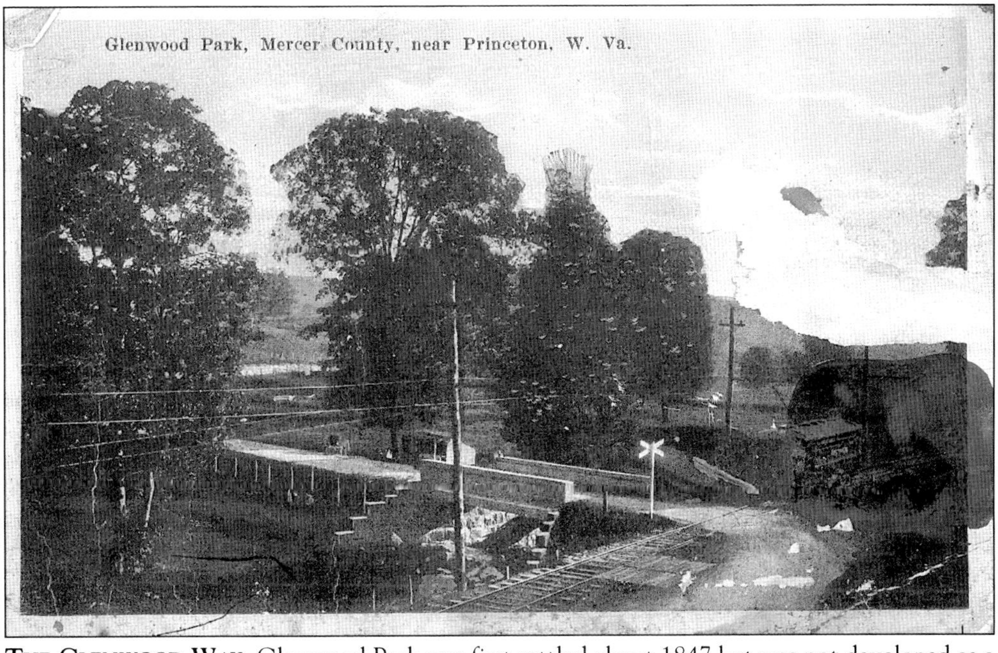

THE GLENWOOD WAY. Glenwood Park was first settled about 1847 but was not developed as a recreation area until about 1916 when Sam Evans built a pool there for swimming and boating. An accidental drowning not long after the pool opened forced officials to drain the pool. The area was acquired by the county in 1935 and developed as a 4-H Camp. (Courtesy of Rick and Jeanie Owens.)

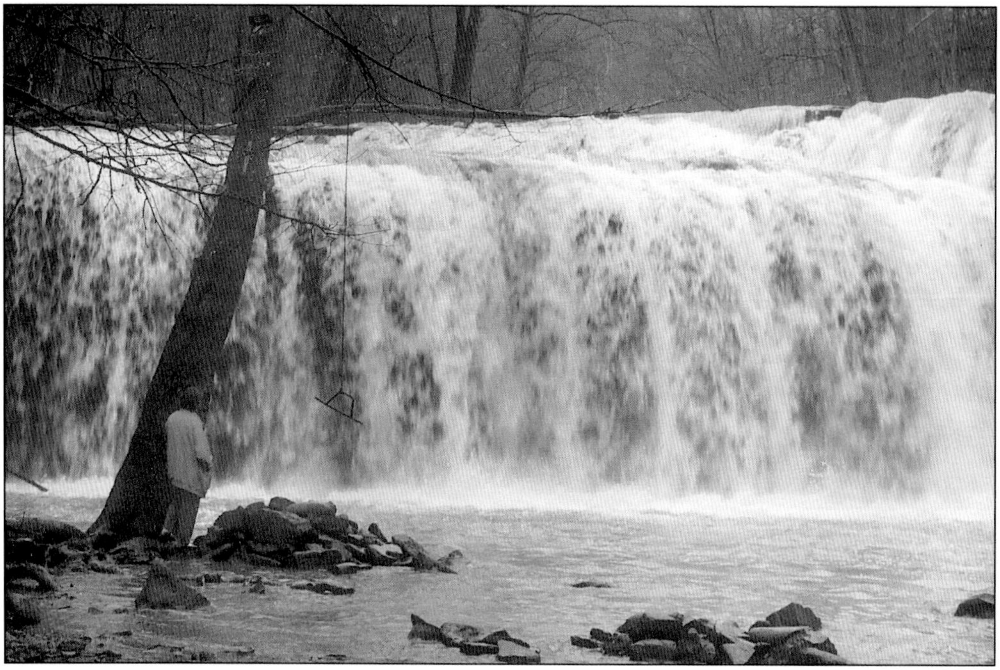

POWERFUL WATERS. Brush Creek Falls is one of Mercer County's most spectacular attractions that remains essentially undeveloped. Accessible by a rough, unimproved road, the 30-foot-high falls is within a quarter mile of I-77. The last commercial operation there was a gristmill that went out of business *c.* 1910. (Photo by the author.)

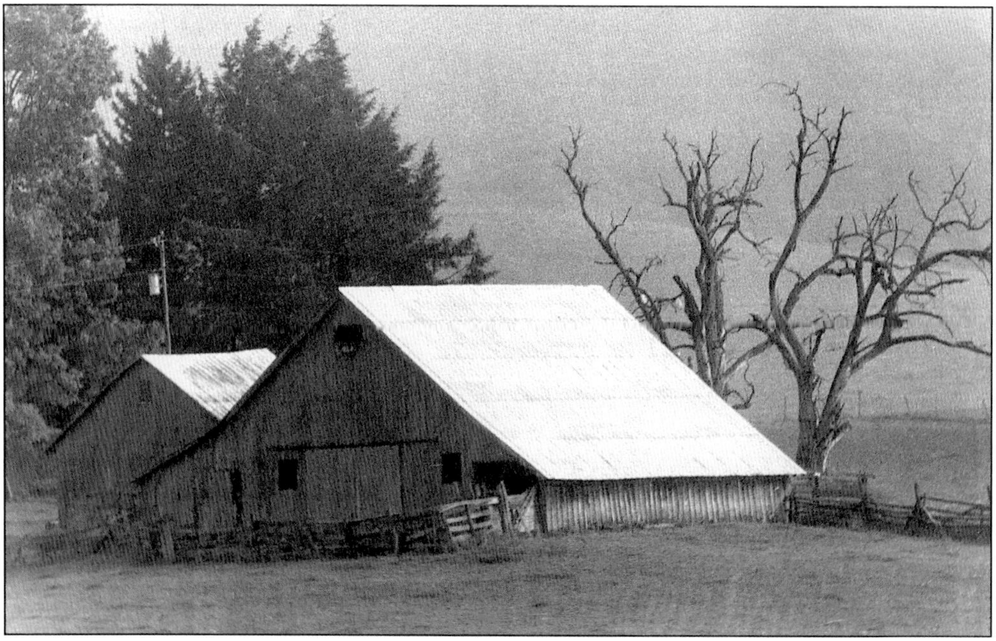

BARN DANCE. While timber and coal attracted the most migration into Mercer County, the first settlers came to develop the region's farmland. There is still a respectable farming community in the county and a decent trade at the local farmers' market each Saturday in Princeton. (Photo by Evonda Archer.)

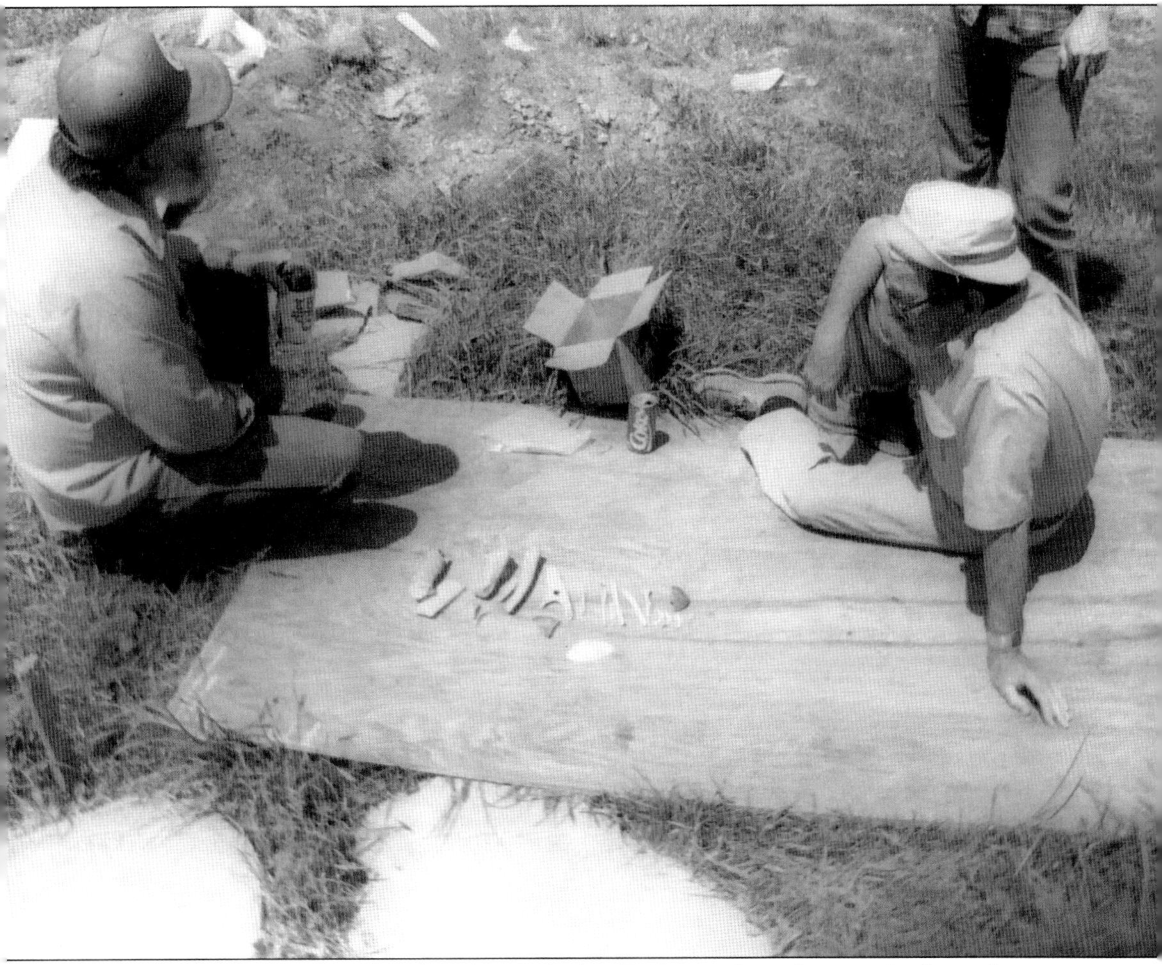

CAN YOU DIG IT? Noted local archaeologist, the late E. Eugene Jones Jr., seated right, is shown examining some of the Native American artifacts discovered during a 1988 excavation of the Snidow Site at Lake Shawnee. Local archaeologists—often aided by professors and students from Marshall University and elsewhere—were able to make incredible finds at the site that provided new insights into the pre-Columbian settlers of Mercer County. Jones is shown above with property owner Gaylord White Sr. (Photo by Evonda Archer.)

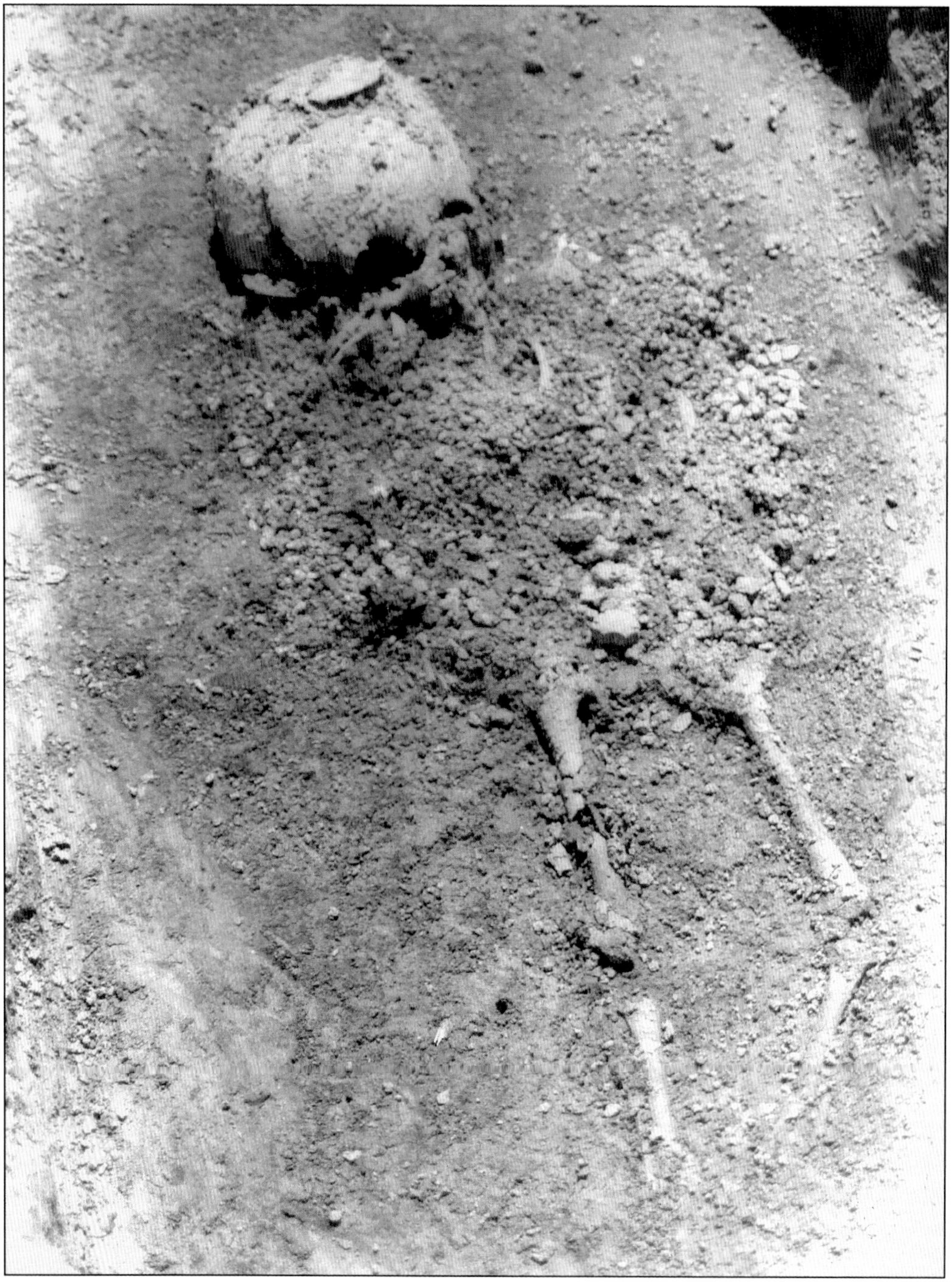

KNOWN BUT TO GOD. In 1671, when Thomas Batts and Robert Fallon made their initial exploration of what is now Mercer County, they found recently abandoned Indian villages but no native people. For years, historians believed there were no indigenous people living in West Virginia when Columbus arrived in the New World, but Gene Jones's findings at the Snidow Site on the banks of the Bluestone River shattered that myth. Glass beads and trade goods found at the site indicate contact between native people as recently as Fort Ancient culture, which thrived from 1100 to 1650. (Photo by Evonda Archer.)

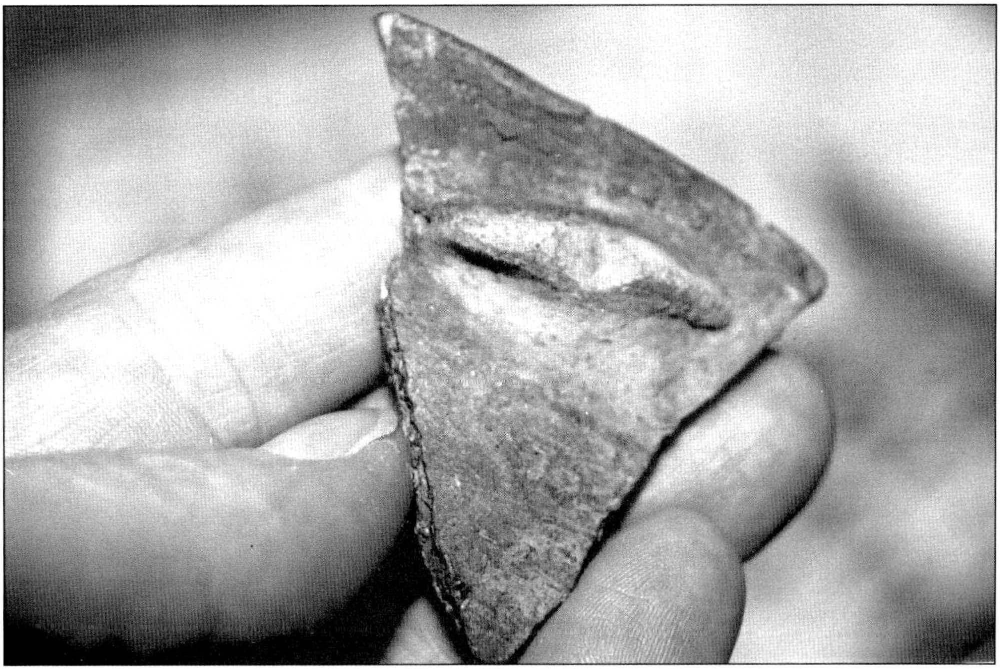

UNCOMMON DENOMINATOR. While searching for Native American artifacts at the Snidow Site in 1989, E. Eugene Jones discovered a pottery chard that was common to the native people living in the immediate vicinity as well as other "tribes" of the Fort Ancient times. (Photo by the author.)

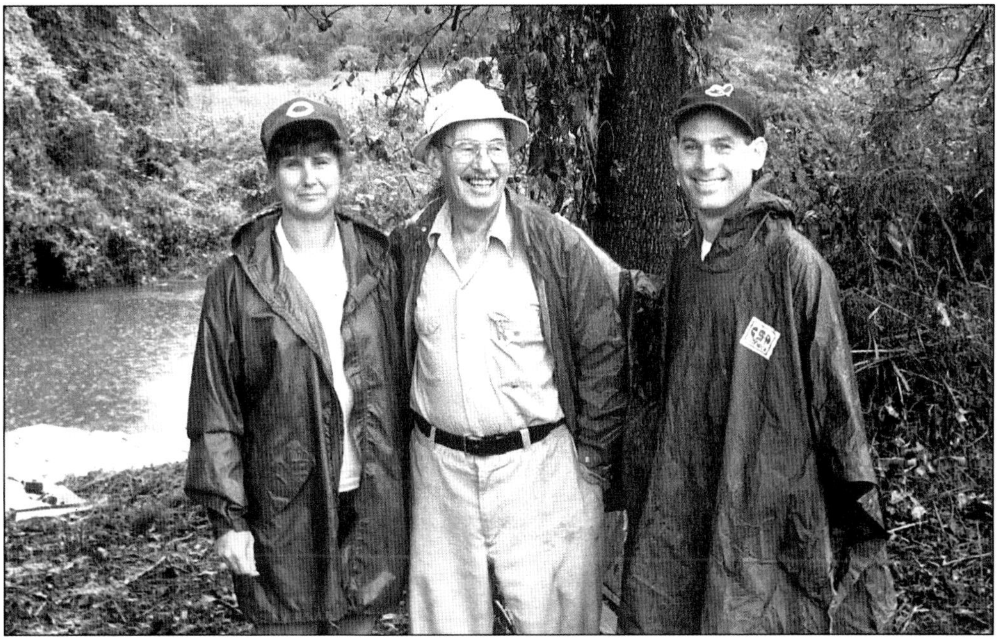

A SHORE BET. Concord College field researcher Faye Vint, local archaeologist E. Eugene Jones, and visiting archaeologist Dr. David Fuerst paused for a photograph on the banks of the Bluestone River at Lake Shawnee during the 1989 dig. Dr. Fuerst was among the last to mount an effort to launch a large-scale excavation at the site. (Photo by the author.)

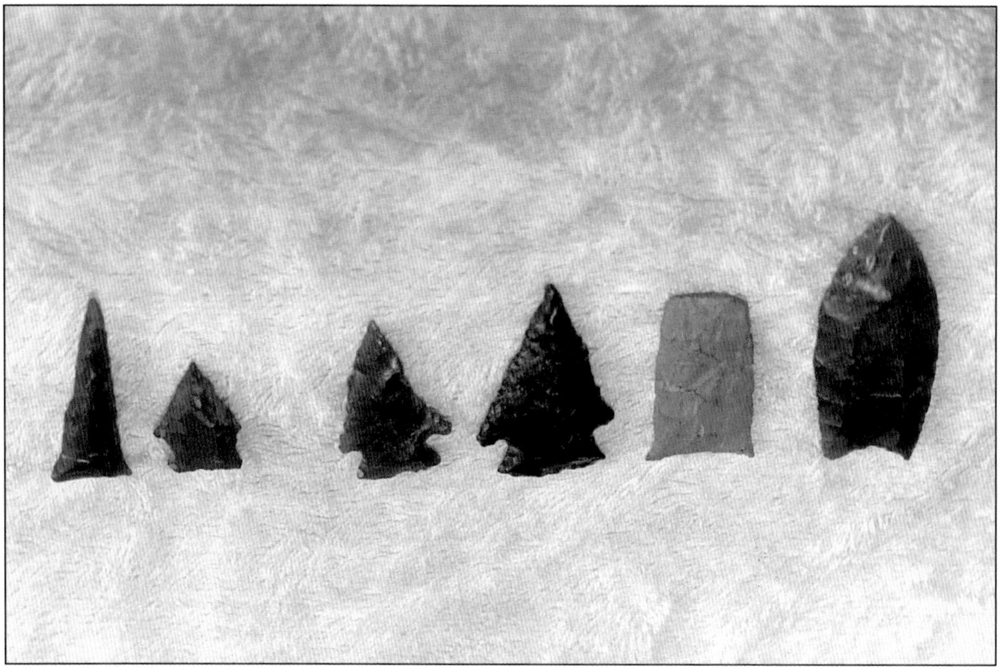

POINTS OF INTEREST. E. Eugene Jones Jr. discovered a wealth of Native American projectile points at the Snidow Site in Mercer County including several examples from the Woodlands Period as well as some earlier points. (Photo by Evonda Archer.)

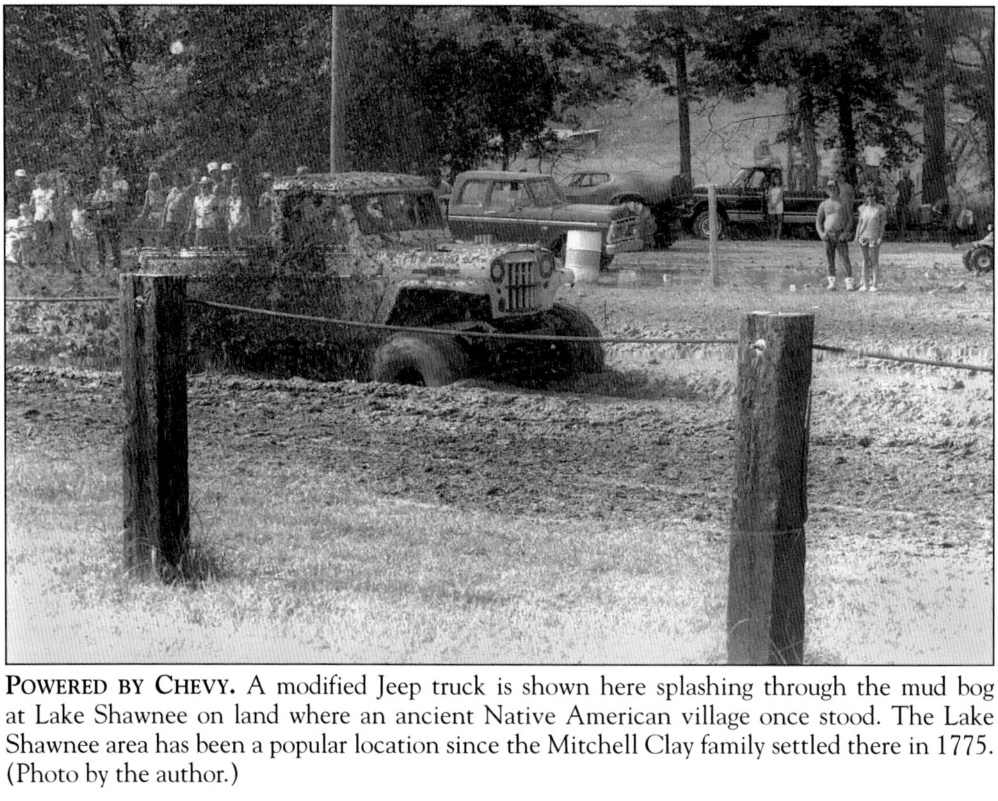

POWERED BY CHEVY. A modified Jeep truck is shown here splashing through the mud bog at Lake Shawnee on land where an ancient Native American village once stood. The Lake Shawnee area has been a popular location since the Mitchell Clay family settled there in 1775. (Photo by the author.)

LOG CABIN DAYS. The photo above shows a rear view of the Old Davidson Home, one of the few remaining log structures dating from the years before the city was founded. The structure has been restored and is now in Bluefield City Park. (Photo by Evonda Archer.)

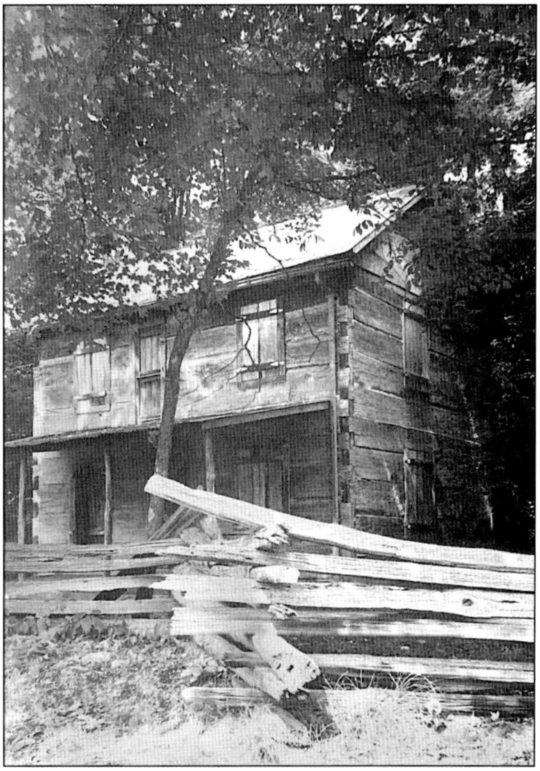

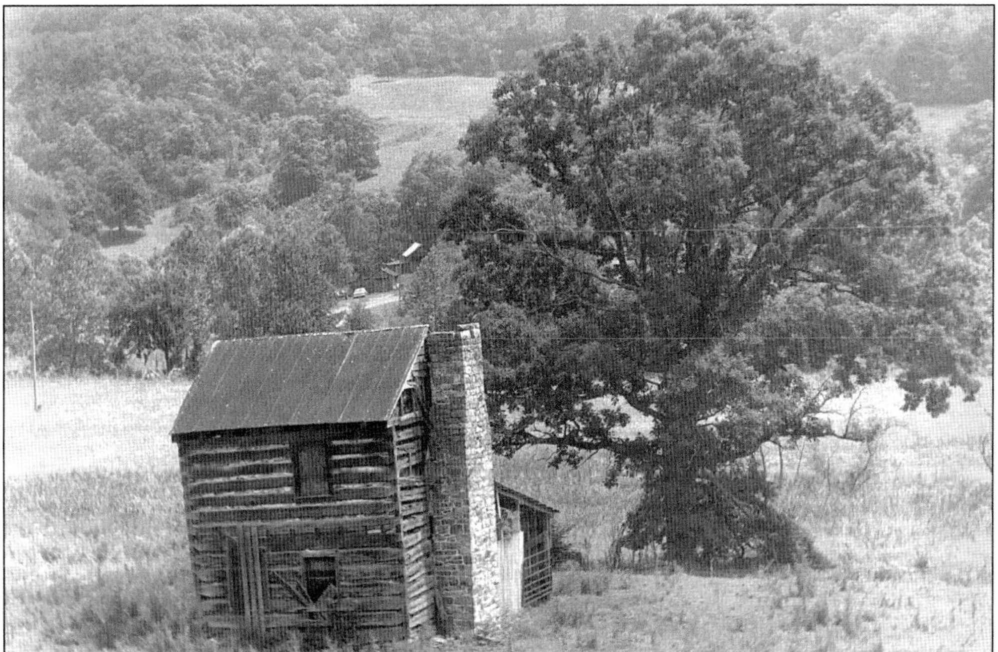

CABIN BY A TREE. There are still some log cabins located in isolated parts of Mercer County, but very few reminders of the region's pioneering past remain. This is the Wall house on Route 20 near New Hope (Photo by Evonda Archer.)

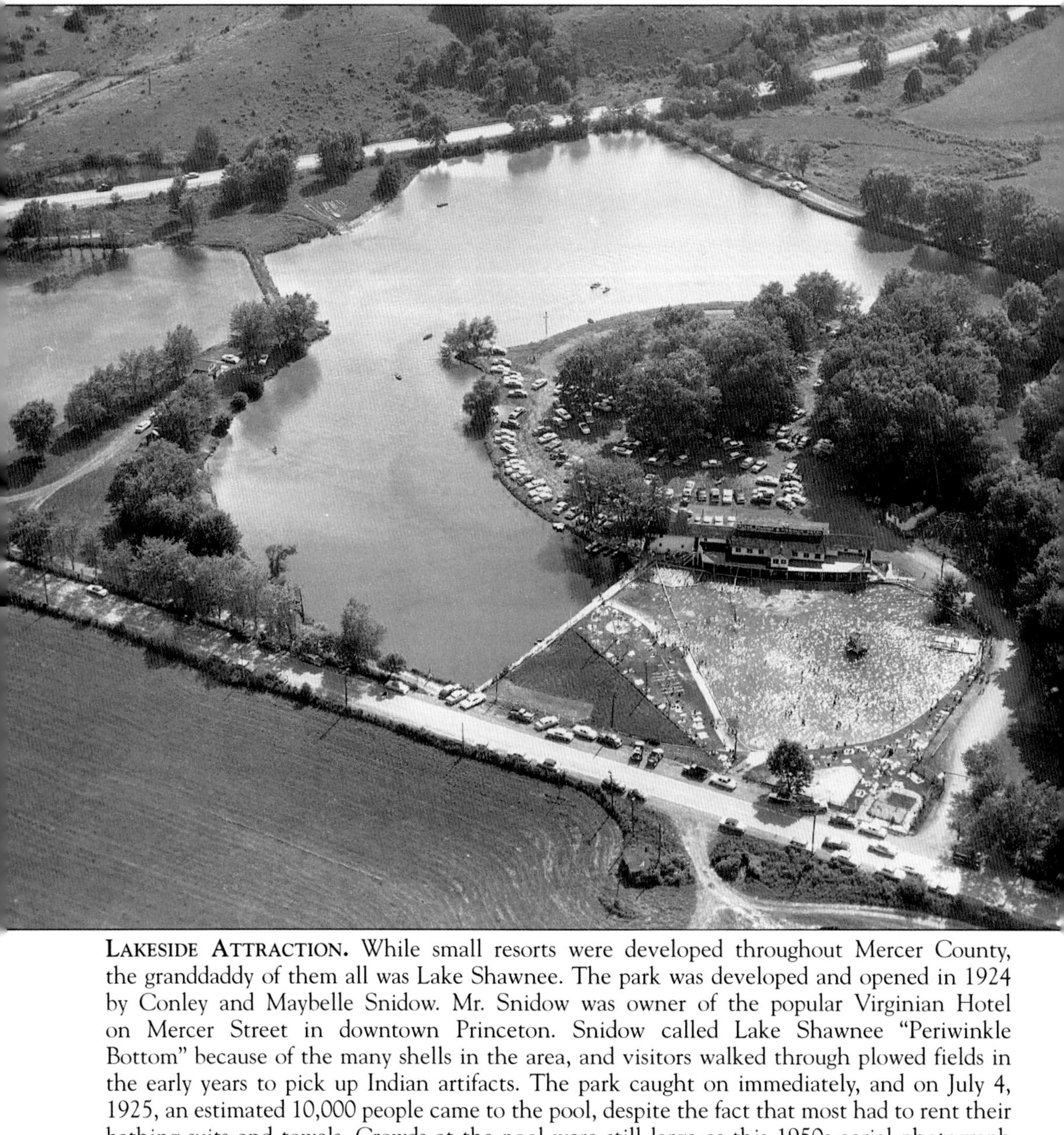

LAKESIDE ATTRACTION. While small resorts were developed throughout Mercer County, the granddaddy of them all was Lake Shawnee. The park was developed and opened in 1924 by Conley and Maybelle Snidow. Mr. Snidow was owner of the popular Virginian Hotel on Mercer Street in downtown Princeton. Snidow called Lake Shawnee "Periwinkle Bottom" because of the many shells in the area, and visitors walked through plowed fields in the early years to pick up Indian artifacts. The park caught on immediately, and on July 4, 1925, an estimated 10,000 people came to the pool, despite the fact that most had to rent their bathing suits and towels. Crowds at the pool were still large as this 1950s aerial photograph shows, but soon after, improved highways made other resort locations more accessible. (Photo by Mel Grubb.)

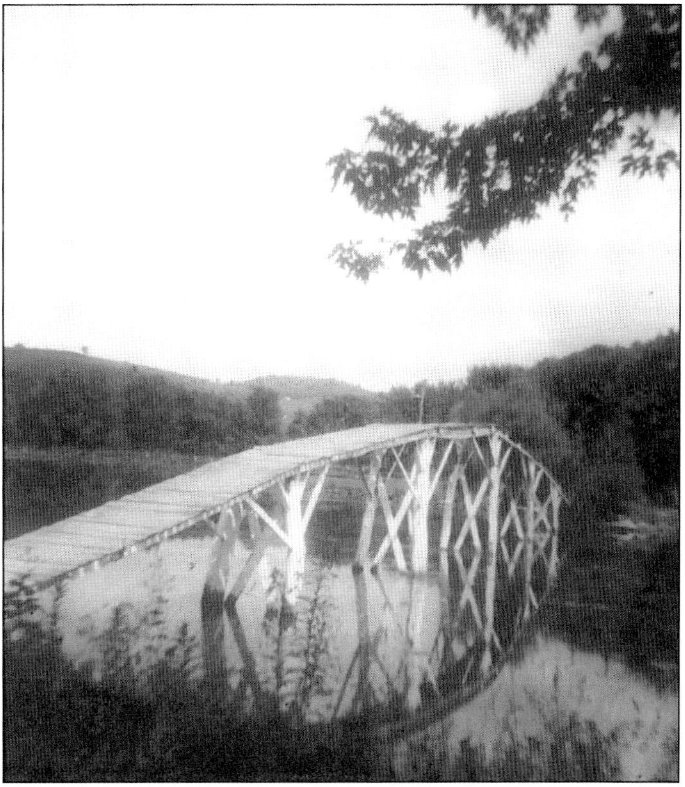

Board Walk. The wooden footbridge across Lake Shawnee was just one of several new attractions in the early 1940s that brought tourists to the lake. (Courtesy of Doug Campbell.)

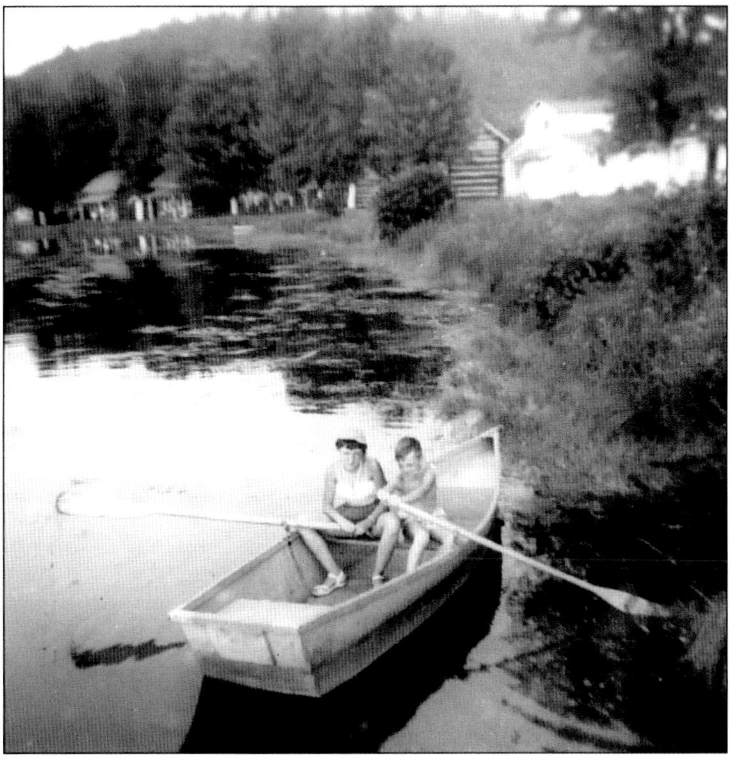

Boat People. Lois Campbell and her son, prominent local attorney Doug Campbell, are shown paddling around Lake Shawnee in a rowboat c. 1945. (Courtesy of Doug Campbell.)

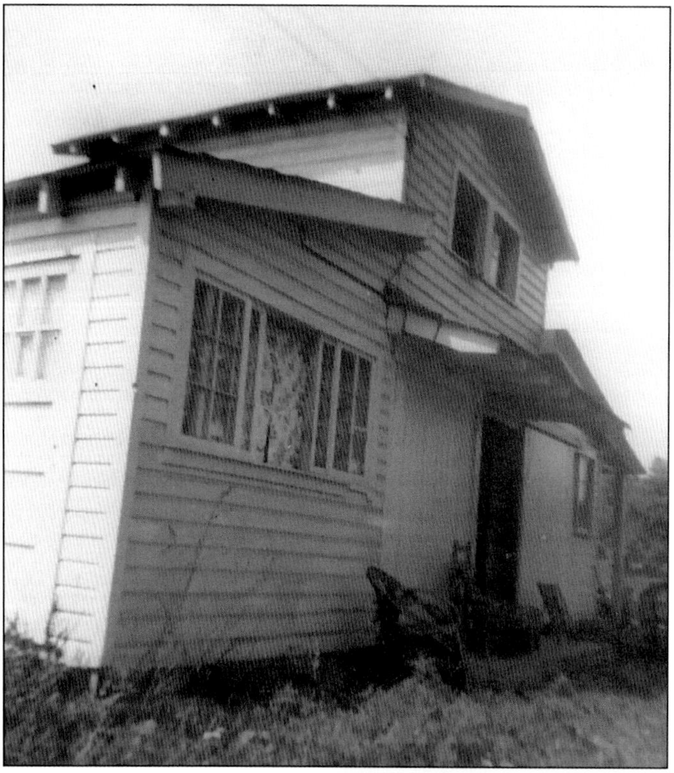

By the Sea. Lake Shawnee cottages like the one shown above were available for rent throughout the summer season. At the height of Lake Shawnee's popularity, there were a total of 17 rental cottages that went for a cost of $10 per week. The resort also featured a lodge. (Courtesy of Doug Campbell.)

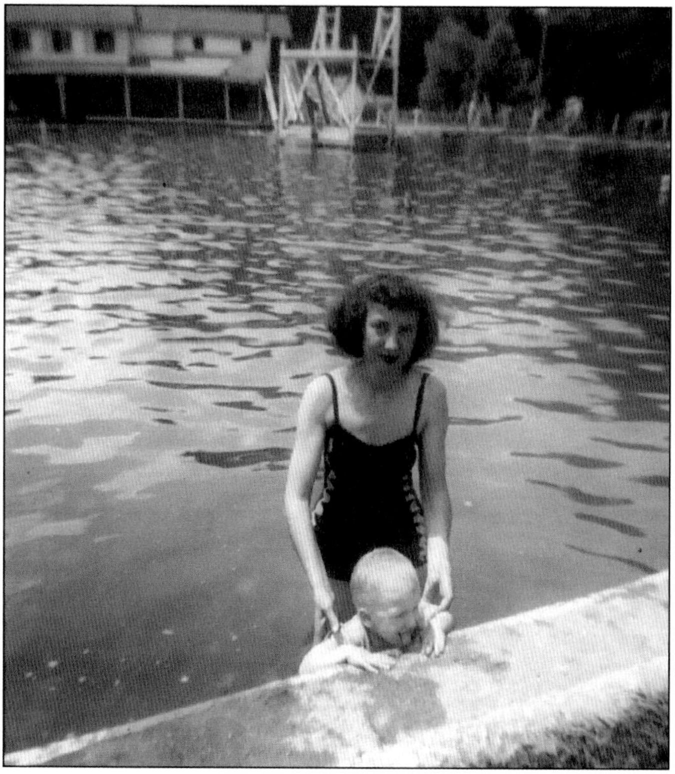

Poolside. Helen VanCuron is shown above in the Lake Shawnee pool with her daughter, Joyce Sue VanCuron, c. 1945. Helen's husband is editor of the *Harlan Daily Enterprise* newspaper. (Courtesy of Doug Campbell.)

Four

PEOPLE

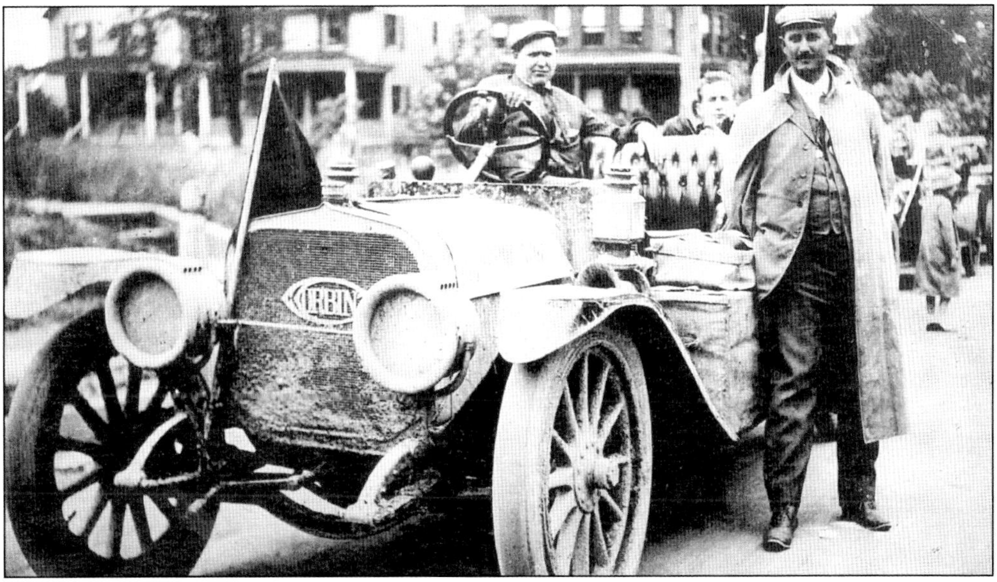

POWER PIONEER. Tom Cooper is shown here standing beside the touring car he used in an endurance race from Atlanta to New York City in 1910. Tom's brother, John Cooper, developed the Mill Creek Coal Mine in 1884—the first mine in Mercer County, but Tom's arrival in Bramwell in 1910 was said to have created quite a stir.

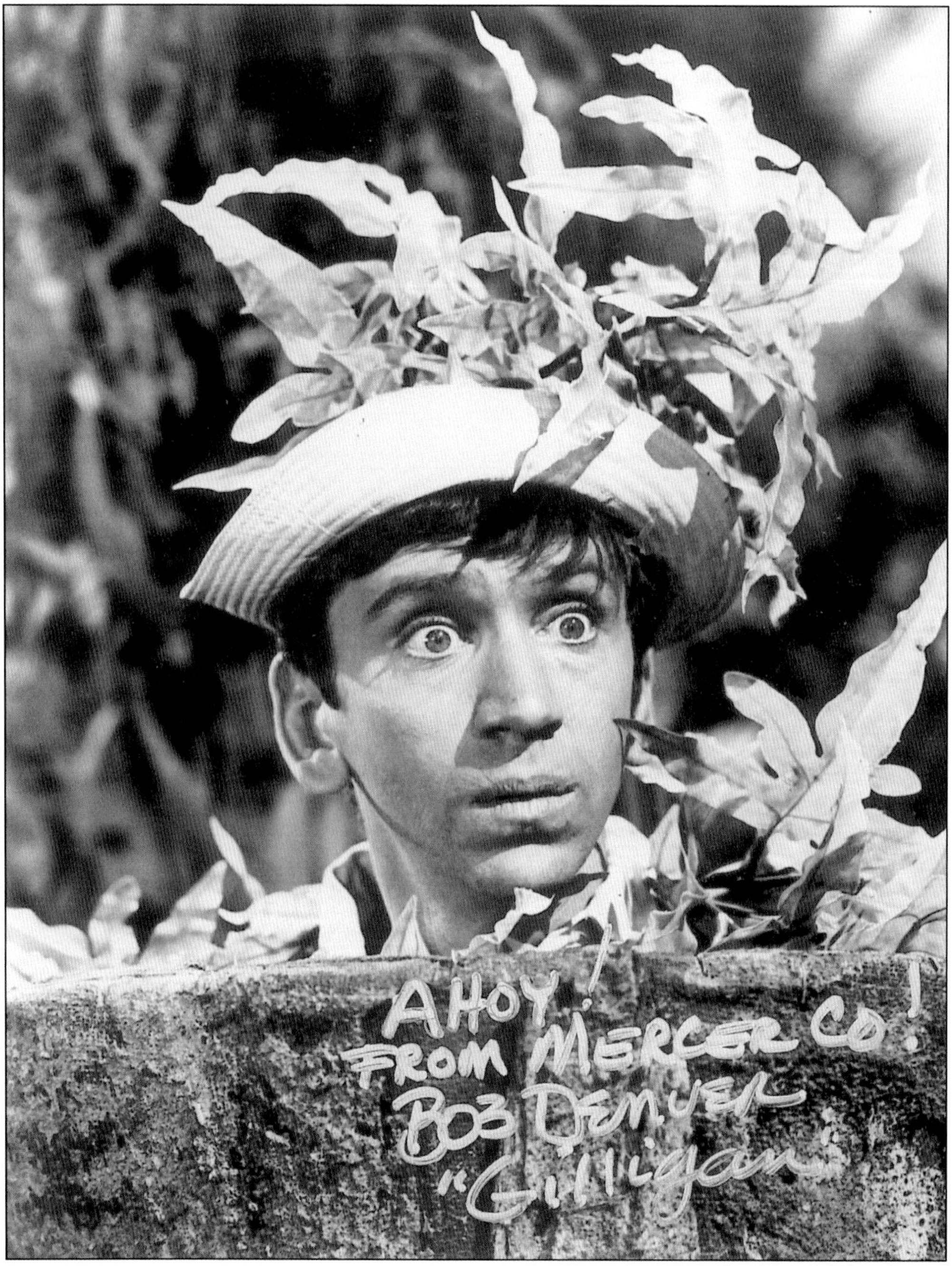

LIKE, HI MAYNARD. Bob Denver, shown above, played Maynard G. Krebs in the popular 1959 television show *Dobie Gillis*, then followed that by playing the title character of Willy Gilligan in the still popular *Gilligan's Island* series of 1964. Bob met his wife, Dreama Denver, while performing together in a summer stock theater. They, along with their son Colin, moved to Princeton in 1991, and have become active participants in programs that benefit the community. (Courtesy of Bob Denver.)

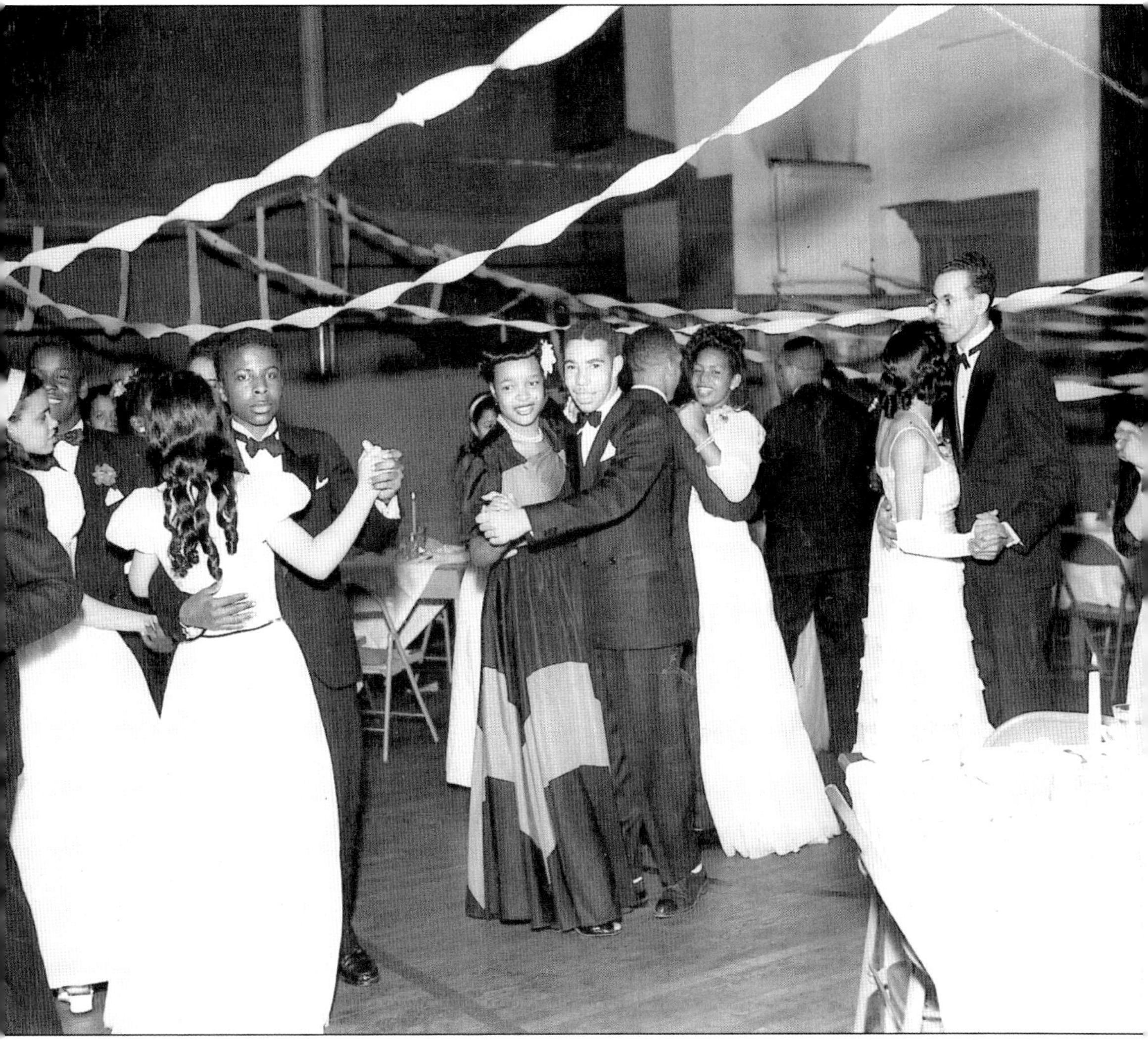

A Formal Affair. Students of Bluefield's Genoa High School are shown here at a formal dance in the school's auditorium. Genoa was a center of activity in the community for many years. The school was closed after the new Park Central High School was opened on the city's North Side. (Courtesy of Juanita Willis.)

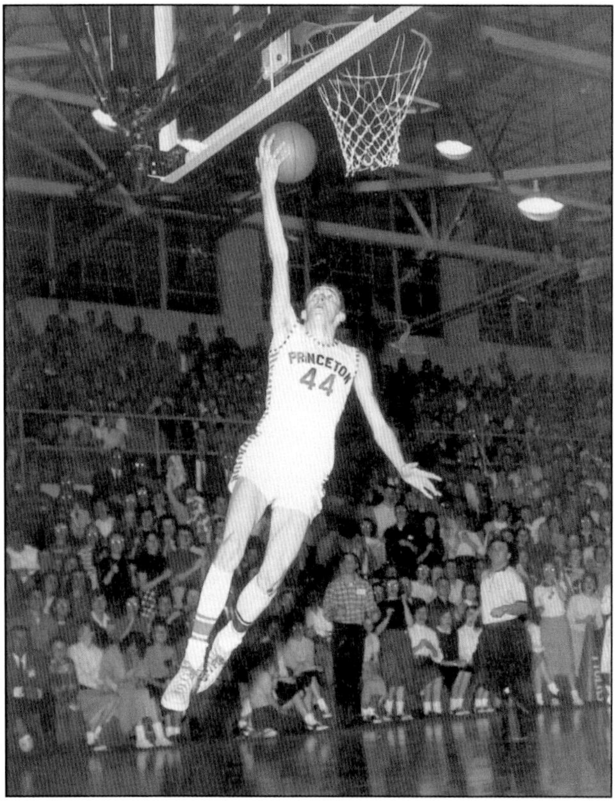

Highest Height. Rod Thorn graduated from Princeton Senior High School in 1959 after earning All-State honors for three consecutive years and scoring an incredible 2,241 points in his high school career. He went on to earn All-American honors at West Virginia University, and after a successful professional career, he became a coach. He was the coach of the Chicago Bulls who drafted Michael Jordan into the NBA. (Courtesy of Joe and Jackie Thorn.)

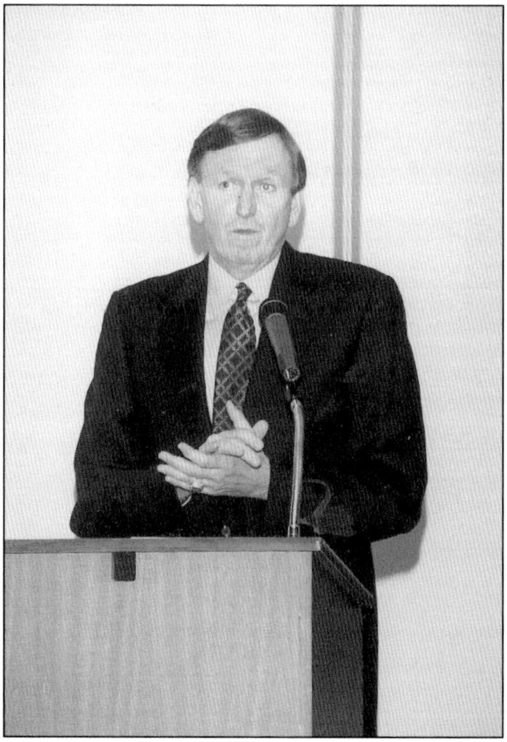

Back at Home. Rod Thorn returned to his Princeton home in 1999 to serve as speaker for the 72nd annual dinner meeting of the Princeton/Mercer County Chamber of Commerce. At that time, he was vice president of operations for the NBA. He has since become president of the New Jersey Nets. His parents still live in Princeton. (Photo by Alex Crookshanks.)

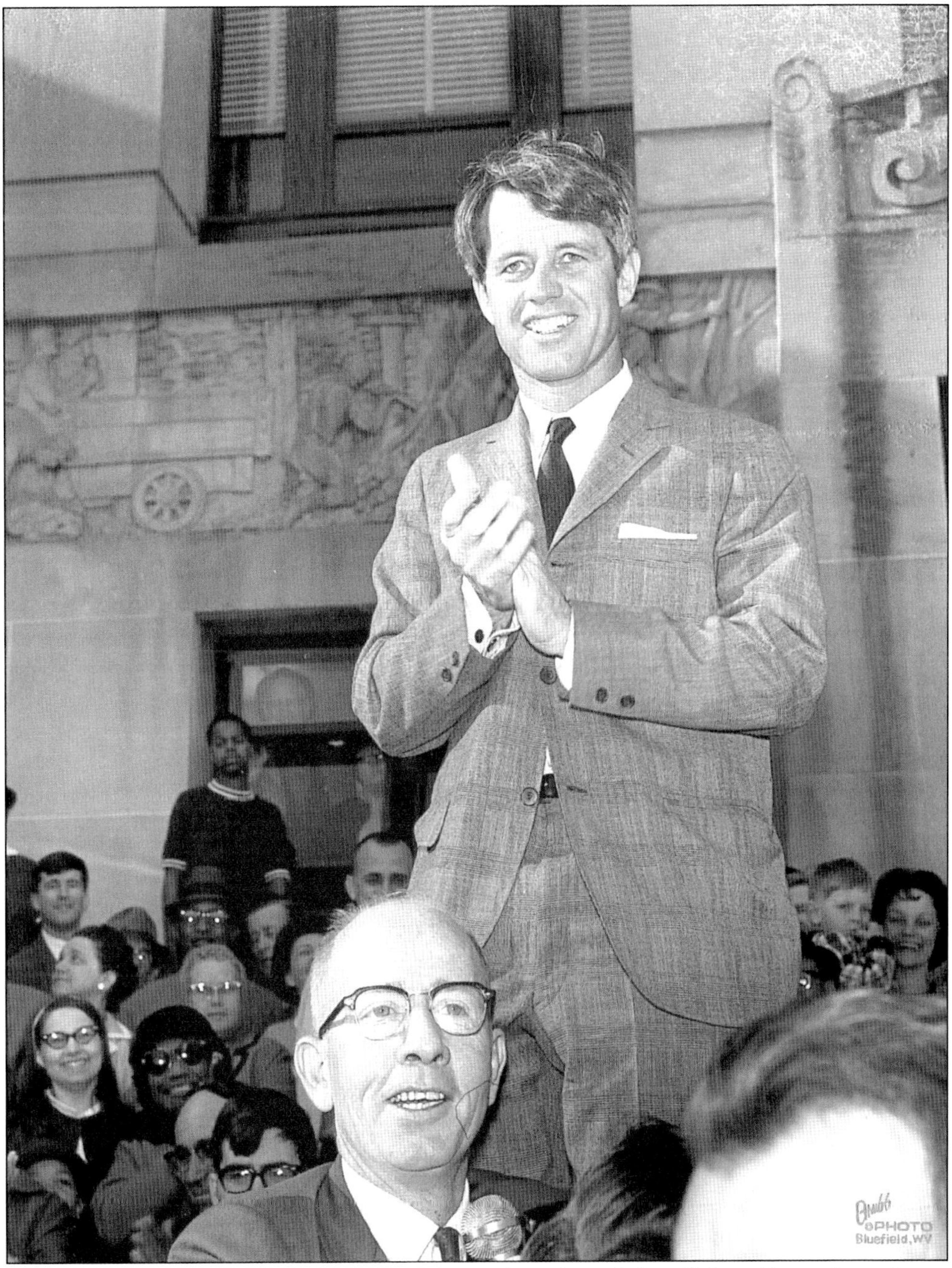

MAN OF THE MOMENT. Democratic Party presidential candidate Robert Kennedy is shown here campaigning on the steps of the Mercer County Courthouse prior to the West Virginia Primary in 1968. At the time, Kennedy was on his way to becoming the frontrunner for the nomination. An assassin cut Kennedy's life short a few weeks after his appearance in Princeton. Local photographer Mel Grubb loaned Kennedy his ladder so he could stand and address the crowd. Judge Howard M. Jarrett is shown in the foreground. (Photo by Mel Grubb.)

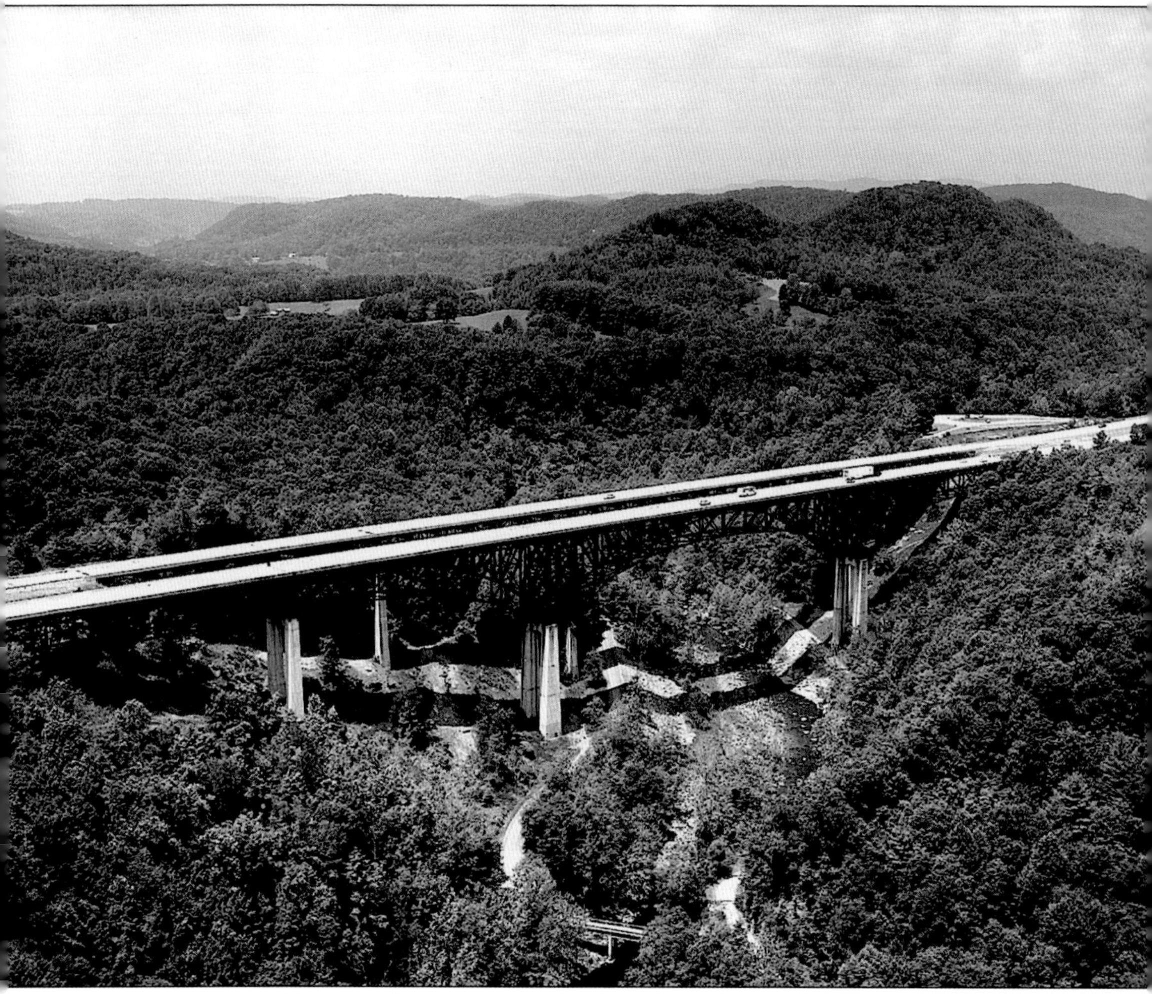

BRIDGE TO THE FUTURE. The opening of the Cornelius Charlton Bridge on the West Virginia Turnpike and the subsequent dedication of the highway on September 2, 1954, signaled an absolutely new age in southern West Virginia travel. Special ceremonies were held in Princeton and in Beckley. Brig. Gen. Charles R. Fox gave the dedication speech at the bridge, with "Taps" performed by Clarence Edmundson and Wayland Redden. Sergeant Cornelius H. Charlton was awarded the Congressional Medal of Honor for valor in action on June 2, 1951, near Chipo-ri, Korea. He was born in East Gulf but had lived in several area coal camps during his youth. (Photo by Mel Grubb.)

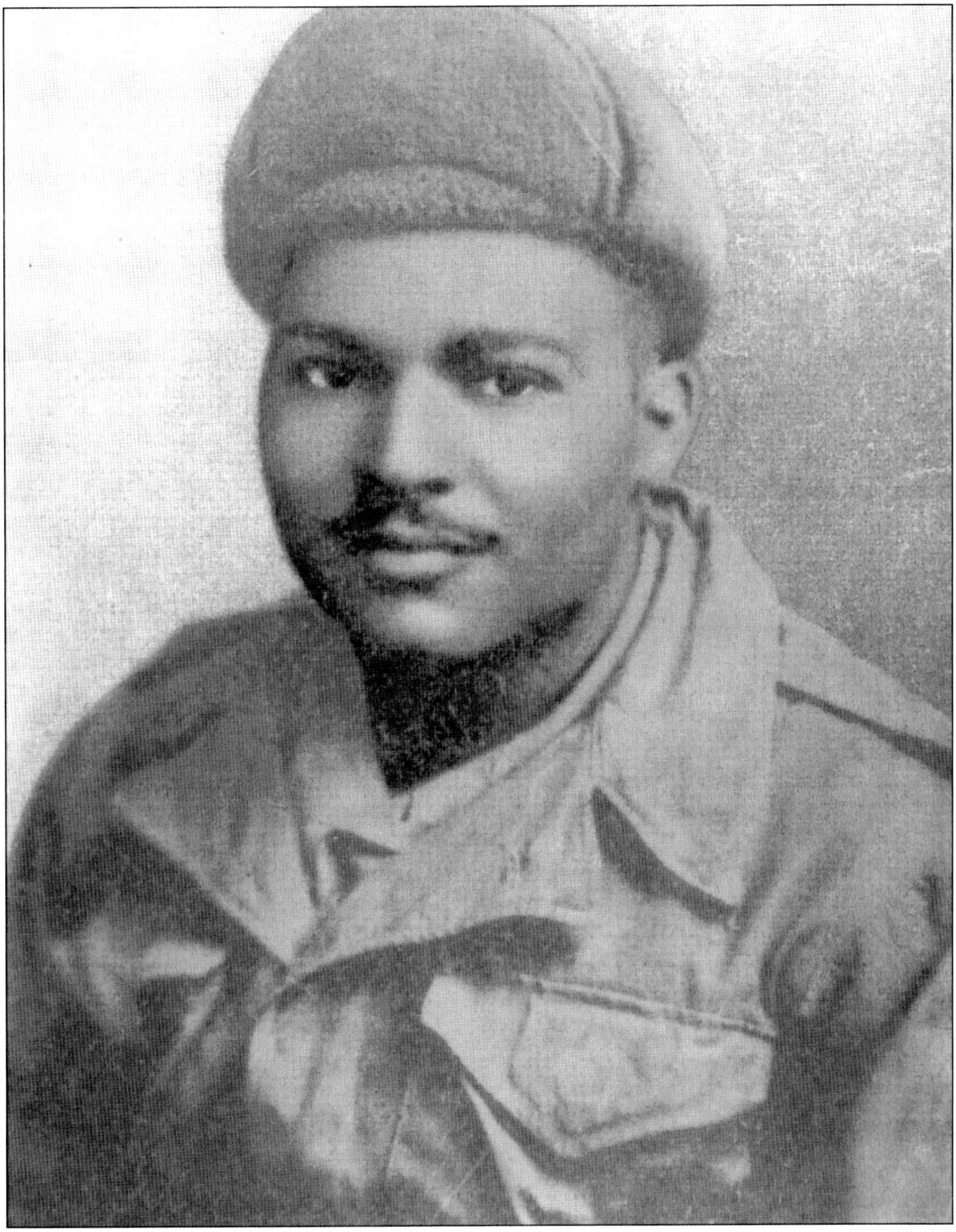

HERO. Sgt. Cornelius Charlton was one of two African-American soldiers who received the Congressional Medal of Honor during the Korean War. While he fought in an integrated U.S. Army, many of the institutions at home remained segregated—including Arlington National Cemetery where Congressional Medal of Honor recipients are often buried. Charlton's remains were brought to the Bryant Cemetery, a black cemetery near Bramwell, where he was interred until his body was removed and taken to Beckley's American Legion Cemetery on March 10, 1990. The U.S. Army would later call the situation involving Charlton's burial an "administrative error." Charlton was one of 43 West Virginians to have received the nation's highest honor for valor in combat. (Courtesy of Mr. and Mrs. Arthur Charlton.)

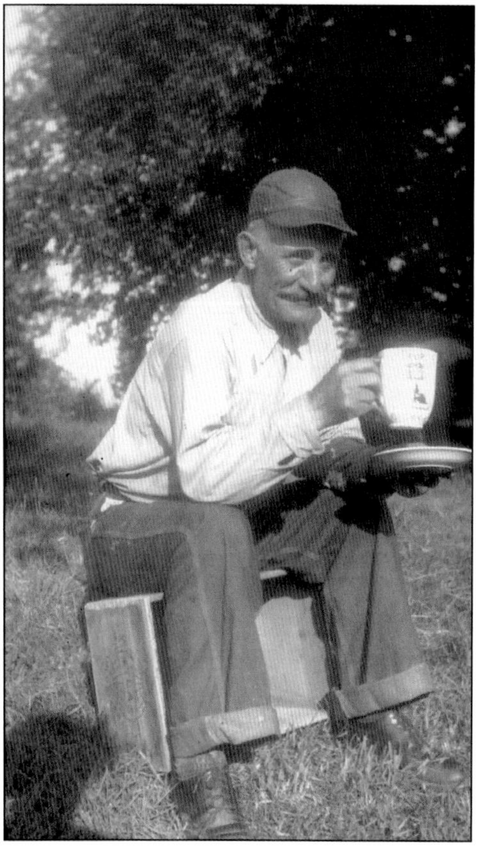

Mighty Good Coffee. Oscar Levi Harman, a longtime Mill Creek Coal & Coke Company employee and resident of Coopers, is shown here enjoying a relaxing moment. (Courtesy of Betty Goins.)

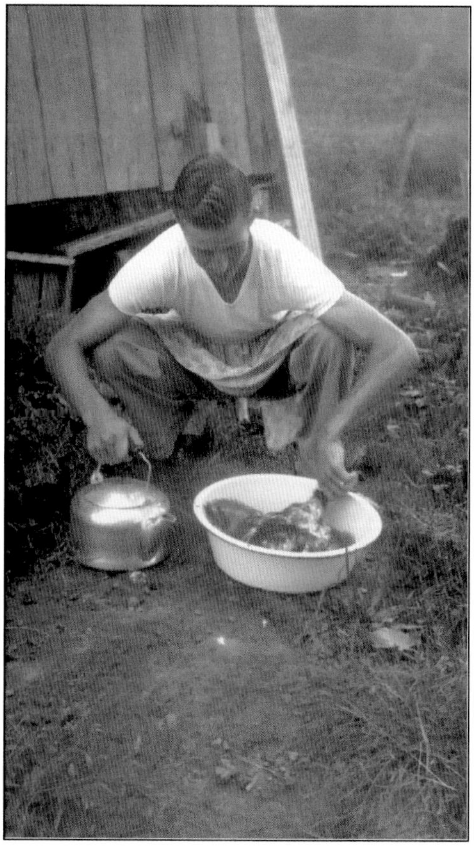

Chicken and Dumplings. Tom Harman of Coopers, a third-generation coal miner, is shown here preparing a meal. The people who came to work in the southern West Virginia coalfields learned to do a little bit of everything. When it comes to chicken, just add scalding hot water, pluck, and singe. (Courtesy of Betty Goins.)

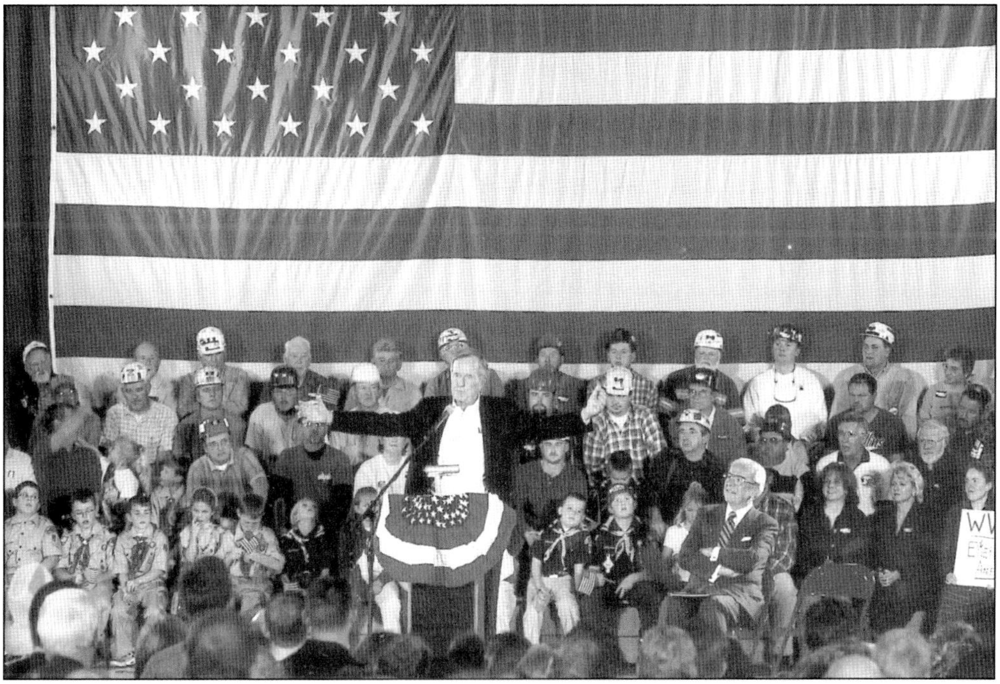

LANDING THE BIG ONE. Former Pres. George Bush appeared at the National Guard Armory at Brushfork on October 30, 2000, on the campaign trail for his son George Walker Bush. Gov. Cecil Underwood, seated to Bush's left, was unsuccessful in his re-election bid. (Photo by Mel Grubb.)

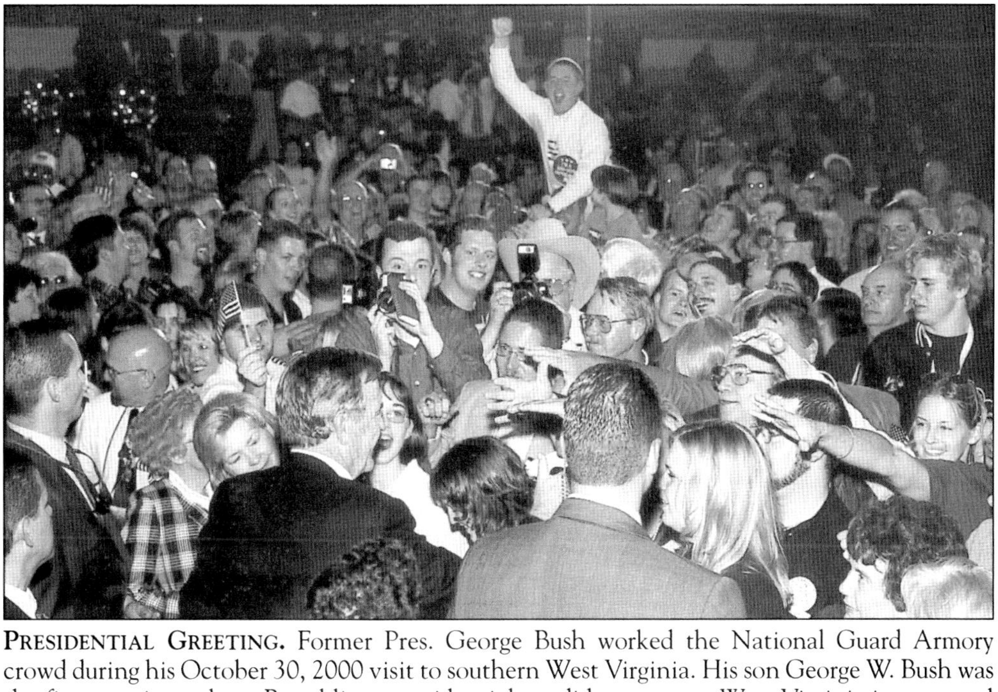

PRESIDENTIAL GREETING. Former Pres. George Bush worked the National Guard Armory crowd during his October 30, 2000 visit to southern West Virginia. His son George W. Bush was the first non-incumbent Republican presidential candidate to carry West Virginia in a general election through the 20th century. (Photo by Mel Grubb.)

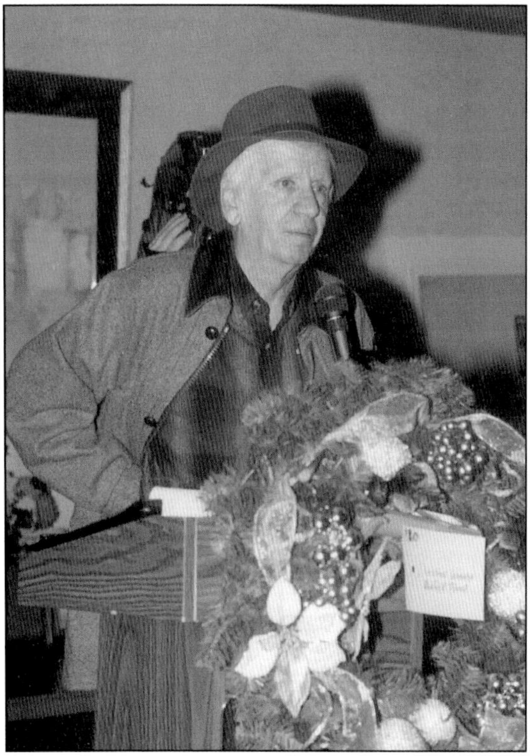

GOOD HEART. Bob Denver has lent his celebrity support to the annual "Share The Blessing" auction to benefit the Bluefield Union Mission since its inception. Denver is a native of New Rochelle, New York, but has been living in Princeton for the past decade. The star of *Gilligan's Island* turned 65 on January 9, 2001. (Photo by Eric DiNovo.)

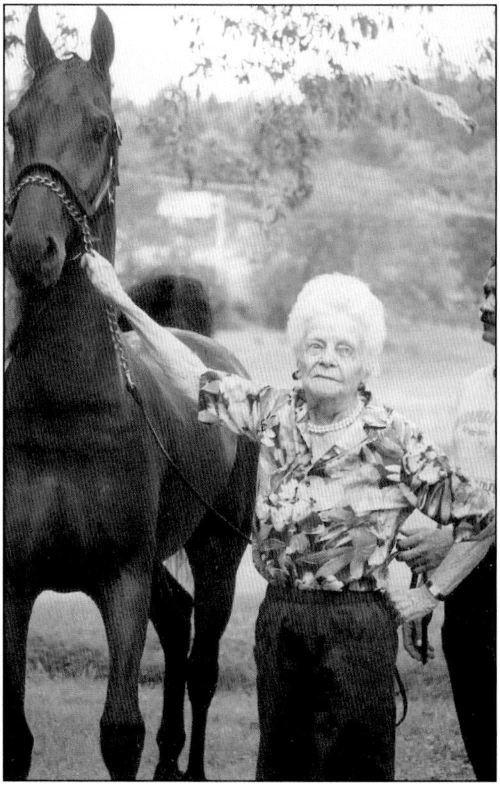

COMMUNITY LEADER. The late Katharine Tierney, shown here with one of her horses at Leatherwood Farms, was one of Mercer County's most dynamic civic leaders of the 20th century. In addition to her financial support of worthy projects, she was a tireless volunteer who gave freely of her time and talents. Ms. Tierney passed away on July 19, 1996, just a few days before the start of the annual Blue-Gray Horse Show, sponsored by the Bluefield Shrine Club. (Photo by the author.)

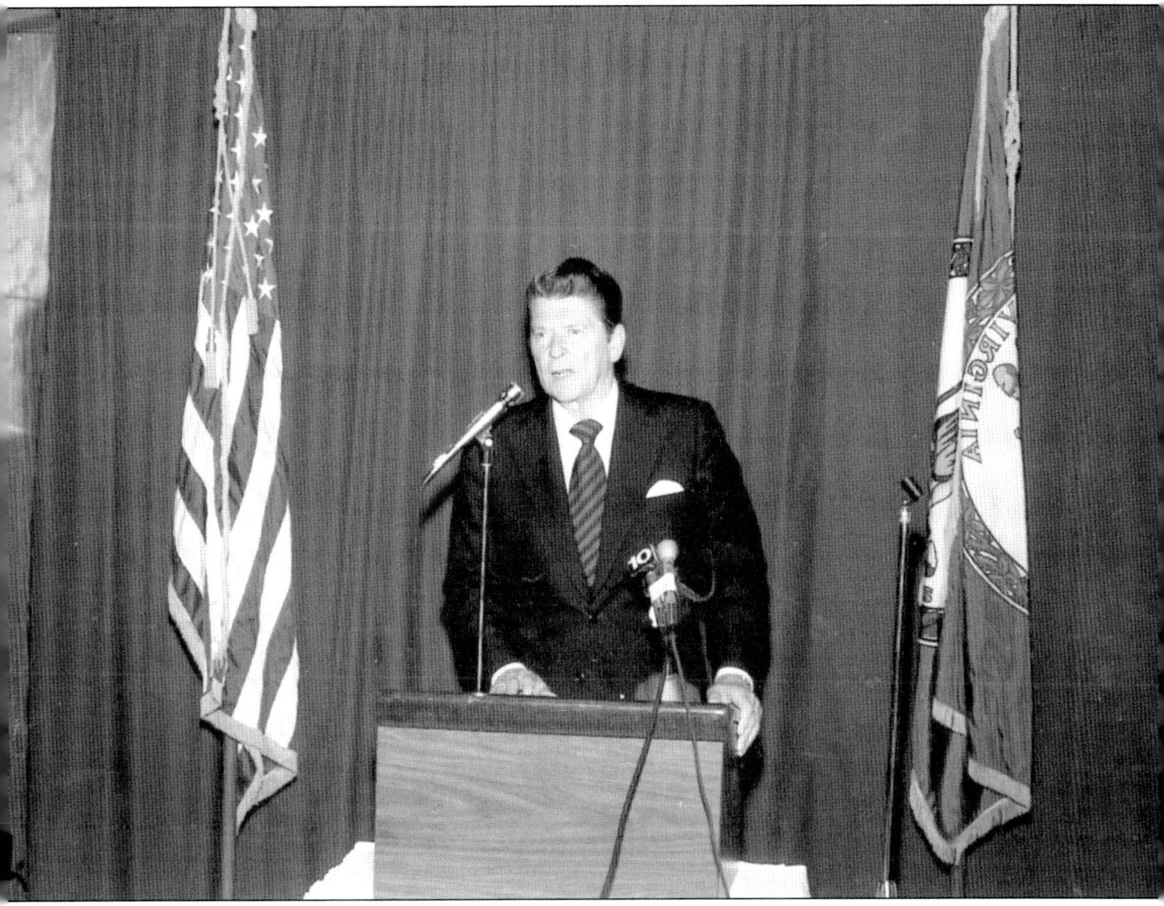

THE GREAT COMMUNICATOR. Former Pres. Ronald Reagan was the guest speaker at the Greater Bluefield Chamber of Commerce Annual Dinner on April 11, 1979. At the time, he was mentioned as a "possible" presidential contender for the 1980 election. However, during the dinner, he was the former governor of California. A huge crowd of more than 1,200 people attended the dinner held at the National Guard Armory in Brushfork. Reagan criticized federal interference in business and personal life during the dinner. (Photo by Mel Grubb.)

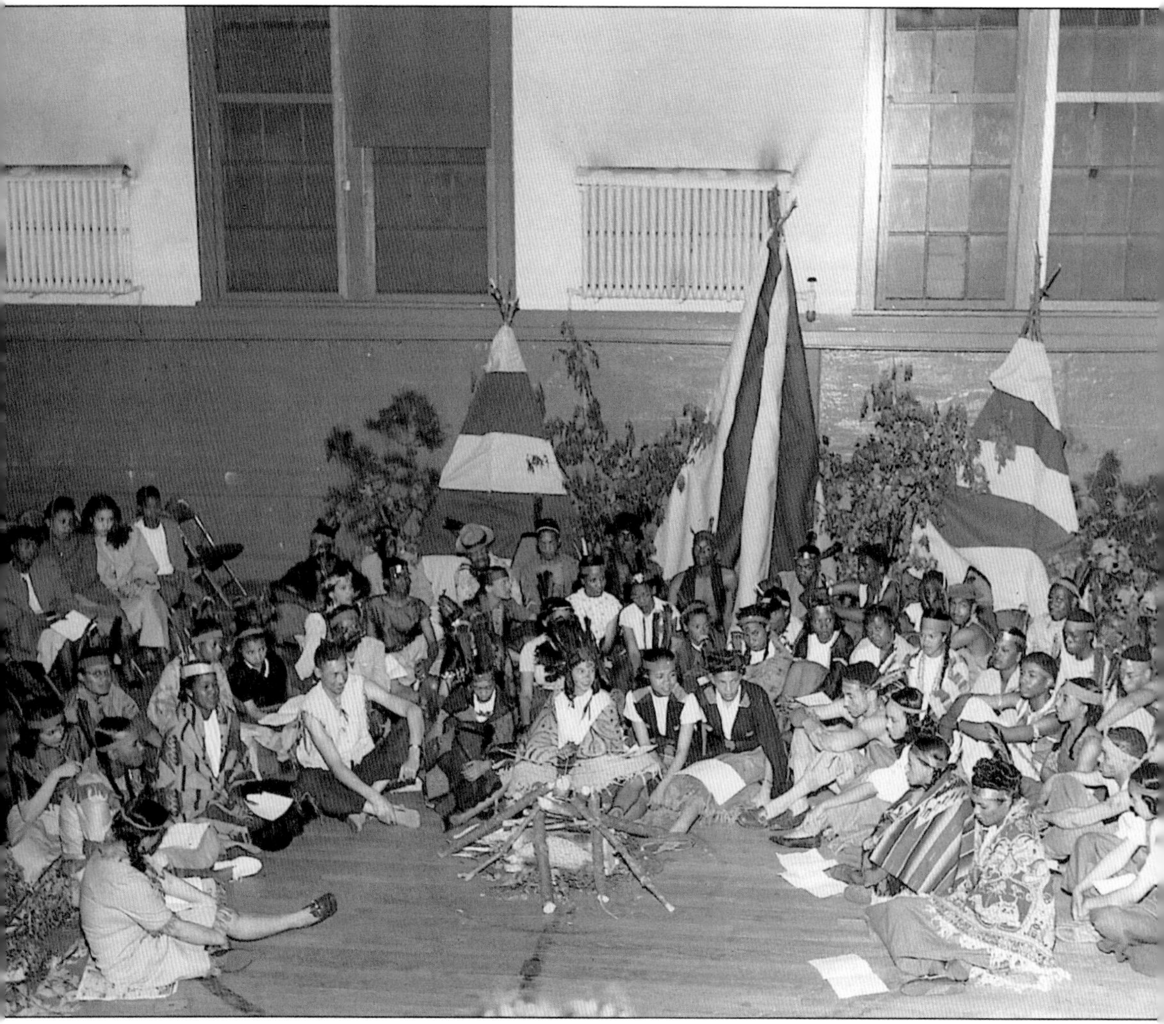

Student Council Fires. Students of Bluefield's Genoa High School are shown here at one of several theme gatherings that brought classmates together for a learning experience. While the concept of "separate but equal" was employed in the African-American public schools of Mercer County, the reality was that the educational resources were limited. Thus, teachers developed creative ways to educate students. (Courtesy of Juanita Willis.)

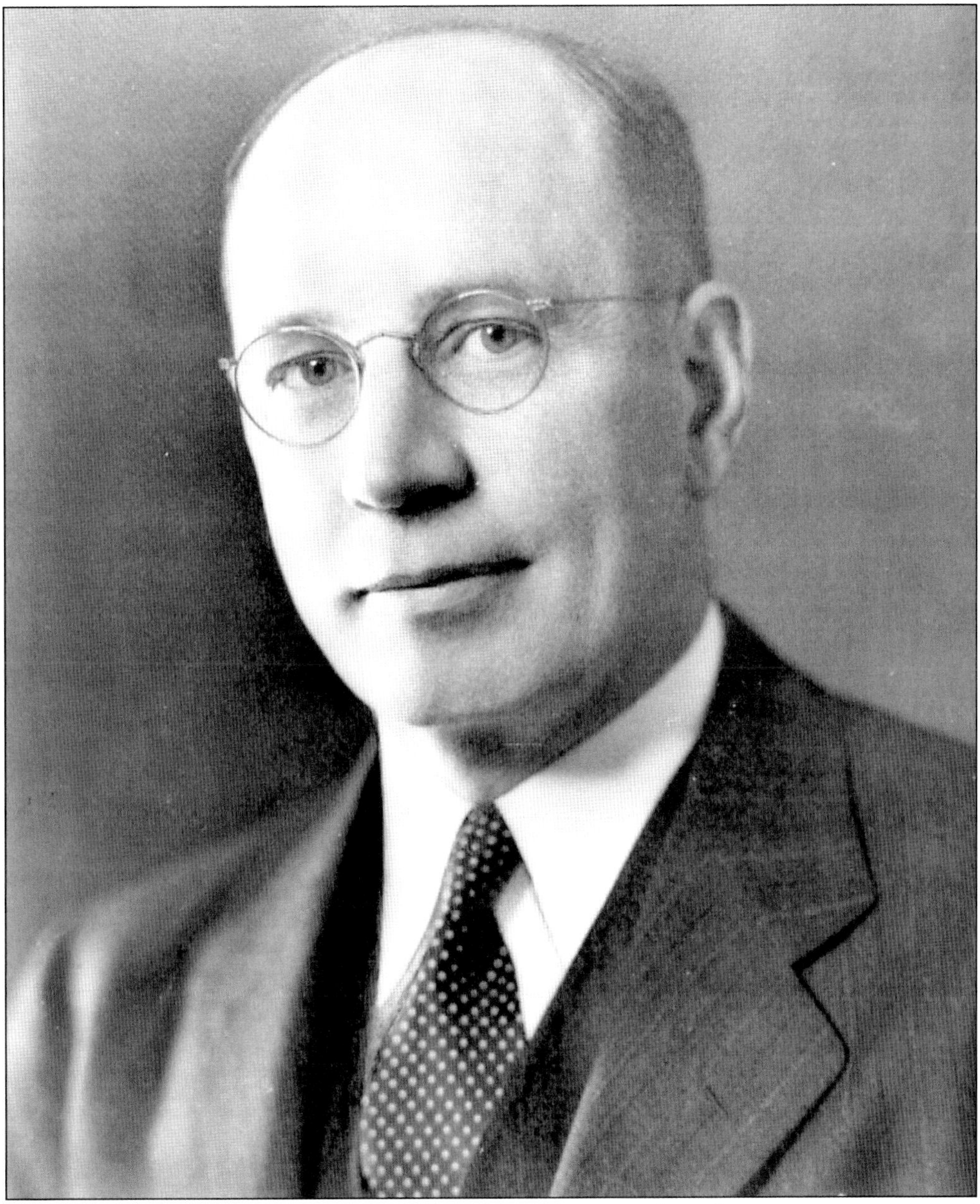

Father of Modern City Management. A trivia question that often comes up at national conventions of city managers is "Where is the only city that Clarence Ridley ever served as city manager?" The answer is Bluefield. Ridley was born in Armada, Michigan, and after receiving his master's degree at Columbia University in 1921, he accepted the position as Bluefield's first city manager where he served until 1925. He completed a doctorate degree and worked two years as staff engineer with the National Institute of Public Administration. From 1929 until his retirement in 1956, he served as executive director of the International City Managers' Association, an organization he helped shape from its infancy. Following the end of World War II, he lent his considerable administrative skills to the process of rebuilding European cities destroyed by war. His faith in the council-manager form of city government was a constant through his distinguished career. (Courtesy of The City of Bluefield.)

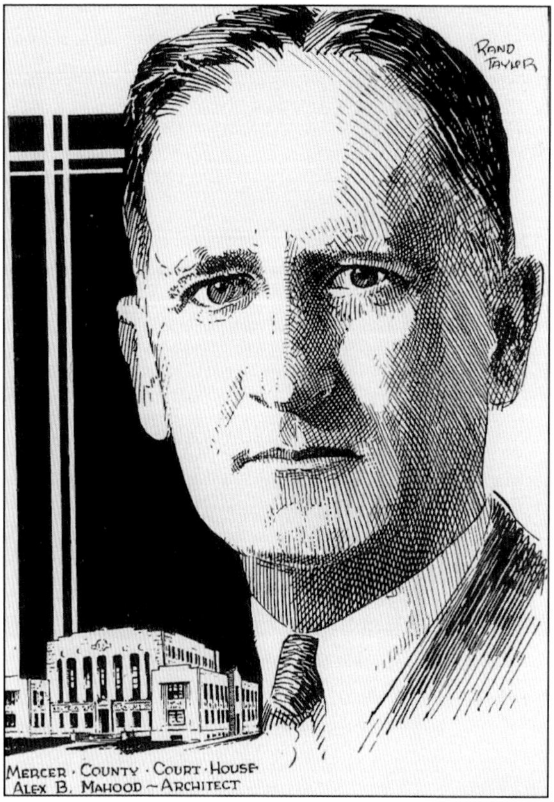

GRAND DESIGNS. Alex B. Mahood was Mercer County's most well-known architect. Among the many designs he left behind was the Mercer County Courthouse in Princeton dedicated August 8, 1931. The image here is taken from a Rand Taylor sketch. (Courtesy of the Mahood family.)

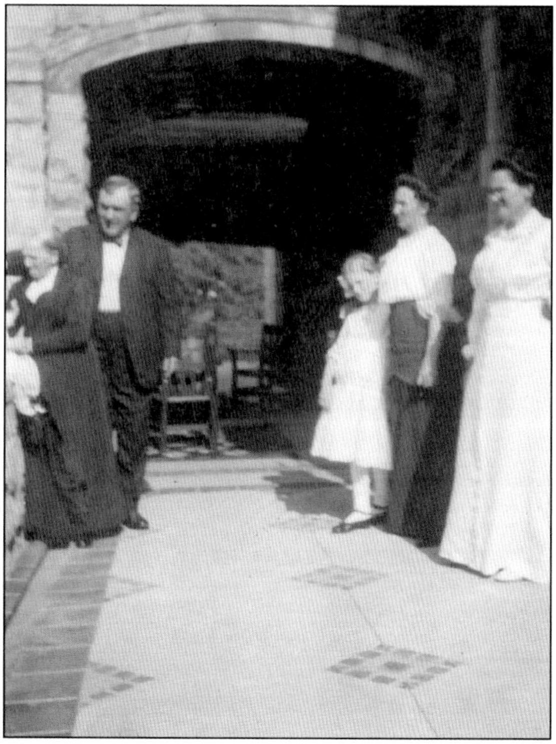

THOMAS MANSION. A reception line is shown forming at the Thomas mansion in Bramwell. From left to right are Maria Cooper, Col. W.H. Thomas, Lara Jessamal, Sallie Cooper, and Annie Cooper. (Courtesy of Eve Cooper Murphy.)

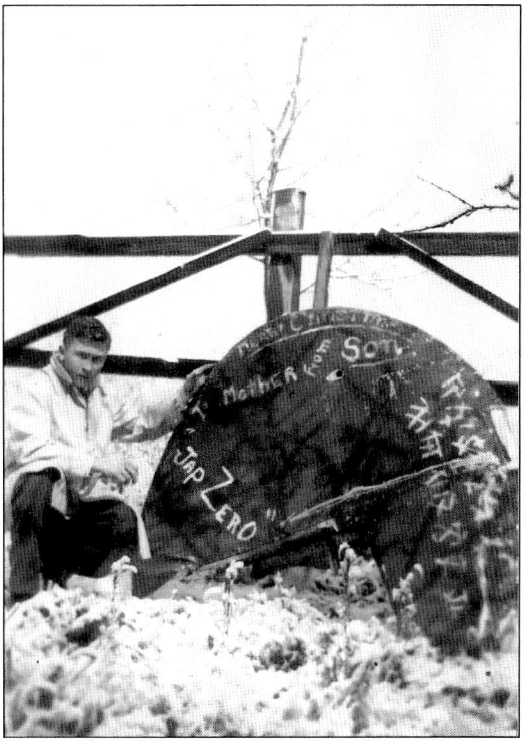

PIECE OF HISTORY. Bud Coppinger is shown here with a piece of a B-24 that was being transported to Europe during World War II but crashed on East River Mountain on February 7, 1943. The crash was discovered on April 22, 1943, about two months after the plane went down. The crew was taking the B-24 from Nashville, Tennessee to a base in England. All three members of the crew perished in the crash. (Courtesy of Bud Coppinger.)

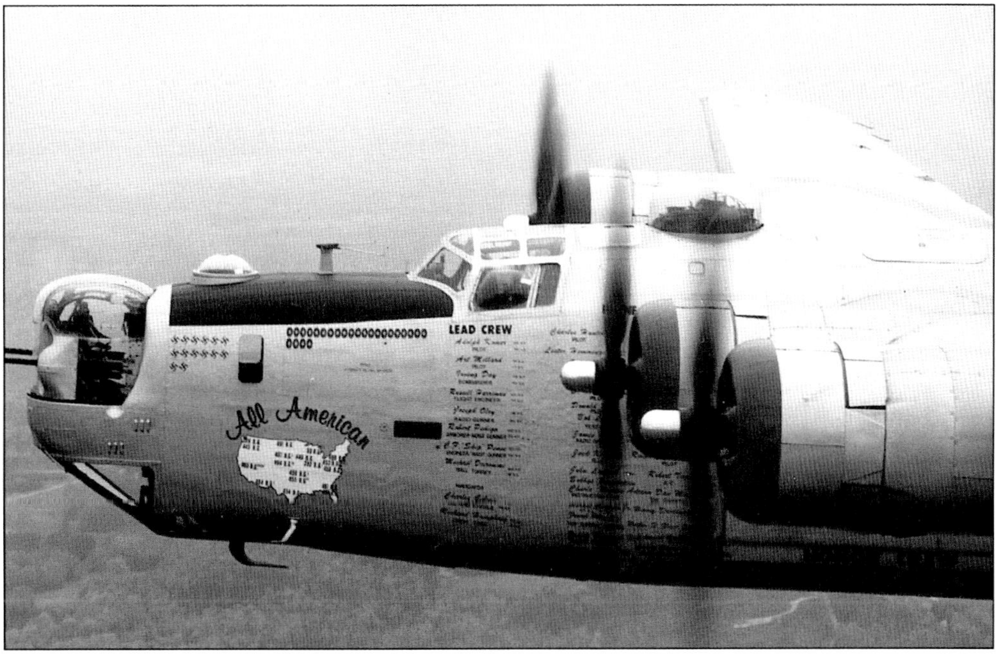

THE LIBERATOR. After the B-24 (like the one shown here coming to an air show at the Mercer County Airport) was discovered, the U.S. Army retrieved the remains of the crewmen, the engines, and the landing gear and left the rest of the plane on the mountainside. Much of the fuselage and wings were brought off the mountain and sold as scrap or kept as souvenirs. (Photo by the author.)

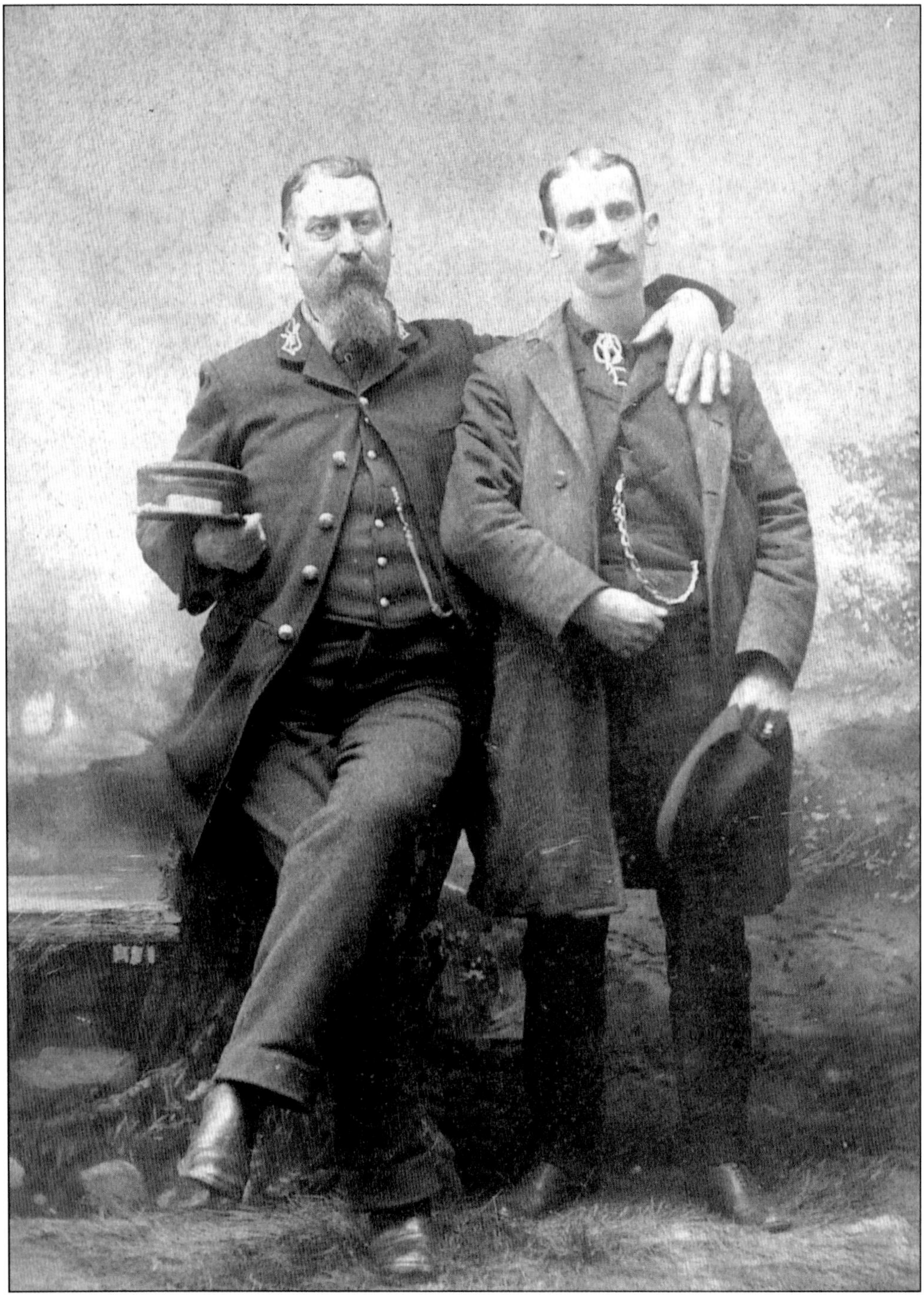

BEST FRIENDS. Capt. George W. Thomas, left, of Bluefield and Doc Goodwill of Bramwell were said to be the best of friends. Goodwill had interest in the coal industry, but after lending his name to a Mercer County coal camp, he got out of the coal business and into the theater business. Goodwill Theater Corporation owned and operated motion picture houses throughout the coalfields. (Courtesy of Wayne Wright.)

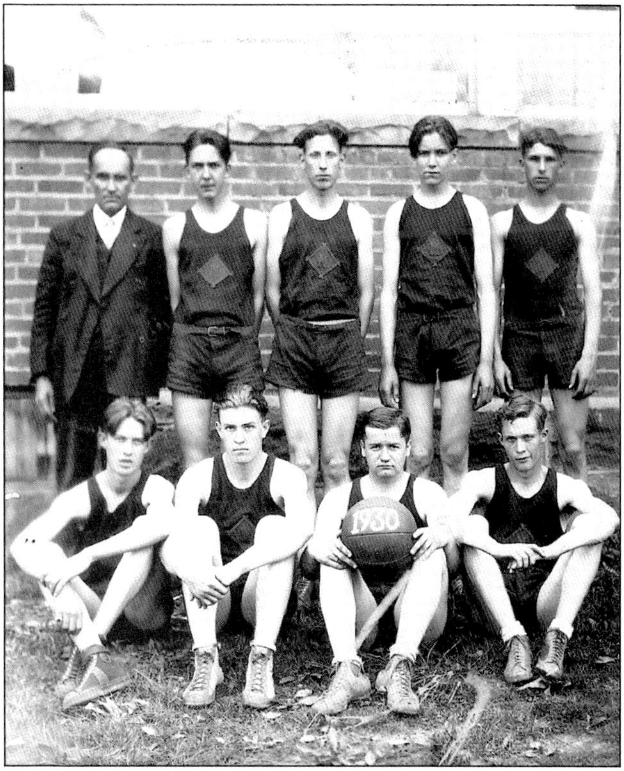

Montcalm Cagers. The members of the 1930 Montcalm basketball team, shown here from left to right, are (front row) Elliott Pierce "E.P." Garrett, Homer Bibey, Paul Fannings, and Kenneth Garrett; (second row) Coach Holston, Garner Virgis, Jason Scott, Pat Pickett, and Clyde Woods. (Courtesy of Dorothy Garrett and the late Elliot P. Garrett.)

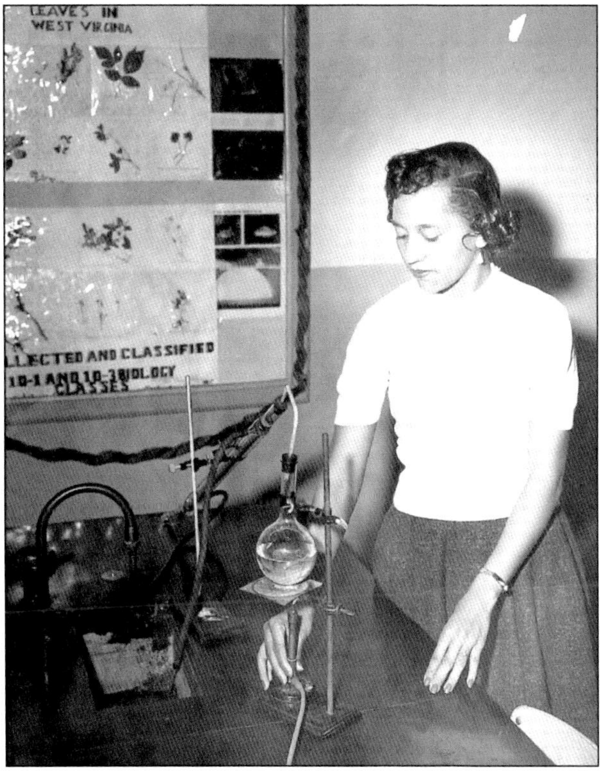

Science Project. Park Central High School student Drexel Wade is shown here conducting an experiment using a Bunsen burner. (Courtesy of Juanita Willis.)

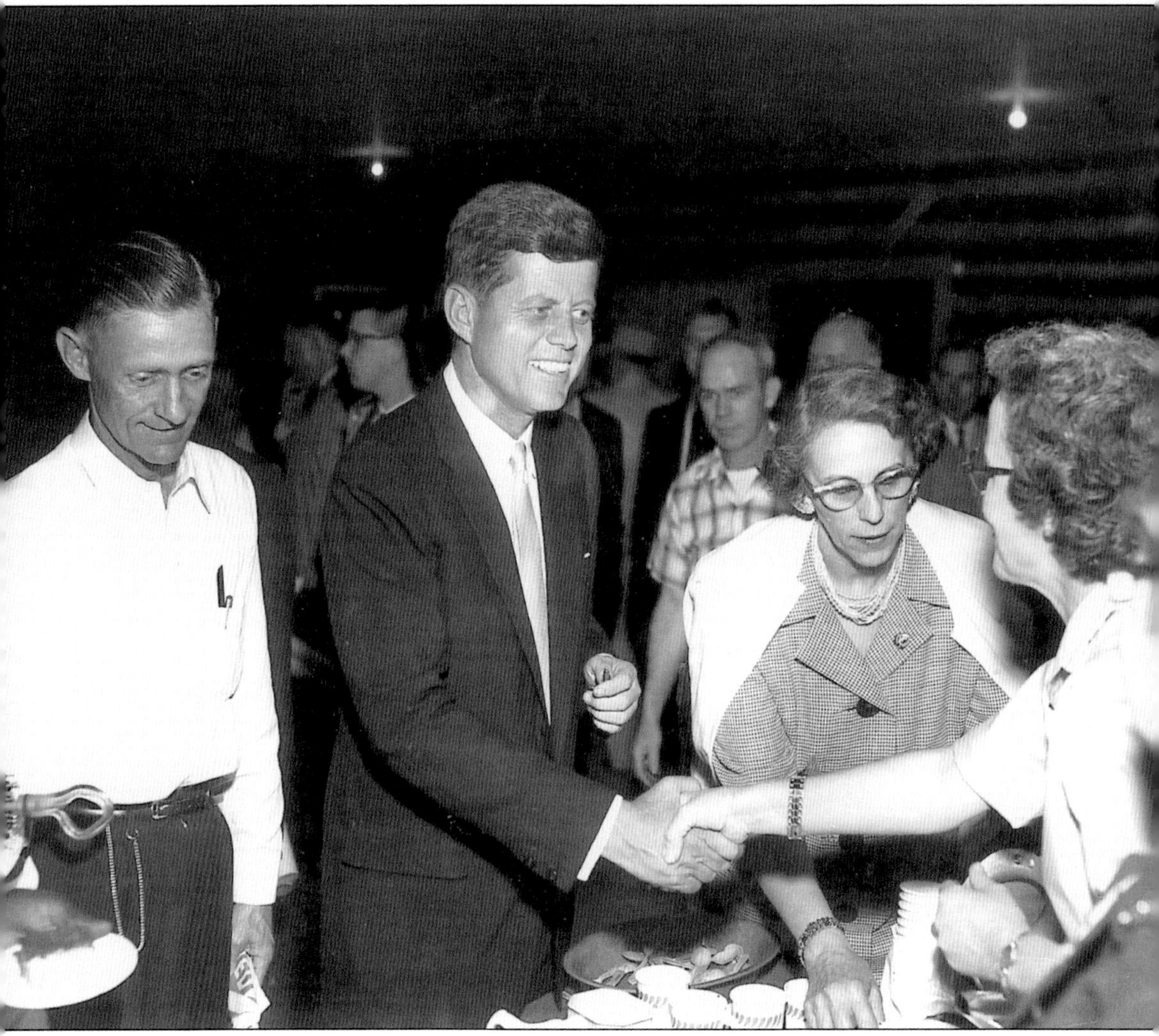

THE PREZ. Pres. John F. Kennedy made several stops in southern West Virginia during his campaign for the Democratic Party's presidential nomination in 1960. Kennedy is shown visiting here with Mercer County Democrats at Glenwood Park on April 28, 1960. The Kennedy campaign was concerned how a Catholic candidate would perform in a Bible-belt state like West Virginia. The state's voters supported Kennedy in the primary and later backed the Kennedy-Johnson ticket in the general election. (Photo by Mel Grubb.)

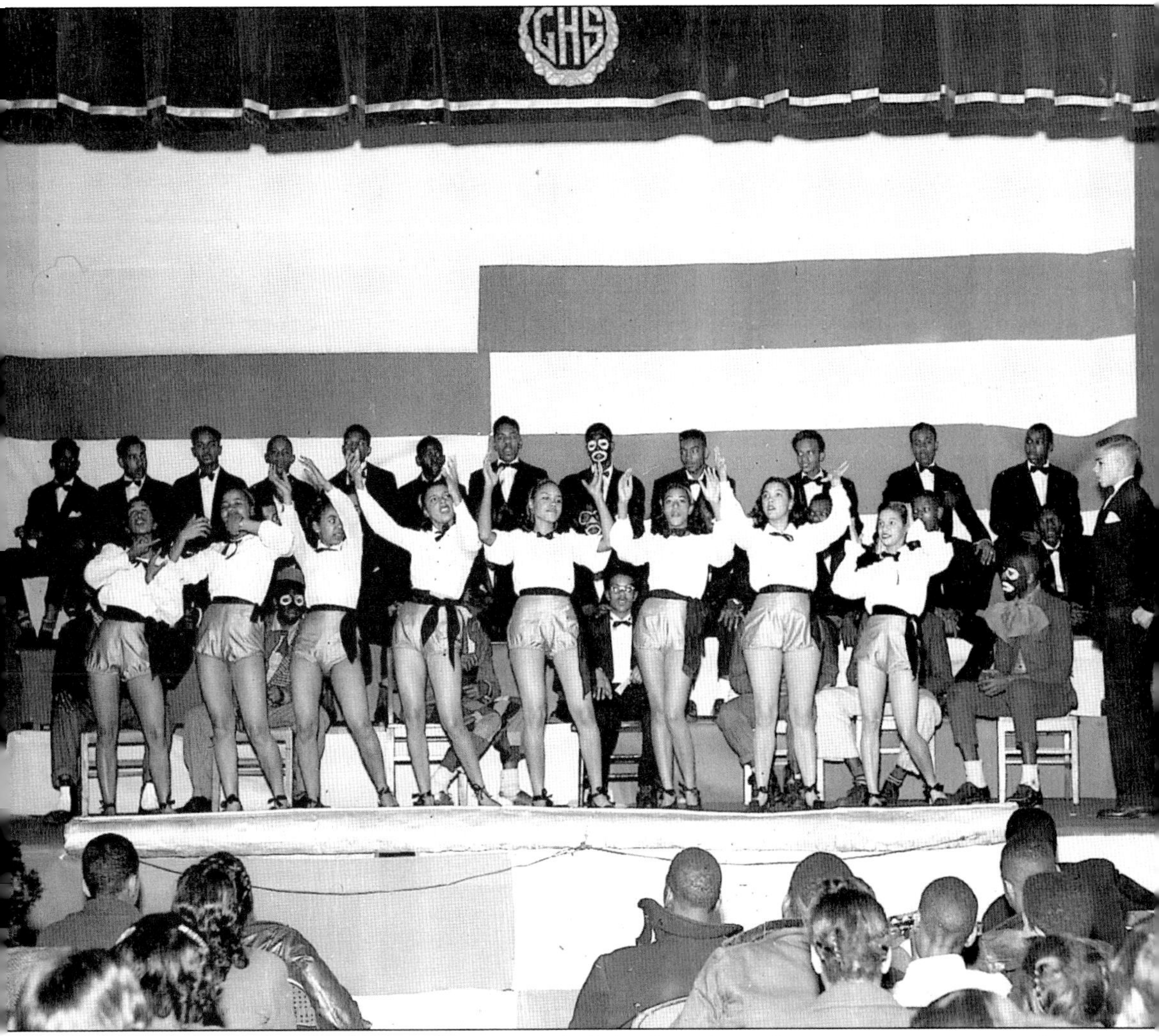

THE WORLD'S A STAGE. Students of Genoa High School are shown here putting on a minstrel show at the high school. Genoa played a part in the early education of such entertainment luminaries as Bobby Benson, composer during the Harlem Renaissance and the original keyboard artist for the Ink Spots; Mable Smalls of Cabin Kids fame; as well as Jacob and Zeke Carey, who would later move to Chicago and form half of The Flamingos, an R&B group whose big break came with their recording of "I Only Have Eyes For You." (Courtesy of Juanita Willis.)

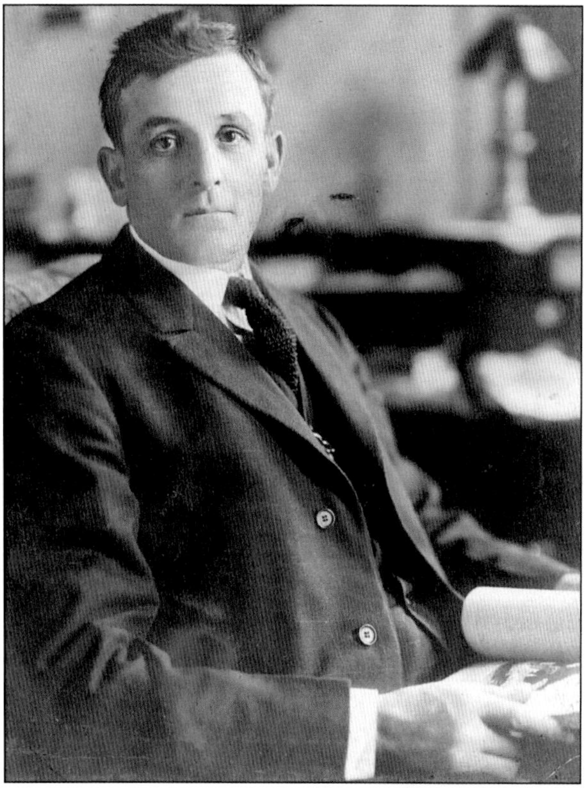

THE GENTLEMAN FROM ROCK. U.S. Rep. Edward Cooper, R-WV, was the only congressman ever to be elected from the Rock District. He was the son of John Cooper of Mill Creek Coal fame and was a graduate of Washington and Lee University, where he earned a law degree in 1893. He ran the family's coal business after his father's death in 1898, and was elected to Congress in 1914 and again in 1918. (Courtesy of Eve Cooper Murphy.)

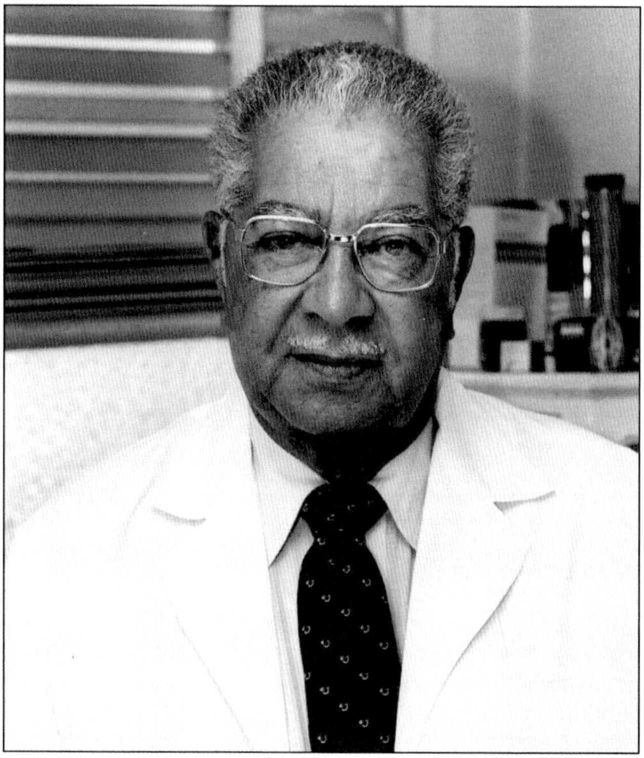

GOOD VIRGINIA NAMES. Dr. Peyton Randolph "P.R." Higginbotham was born in Lynchburg, was educated at Howard University, and came to Bluefield in 1923 to open his medical practice. In addition to being a brilliant diagnostician, Dr. Higginbotham was active as Bluefield State College physician and was instrumental in developing a well baby clinic through the Carolina Community Home, now known as the Bluefield Community Center. (Photo by Fred Brown.)

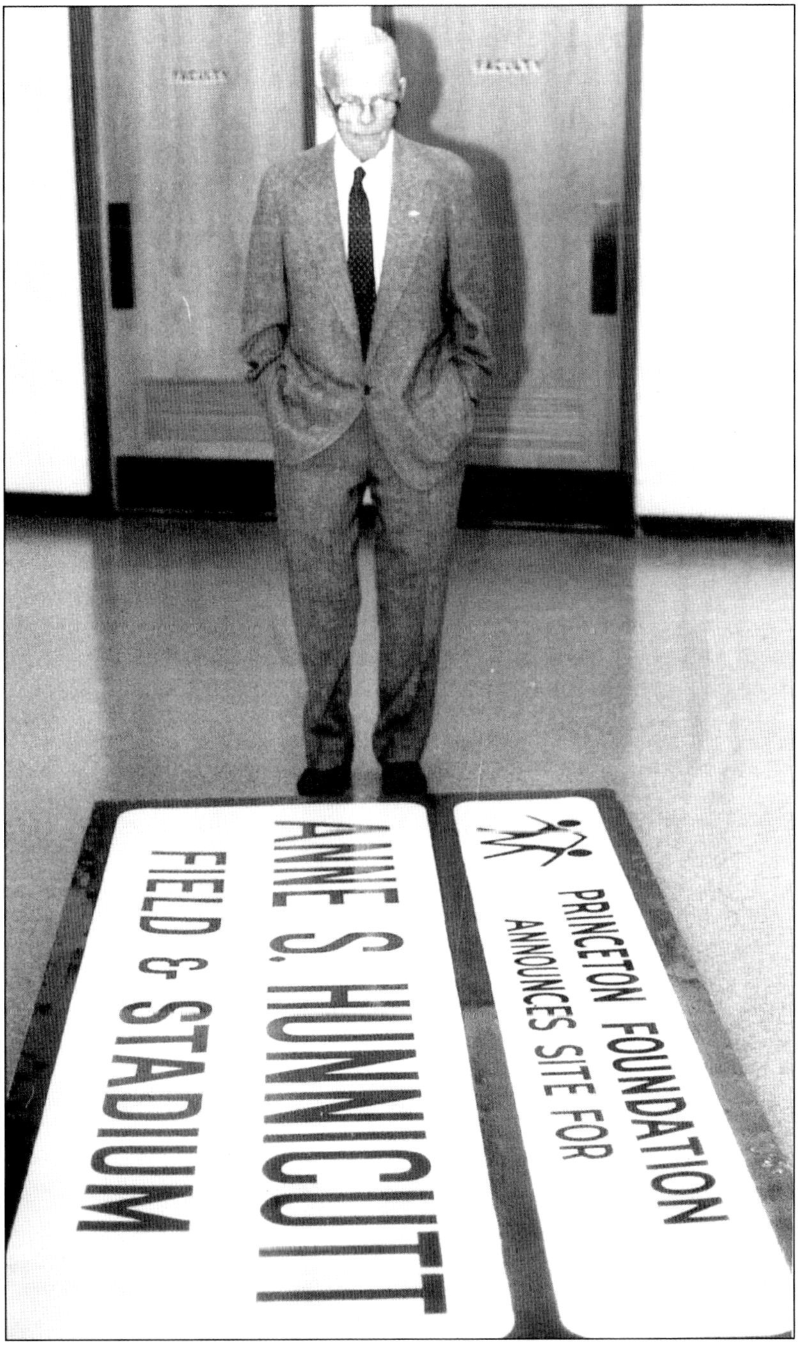

JOY OF PEPSI. H.P. Hunnicutt held the Pepsi Cola Bottling franchise in Princeton for several years. When the company went around the country buying up its franchises, Mr. Hunnicutt was reluctant to part with a product with which he enjoyed working. Eventually, Hunnicutt gave in and sold the franchise, but by that time, its value had increased a great deal. Through the Hunnicutt Foundation, he was able to serve Princeton, Mercer County, and southern West Virginia. Among the most visible of the foundation's projects are the Anne S. Hunnicutt Field and Stadium complex in Princeton. (Photo by Fred Brown.)

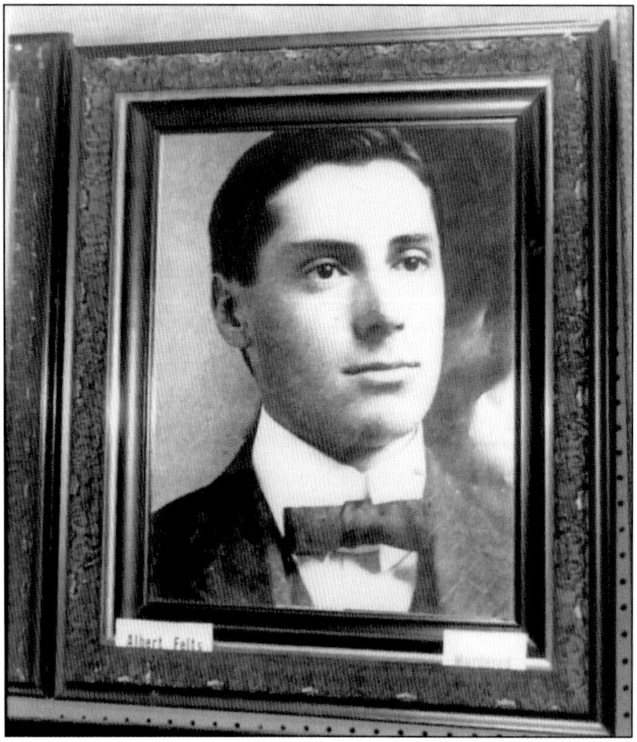

CHIEF OF DETECTIVES. Albert Felts was living in a new home on Bland Street in Bluefield and was head of the Baldwin-Felts Detective Agency when on May 19, 1920, he and his brother as well as five detectives were gunned down by striking coal miners in Matewan, Mingo County. (Photo reproduction by Evonda Archer.)

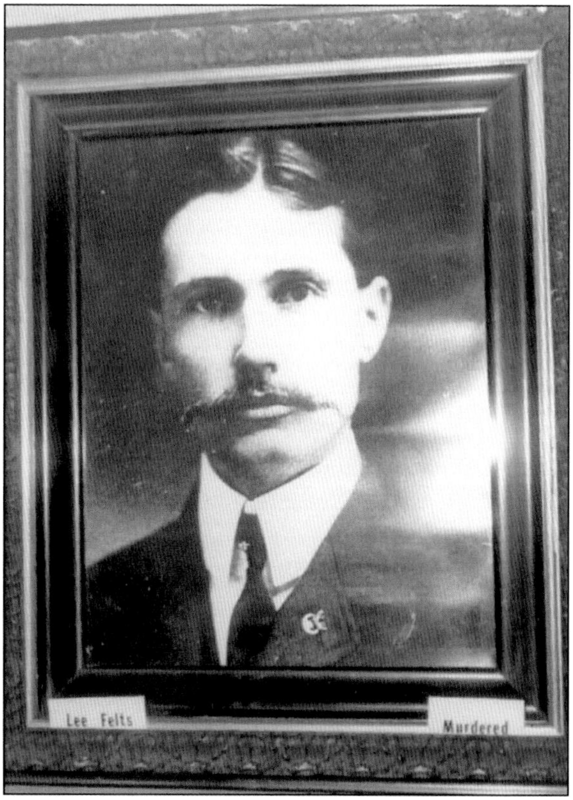

VIOLENT END. Lee Felts was already out of the detective business when his brother Albert asked him to travel along to Matewan to help with evicting striking coal miners from their company-owned homes. (Photo reproduction by Evonda Archer.)

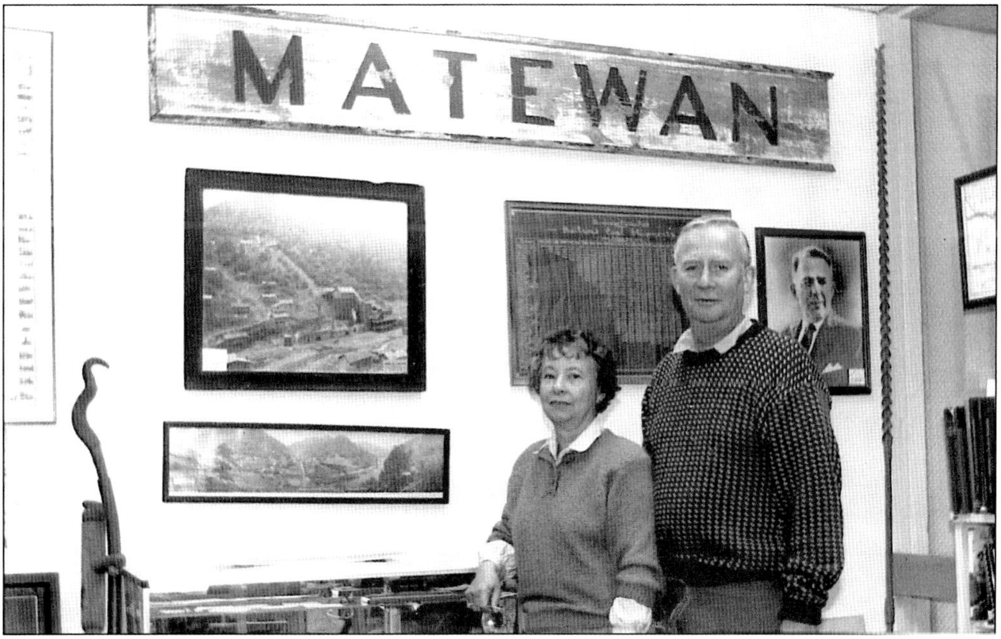

RETURN TO THE SCENE. Claire and Dick Redden of California came back to Bluefield in 1992 to search for their family roots. Dick is the grandson of Albert Felts. His mother was alive at the time of the so-called Matewan Massacre, but she did not speak much about it. The Reddens are shown here at the Eastern Regional Coal Archives of Craft Memorial Library in Bluefield. (Photo by the author.)

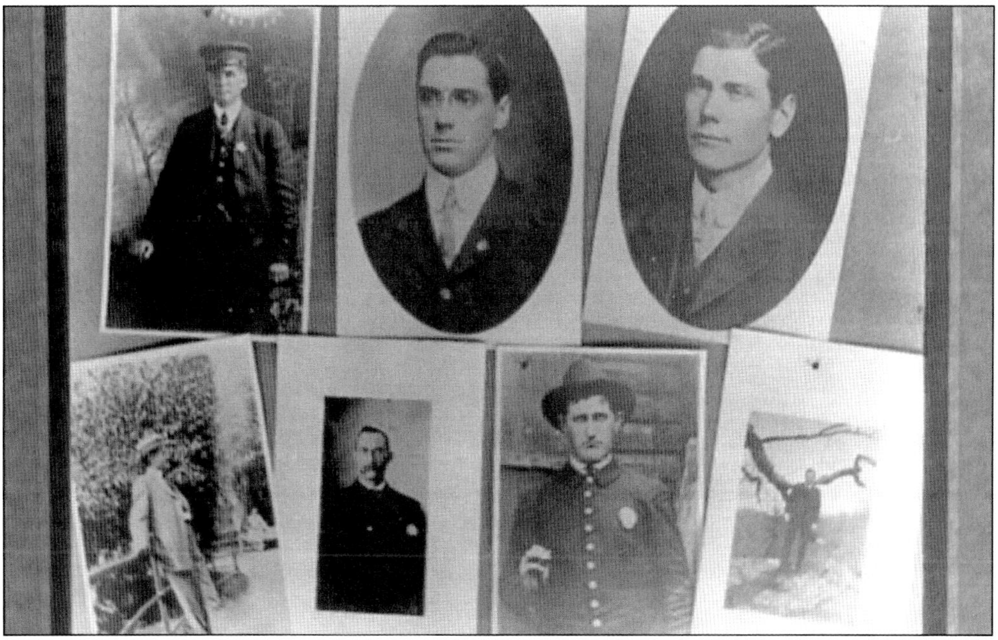

DETECTIVES KILLED AT MATEWAN. The detectives shown here were killed at Matewan in a gun battle with striking coal miners. They are identified, from left to right, as follows: (top row) C.T. Higgins, Albert Felts, and Lee Felts; (bottom row) C.B. Cunningham, A.J. Booker, E.O. Powell, and J.W. Ferguson. (Photo reproduction by Evonda Archer.)

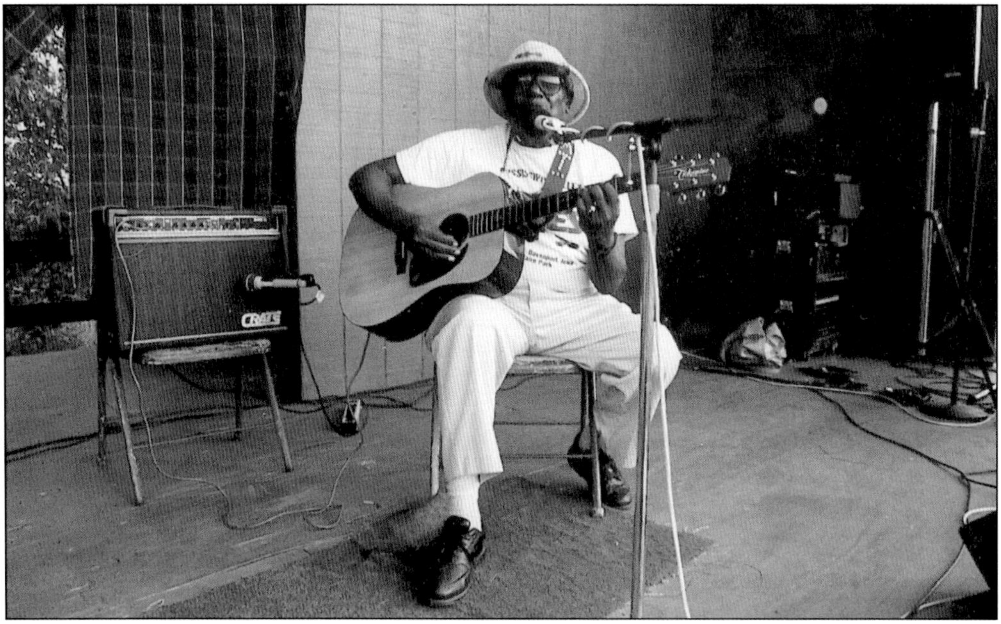

King of the Blues. Legendary blues guitar and vocalist Nat Reese has called Princeton home since his father came to work at the Virginian Railway car shops in 1929. Along with being listed among American Blues Legends, Reese received the West Virginia Cultural Center's Vandalia Award in 1995 for keeping the coalfield blues alive. Reese is still learning, teaching, and playing the blues. (Photo by John Nelson.)

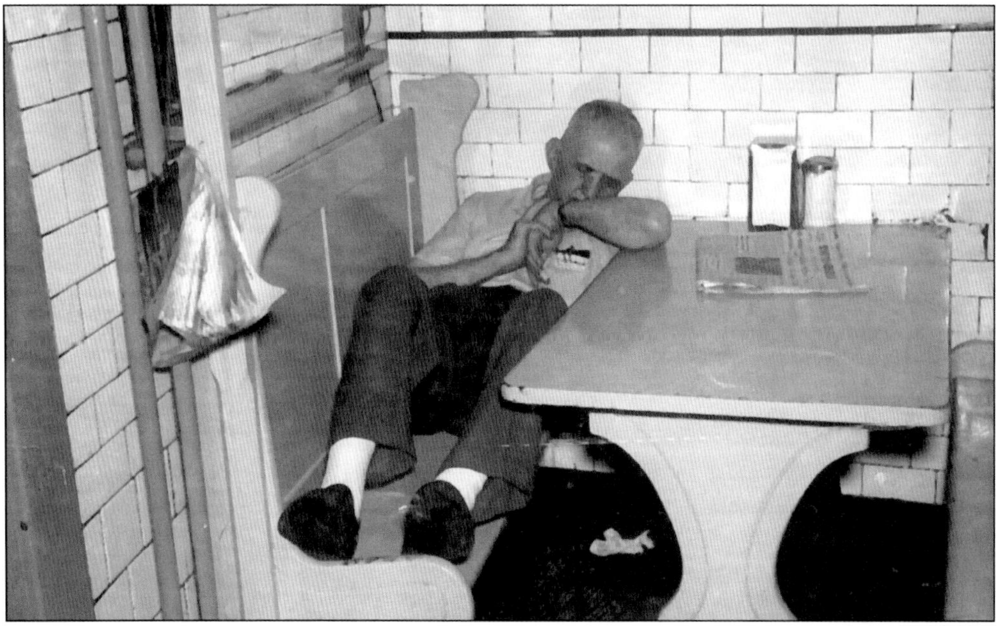

Dough Boy Sam. Sam Nikas and his partner, Gus Theodorou, kept Bluefield's Dough Boy Lunch operating all day, every day. Gus took the 12-hour day shift and Sam took the 12-hour night shift. Sam is shown here taking a nap in this 1962 photo. His death on March 9, 1963, spelled the beginning of the end for the longtime institution. (Photo from the author's collection.)

COOPERS OF BRAMWELL. Edward Cooper Jr., the grandson of Mill Creek Coal founder John Cooper, was not associated with the family's coal business but was active in civic affairs both in Bramwell and throughout the region. He was an avid sportsman and devoted family man. (Courtesy of Eve Cooper Murphy.)

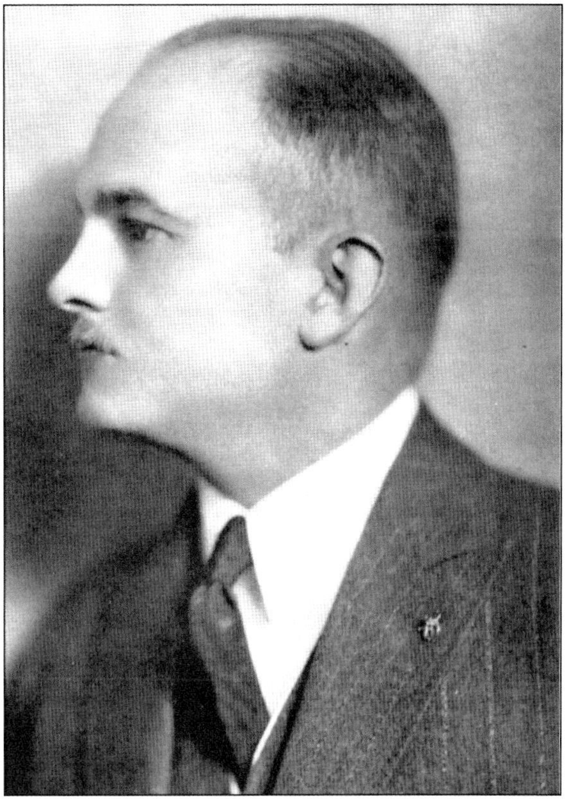

DAYS OF CAMELOT. Jackie and John F. Kennedy are shown together at a 1960 campaign appearance at the Glenwood 4-H Camp. (Photo by Vernon Fields.)

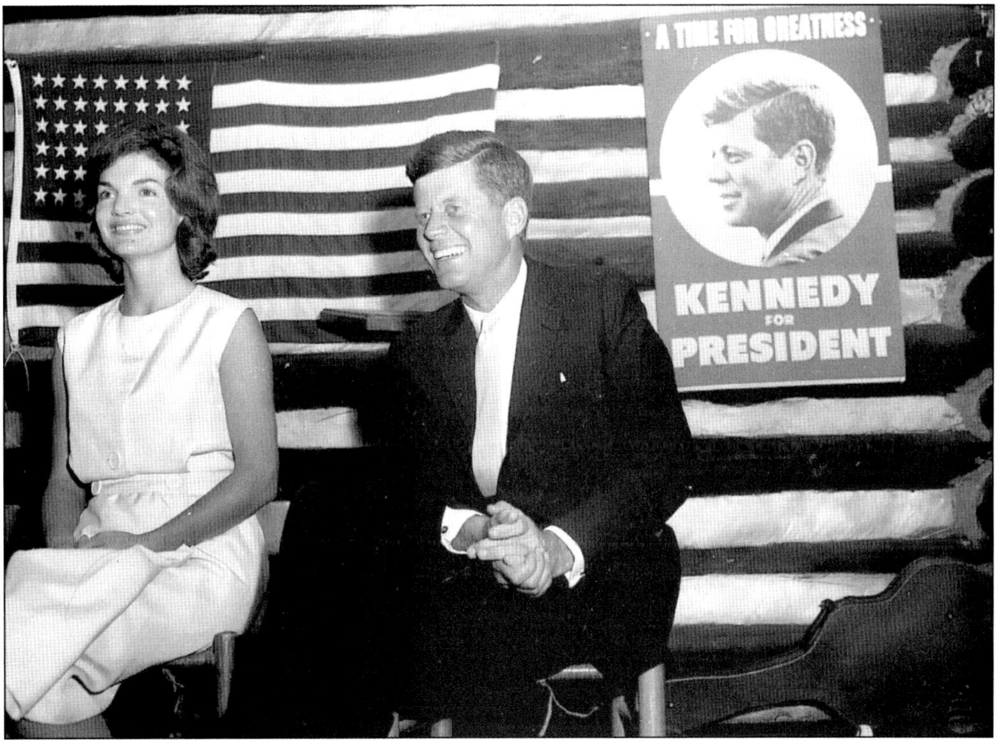

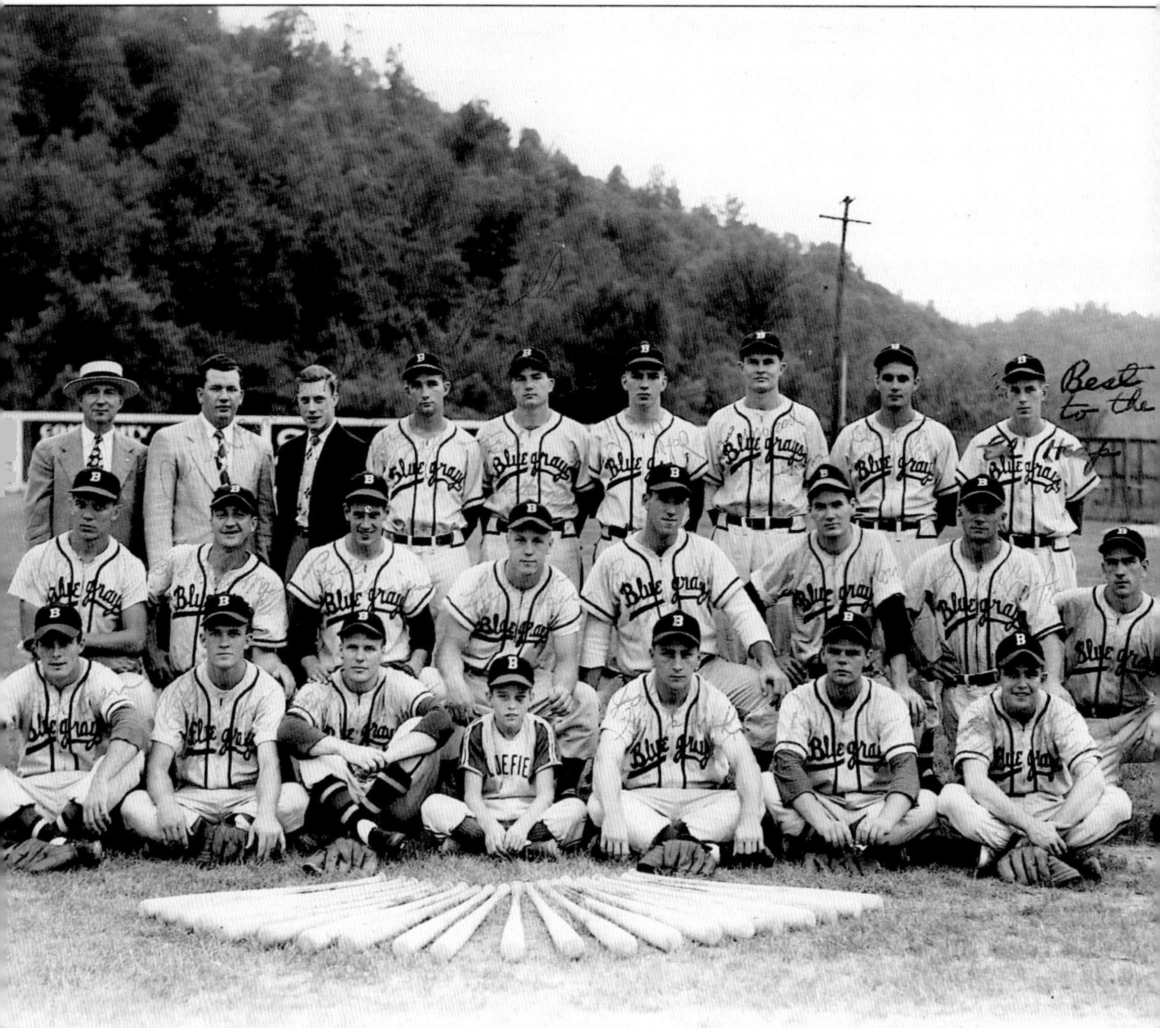

BAD BOYS OF SUMMER. Bob Bowman (second row, second from right) was perhaps the most infamous baseball player to come from southern West Virginia. A fastball hurler from Keystone who got his start with the McComas team, Bowman made it to the majors and was pitching for the Giants on June 20, 1941, when he beaned Ducky Medwick, essentially ending the Hall of Famer's career. Bowman finished out his career with the Bluefield Blue Grays, pictured here. From left to right are (front row) William Green, Melvin Cooper, Robert Schlemmer, Butch Currence (bat boy), John Karpenski, Robert Brown, and George "Mickey" Hennesey; (second row) Ralph Beard, Robert "Bob" Bowman, William Williams, Luther Tucker, Ben Gregory, Jim Herndon, Ernie White (manager), and Joe Roddin; (third row) Clyde Elliott, Austin Brown, Dick Wingfield, Joe Zajac, Robert Pottinger, Jim Pope, Lywood Boehm, Clayton Taylor, and Edwain "Ed" Heap. (Courtesy of Heber Stafford.)

Five

RAIL

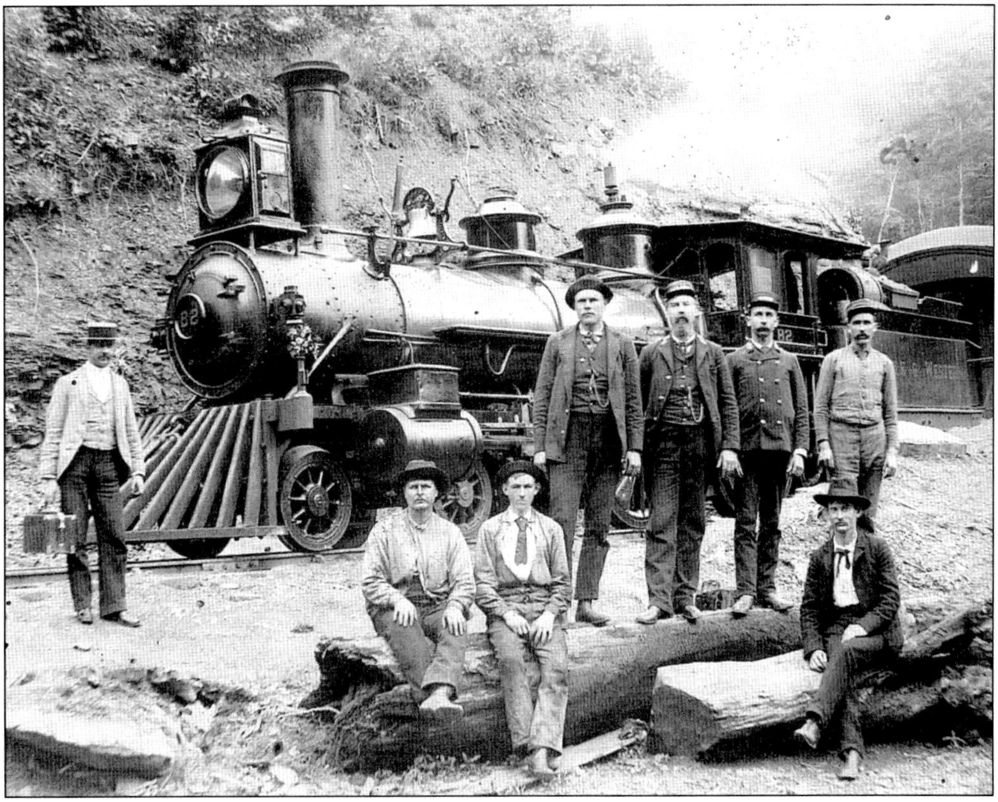

STEAM DREAMS. The history of Mercer County is a saga of the development of the railroad industry. The early Norfolk & Western Railway steam locomotives were rather small when compared to the massive locomotives on the rails when the steam era ended. The man above carrying the suitcase is not identified, but the men standing on the log are Bob Brown, George W. Thomas, Essie Shell, and an unidentified person. The gentlemen seated are Mr. Crowe, an unidentified detective, and Tommy Price. (Courtesy of Wayne Wright.)

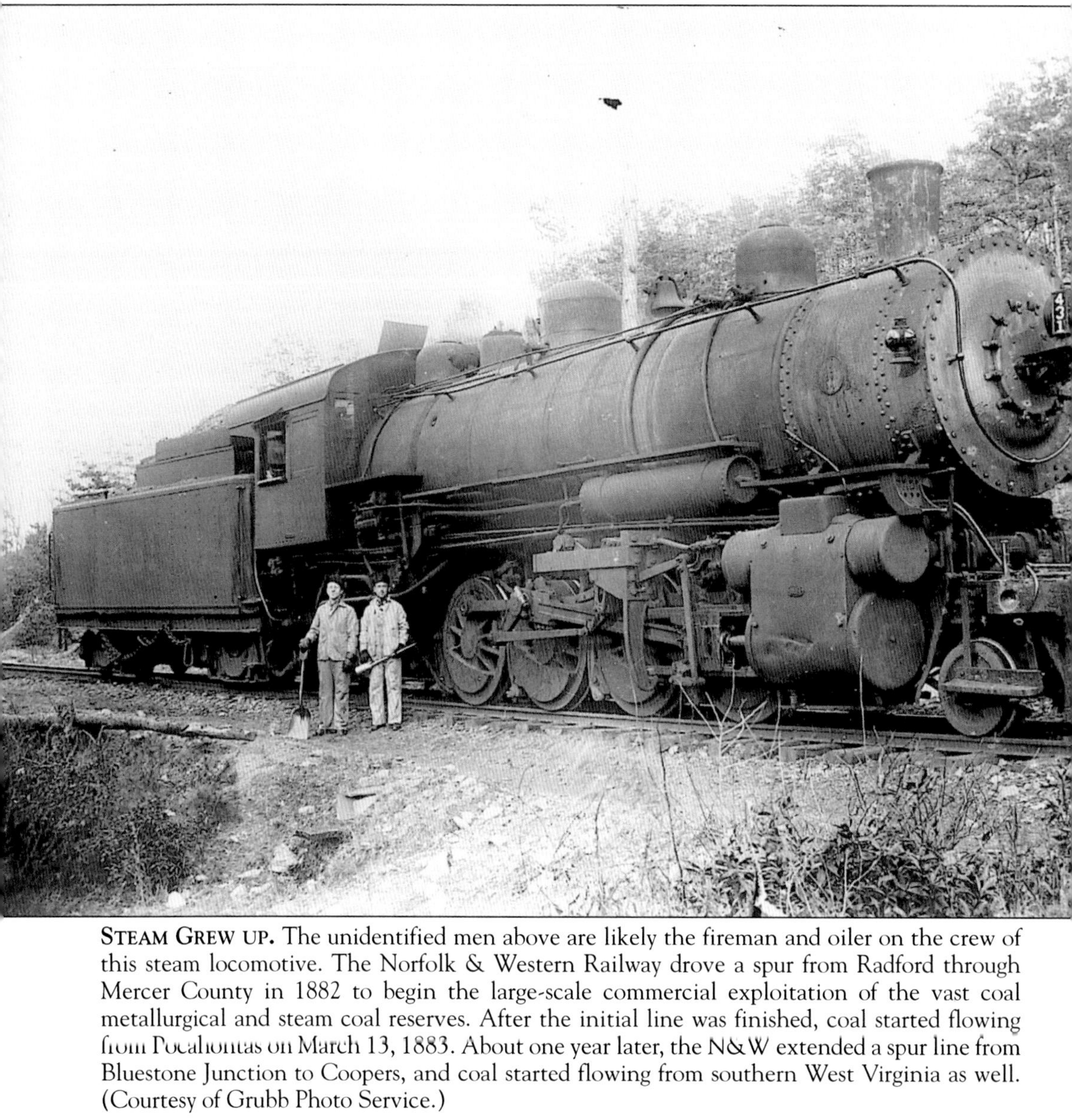

STEAM GREW UP. The unidentified men above are likely the fireman and oiler on the crew of this steam locomotive. The Norfolk & Western Railway drove a spur from Radford through Mercer County in 1882 to begin the large-scale commercial exploitation of the vast coal metallurgical and steam coal reserves. After the initial line was finished, coal started flowing from Pocahontas on March 13, 1883. About one year later, the N&W extended a spur line from Bluestone Junction to Coopers, and coal started flowing from southern West Virginia as well. (Courtesy of Grubb Photo Service.)

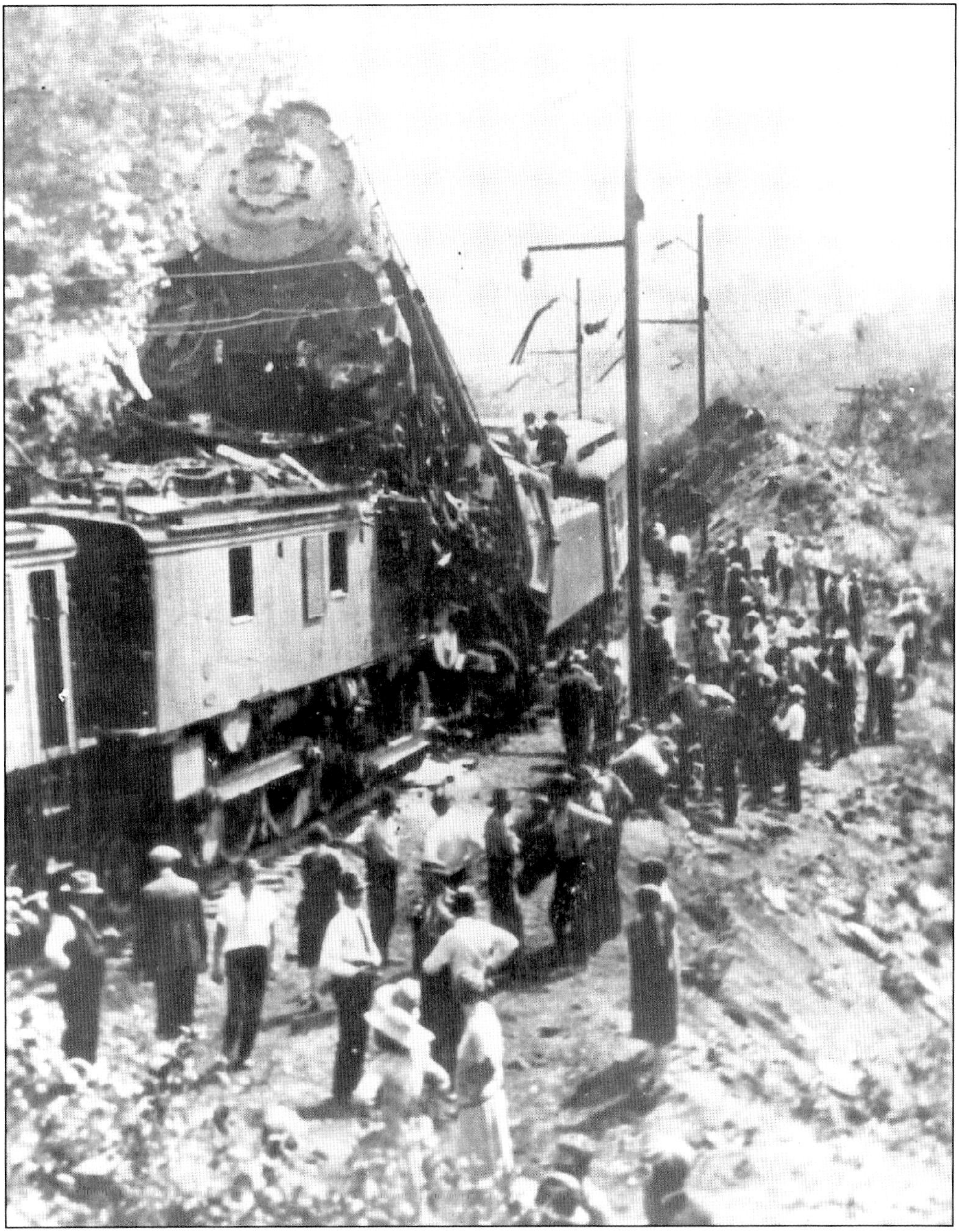

SCALDED TO DEATH BY THE STEAM. This dramatic collision between a westbound steam locomotive and an eastbound electric-powered locomotive occurred May 24, 1927, near Ingleside, Mercer County. E.S. Aldrick, locomotive engineer of Roanoke, Virginia and Frank W. O'Neal, fireman, on the No. 3 westbound passenger train were killed in the accident that left 20 more injured. The westbound train literally climbed the electric locomotive. Both trains were traveling less than 20 miles-per-hour when they collided. The passenger train had just pulled out of the station at Ingleside minutes before the wreck. An investigation later concluded that the crew of the No. 3 passenger train was at fault for failing to obey a "meet" order. (Courtesy of Grubb Photo Service.)

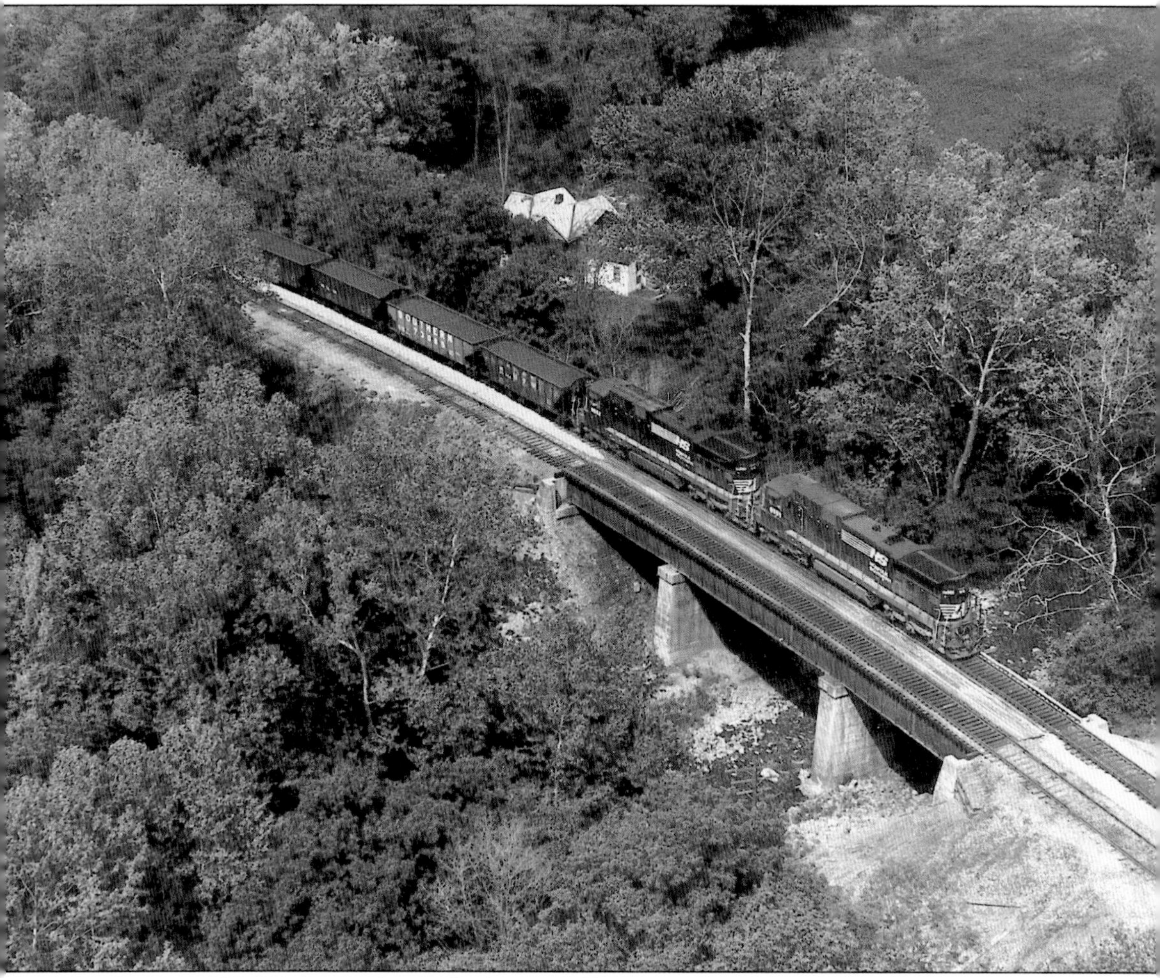

Making Tracks. In order to facilitate traffic east and west, Norfolk & Western Railway, now Norfolk Southern, built a dual-track mainline road. The Bluefield-based NS Pocahontas Division extends from Bluefield west to Portsmouth, Ohio, with about 900 miles of track, 96 tunnels, 823 trestles, and 7,109 culverts. Since NS's acquisition of part of Conrail, the division was expanded to include the Princeton to Deep Water line that connects the region to the Kanawha River. (Courtesy of NS Corporation.)

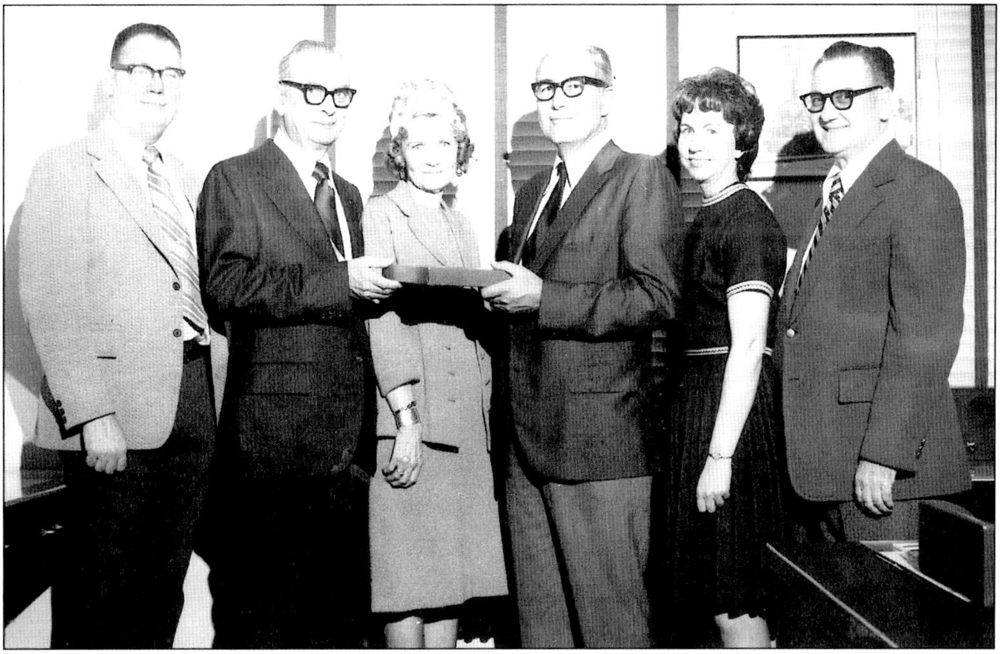

RETIRING MOMENT. P.L. Webber, chief clerk to the Pocahontas Division, is shown in this 1975 photo receiving a plaque of appreciation from Division Superintendent E.E. Nicewonder. Shown from left to right are J.W. King, chief dispatcher; Webber; Mrs. P.L. Webber; Nicewonder; Charlotte Noble, stenographer; and Peery Mooney, chief timekeeper. (Courtesy of Peery Mooney.)

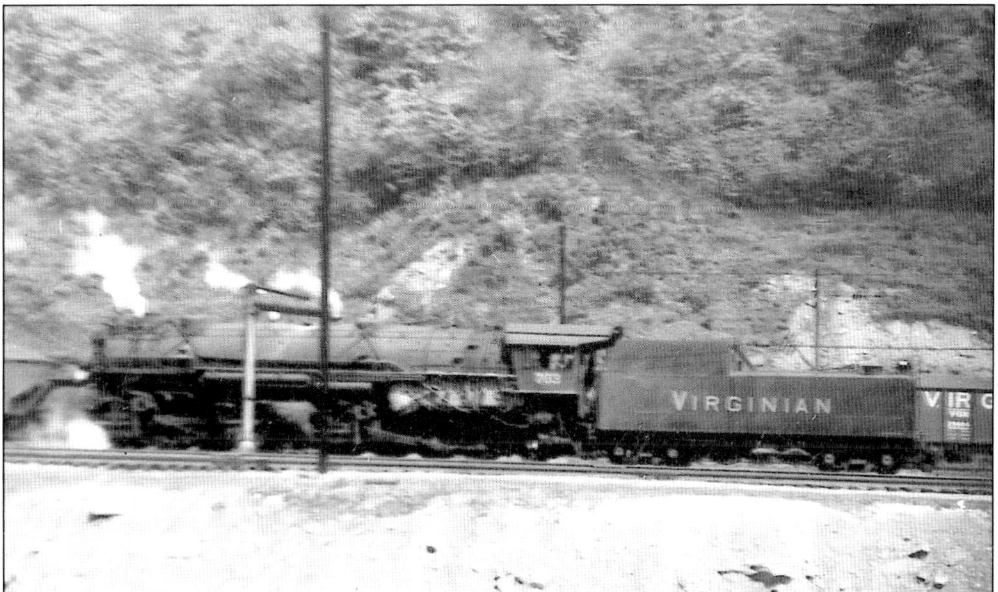

ROCK MOMENTS. The Norfolk & Western, as well as the Virginian Railways, had a battle for competition in the Rock Valley region. The N&W acquired a mill on the Bluestone River at Rock in an attempt to impede the Virginian's progress. The N&W later sold out to their competitor, and the Virginian Railway ruled Rock. (Courtesy of Dollie M. Lawrence.)

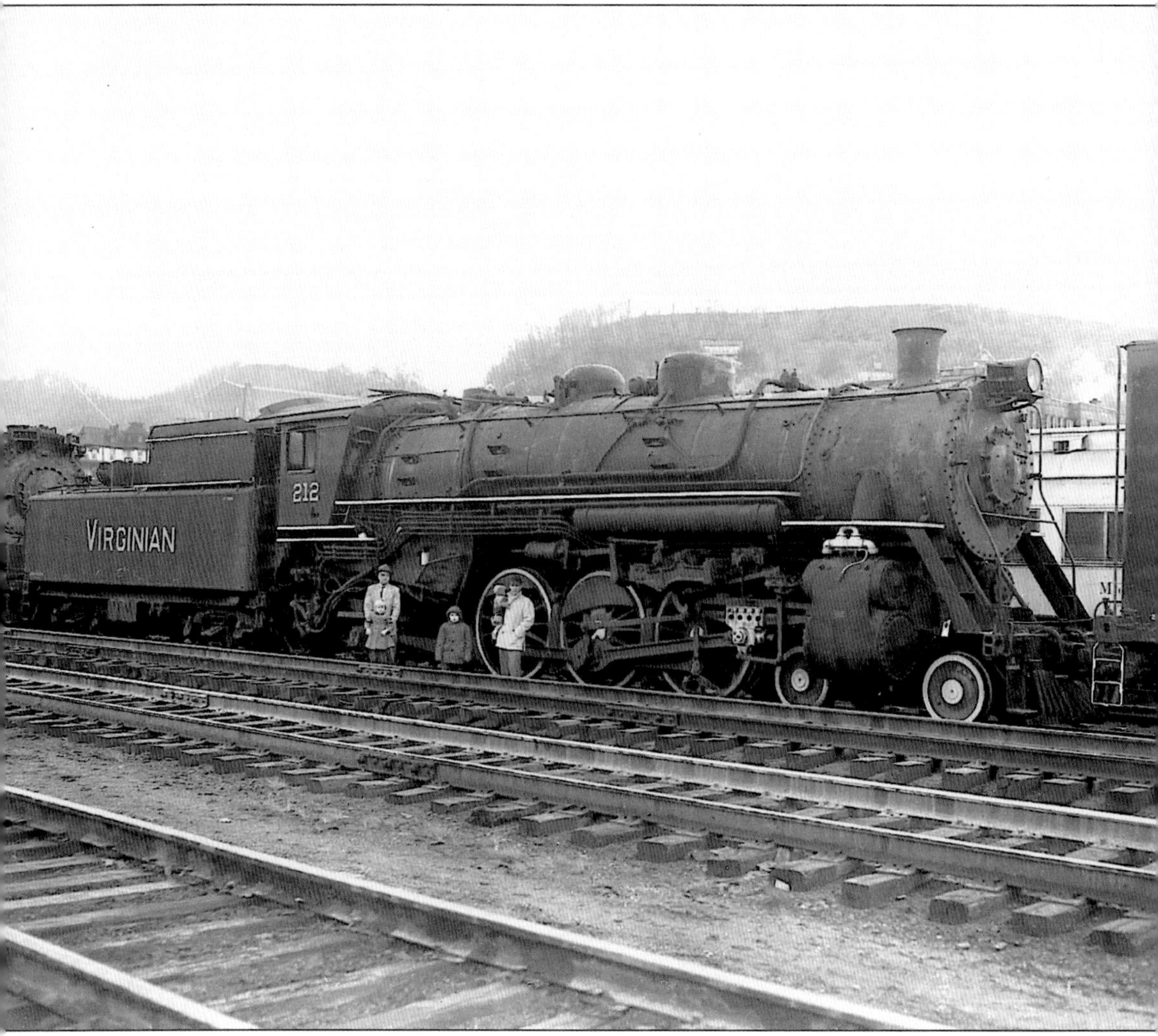

End of the Line. George Martin, a longtime Pocahontas Division locomotive engineer, was among the engineers on the division in the late 1950s responsible for rounding up the old steam locomotives and taking them to be cut up for scrap metal. Martin convinced local photographer Mel Grubb to take a trip with him and photograph the end of an era. Martin is shown to the far left holding Grubb's daughter Lindsey. The other two children and the man are not identified. (Photo by Mel Grubb.)

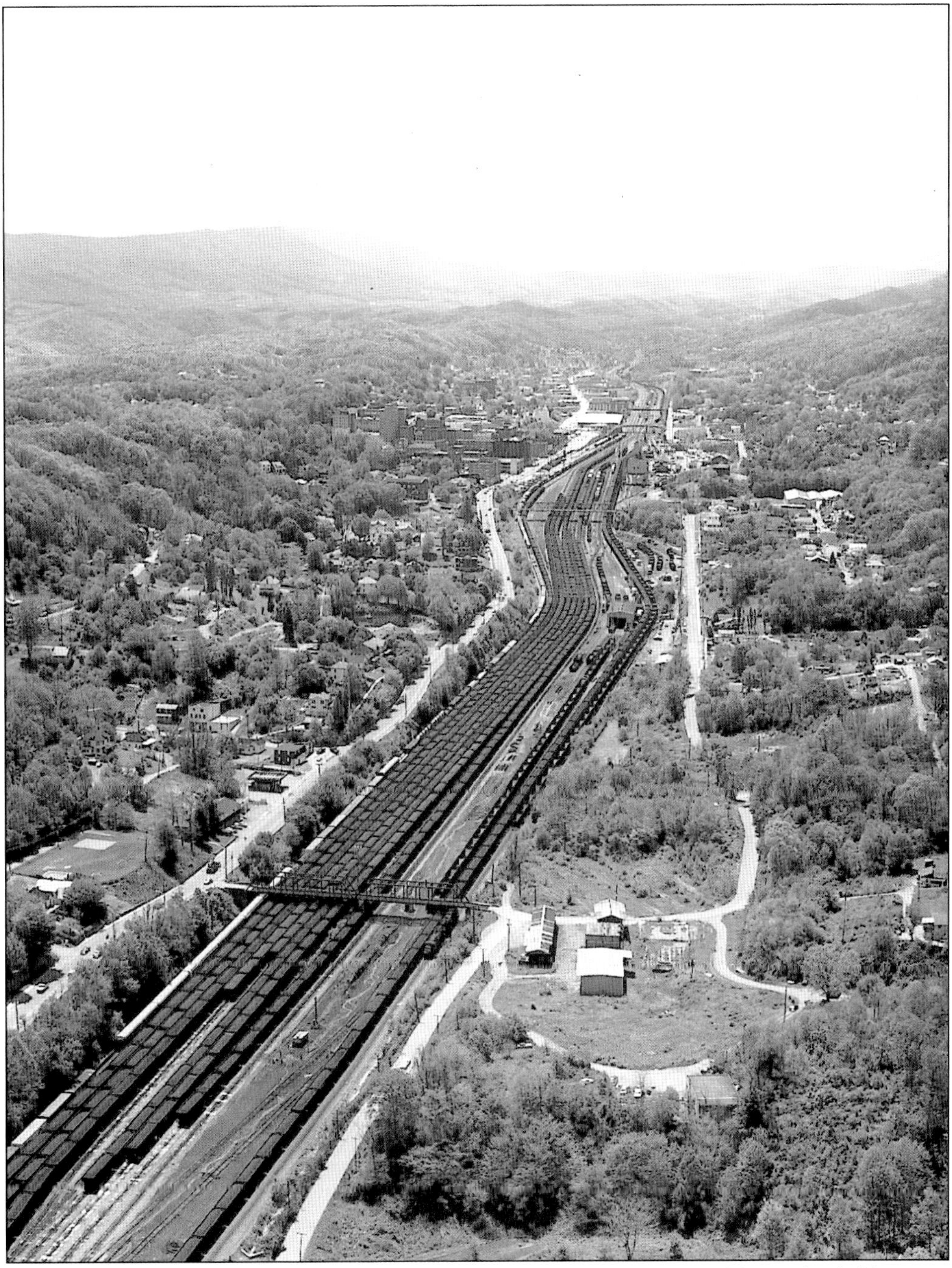

RIVER OF COAL. Since 1883, a steady stream of coal has flowed eastward from Bluefield to Pier No. 6 at Lambert's Point in Norfolk, Virginia. For years, the railroad "draped" coal trains over Bluefield's natural gravity "hump," to prepare them for their eastward journey. Rumor holds that in the 1930s, a former city school superintendent dismissed students when the Bluefield yard was filled with coal cars so that the students could show their appreciation for the industry's role in their community. (Photo by Mel Grubb.)

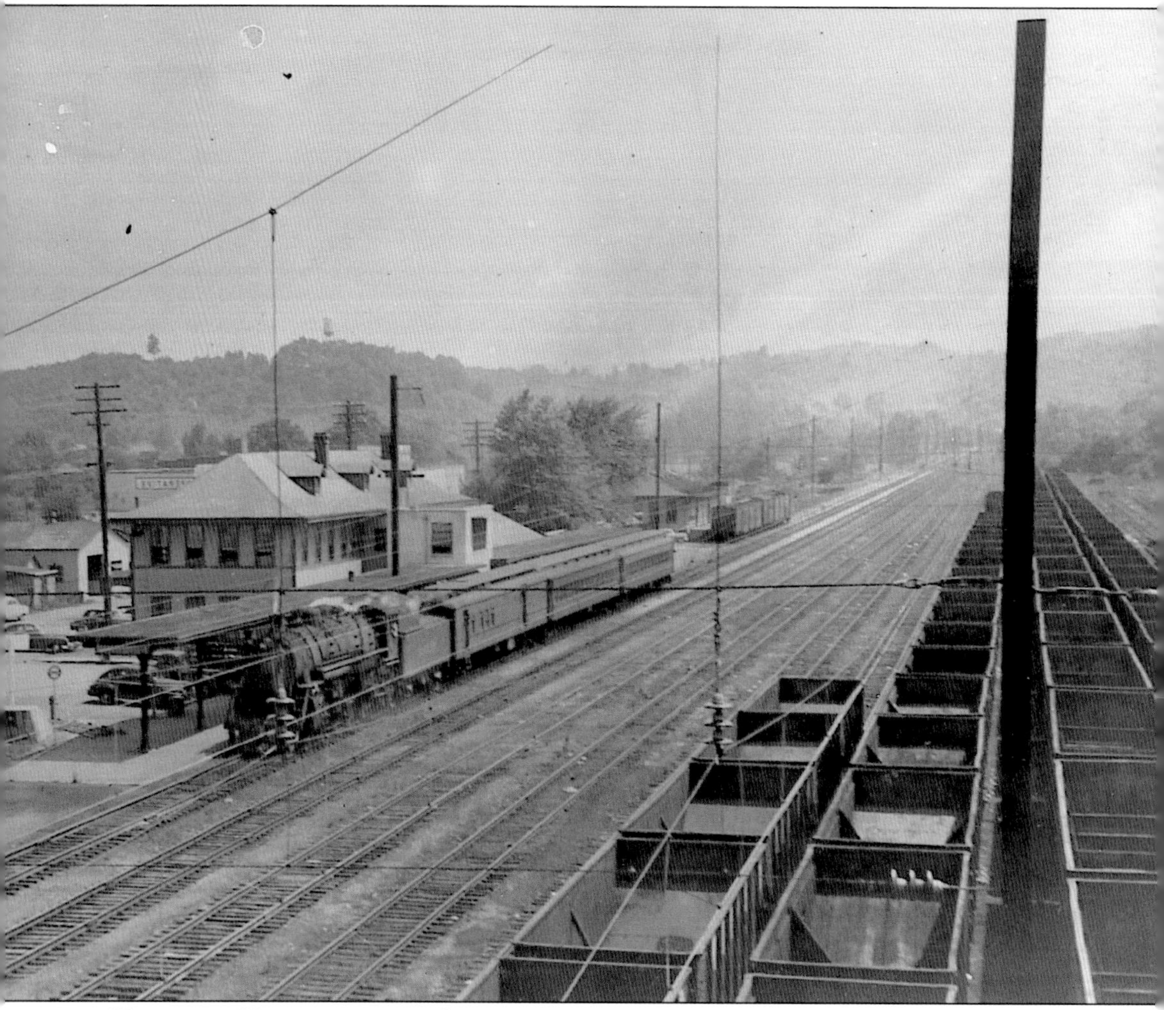

VIRGINIAN HEADQUARTERS. The Princeton passenger station on the Virginian Railway and the division superintendent's office are shown in this 1955 photograph of the last trip for passenger trains No. 3 and No. 4. The Virginian and the old Norfolk & Western are now both part of the Norfolk Southern Railway. The former competitors started dropping their passenger trains in the 1950s after competition from personal vehicles and improved highways started eating away at profits. The Virginian merged with the Norfolk & Western in 1959. (Courtesy of Peery Mooney.)

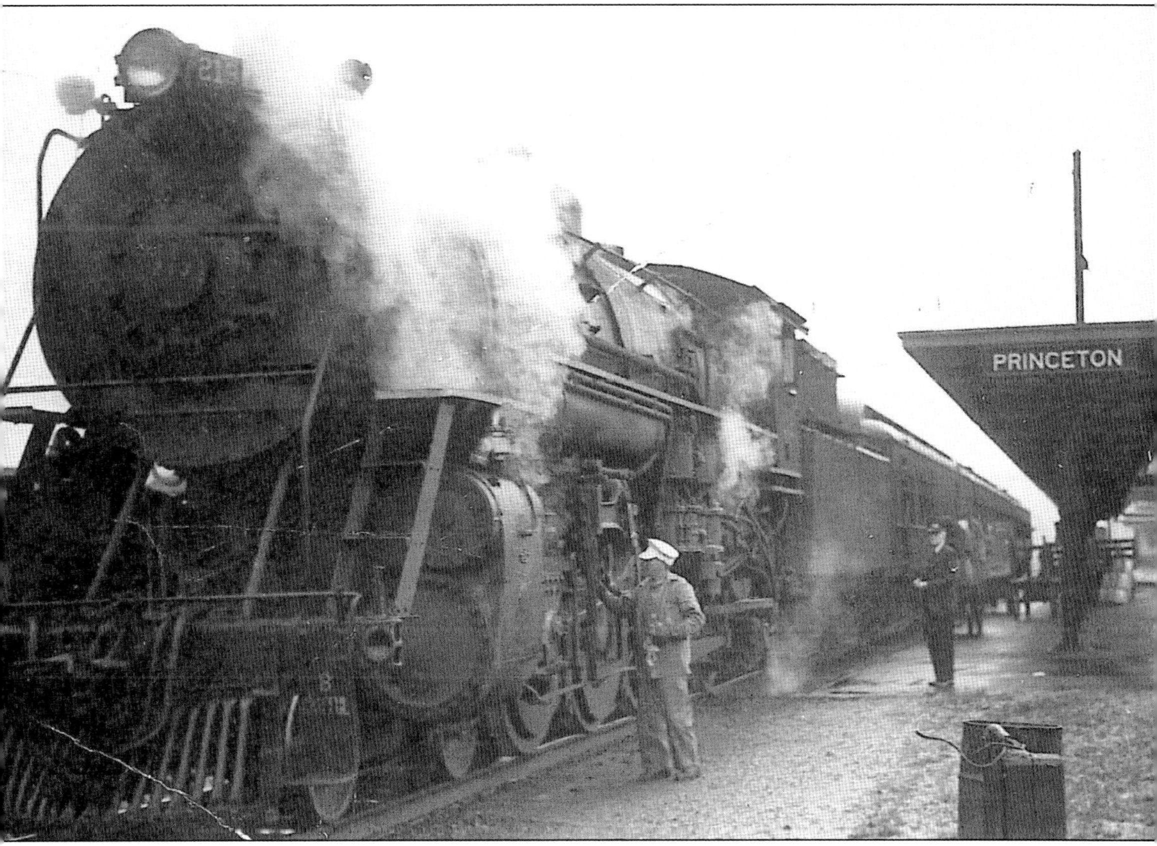

STEAM ON THE RISE. Virginian Railway locomotive engineer A.A. Akers is shown here examining his locomotive in this 1952 photograph as conductor T.J. Henretta looks on. Princeton was a busy station on the Virginian line with scheduled passenger runs to the East Coast as well as a regular route between Princeton and Charleston on the Deep Water track. (Courtesy of Peery Mooney.)

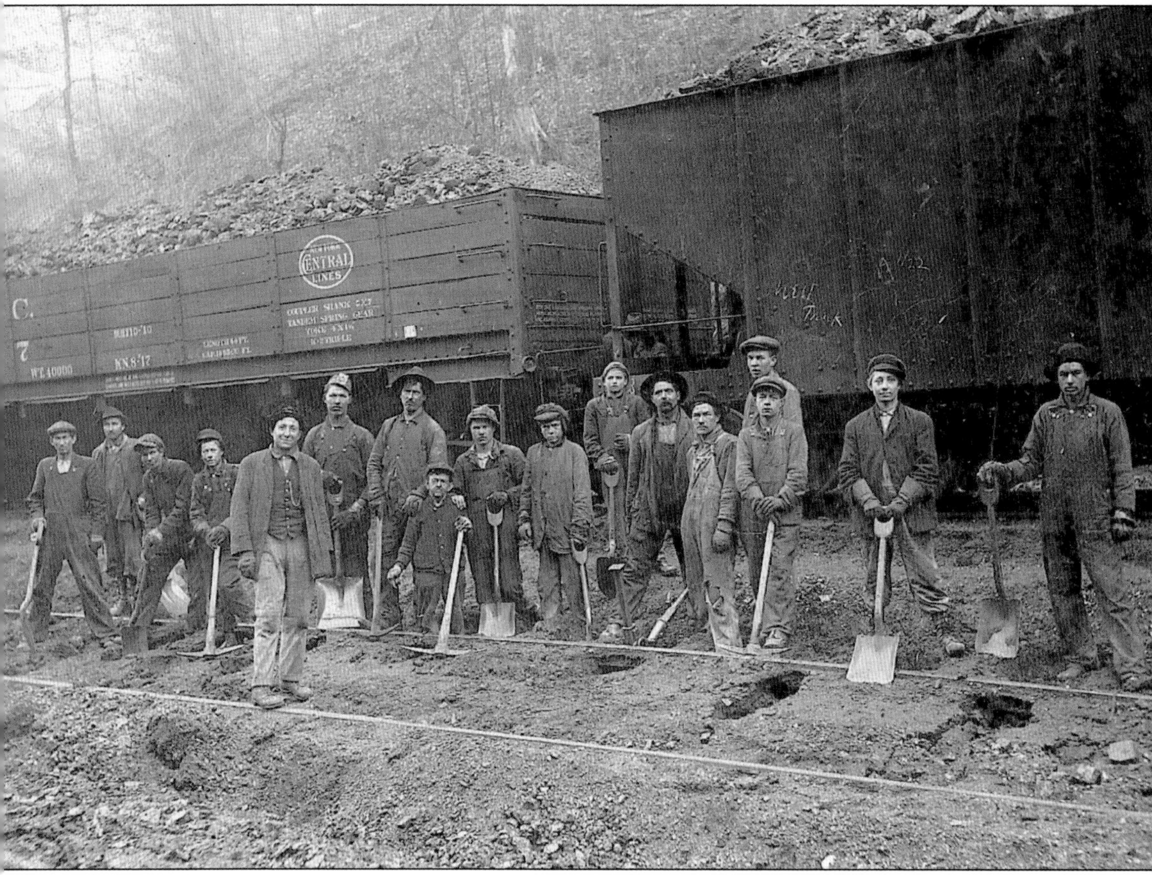

Working on the Railroad. A labor crew is shown here posing for a photograph at an unknown location somewhere within the region. Because there was not a readily available pool of labor in the coalfields region for the railroads to draw on, foreign workers primarily from eastern European countries as well as African-American workers from the South were recruited for the coal and rail jobs. (Courtesy of H. Edward "Eddie" Steele.)

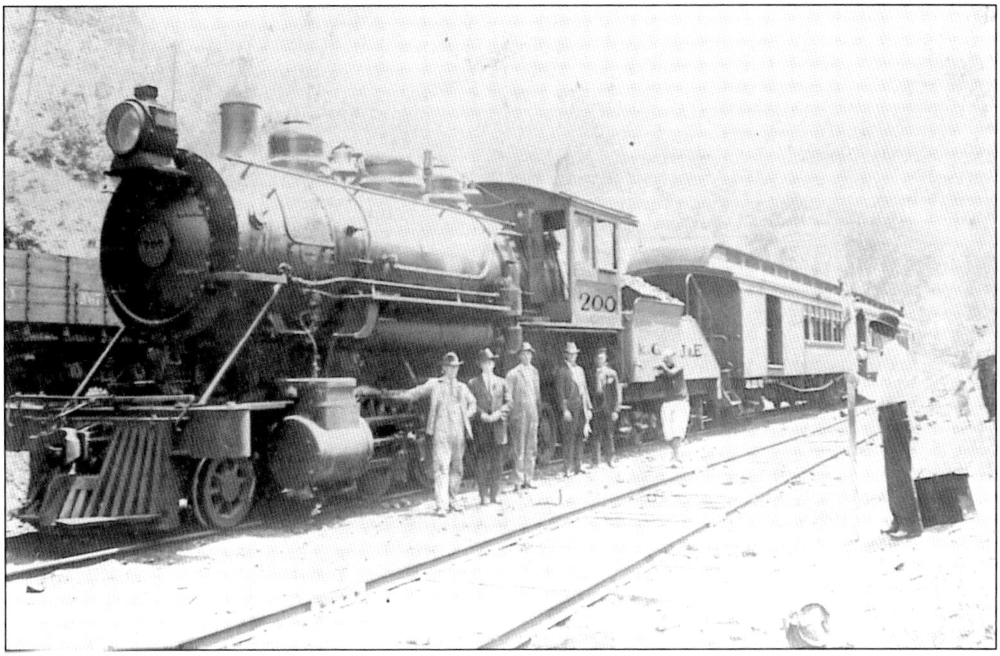

SNAP SHOT. Mercer County's two major railroads made connections with other railroads throughout the region. It appears as though these gentlemen have paused for a publicity shot for a baseball player. (Courtesy of Grubb Photo Service.)

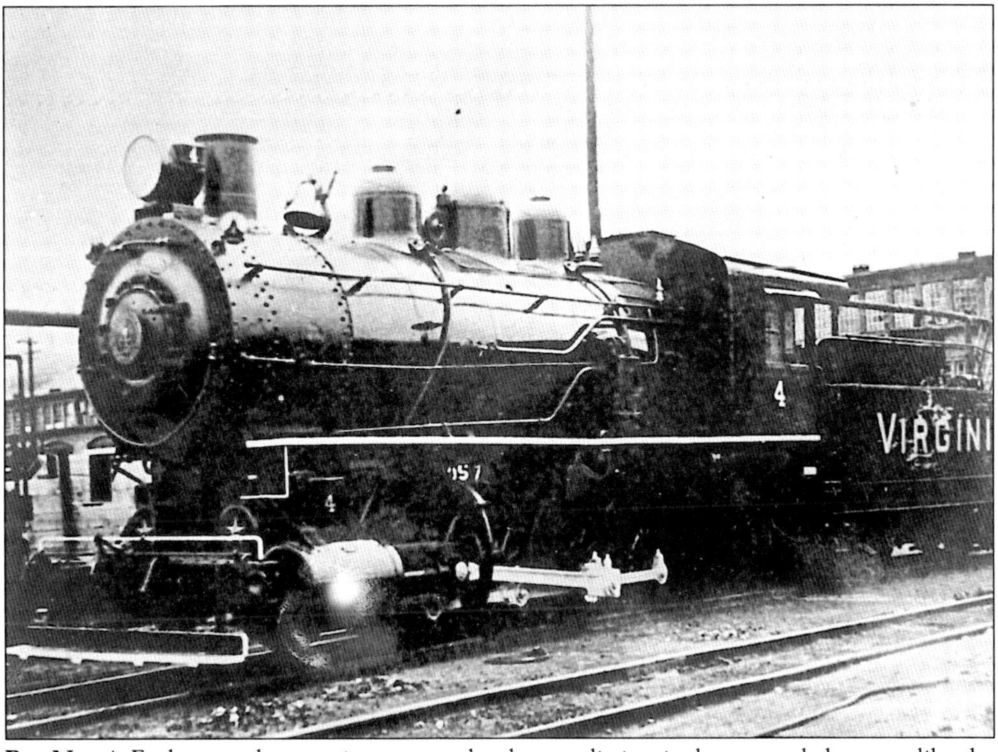

BIG NO. 4. Each steam locomotive appeared to have a distinctively personal character like the No. 4 Virginian locomotive, shown here in Princeton. (Courtesy of Peery Mooney.)

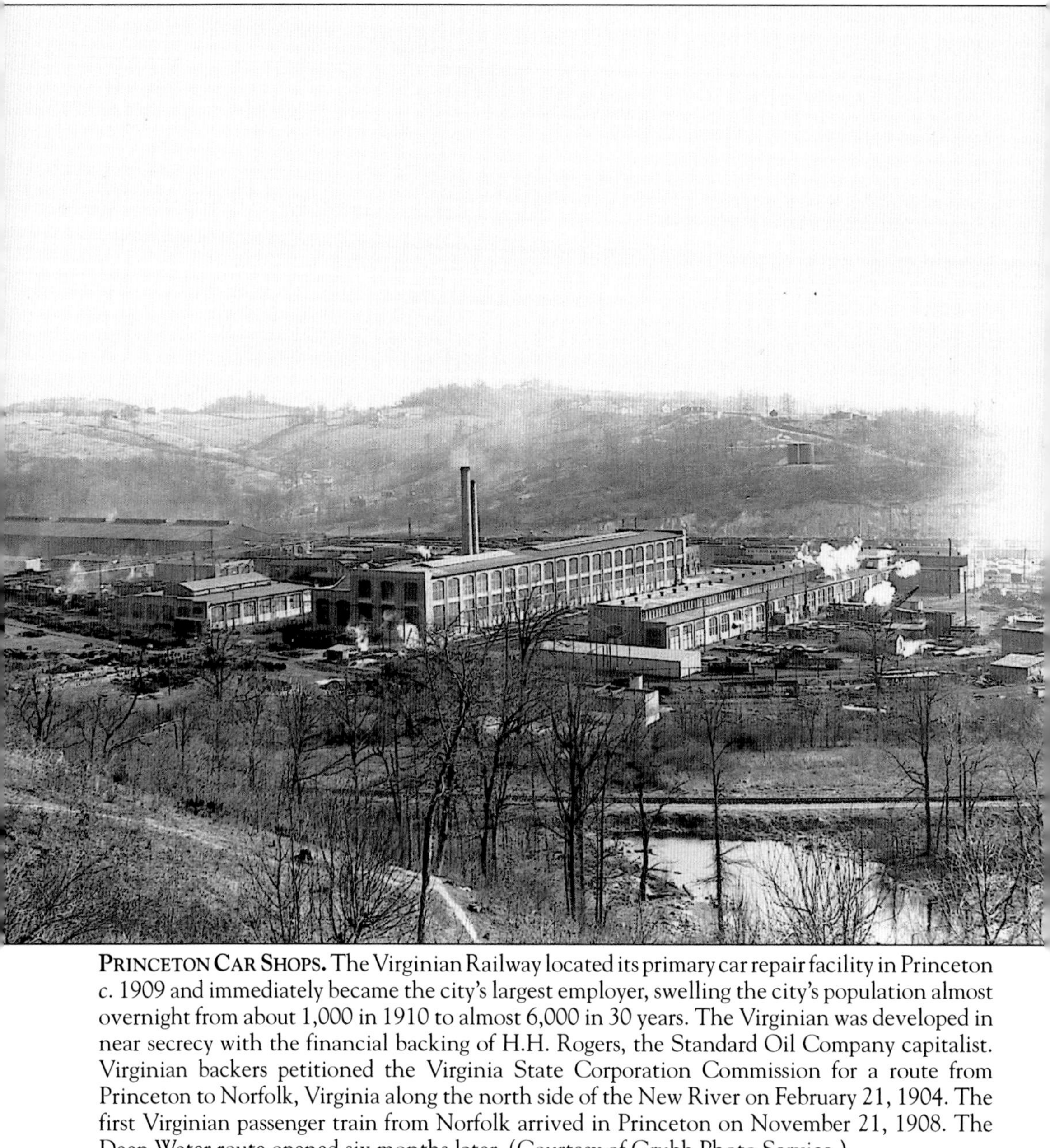

PRINCETON CAR SHOPS. The Virginian Railway located its primary car repair facility in Princeton c. 1909 and immediately became the city's largest employer, swelling the city's population almost overnight from about 1,000 in 1910 to almost 6,000 in 30 years. The Virginian was developed in near secrecy with the financial backing of H.H. Rogers, the Standard Oil Company capitalist. Virginian backers petitioned the Virginia State Corporation Commission for a route from Princeton to Norfolk, Virginia along the north side of the New River on February 21, 1904. The first Virginian passenger train from Norfolk arrived in Princeton on November 21, 1908. The Deep Water route opened six months later. (Courtesy of Grubb Photo Service.)

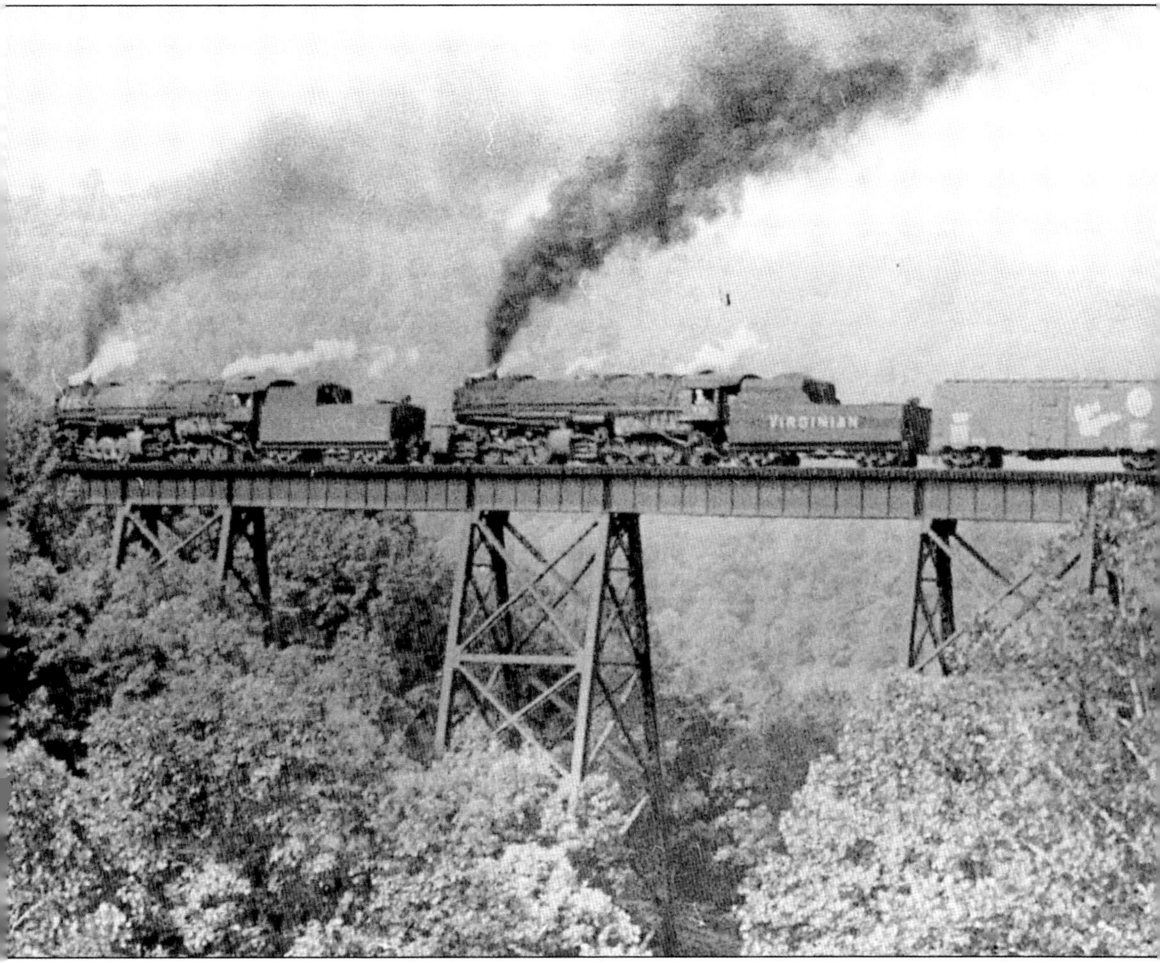

RAILROAD ON STILTS. Like its Norfolk & Western "cousin," the Virginian Railway had to tame some rather challenging geography in order to create manageable grades for its steam, electric, and diesel-powered locomotives to carry freight from the East and coal from southern West Virginia to customers worldwide. Present-day travelers on I-77 between Princeton and Bluefield may notice a scene similar to the one shown here without any steam locomotives. (Courtesy of Grubb Photo Service.)

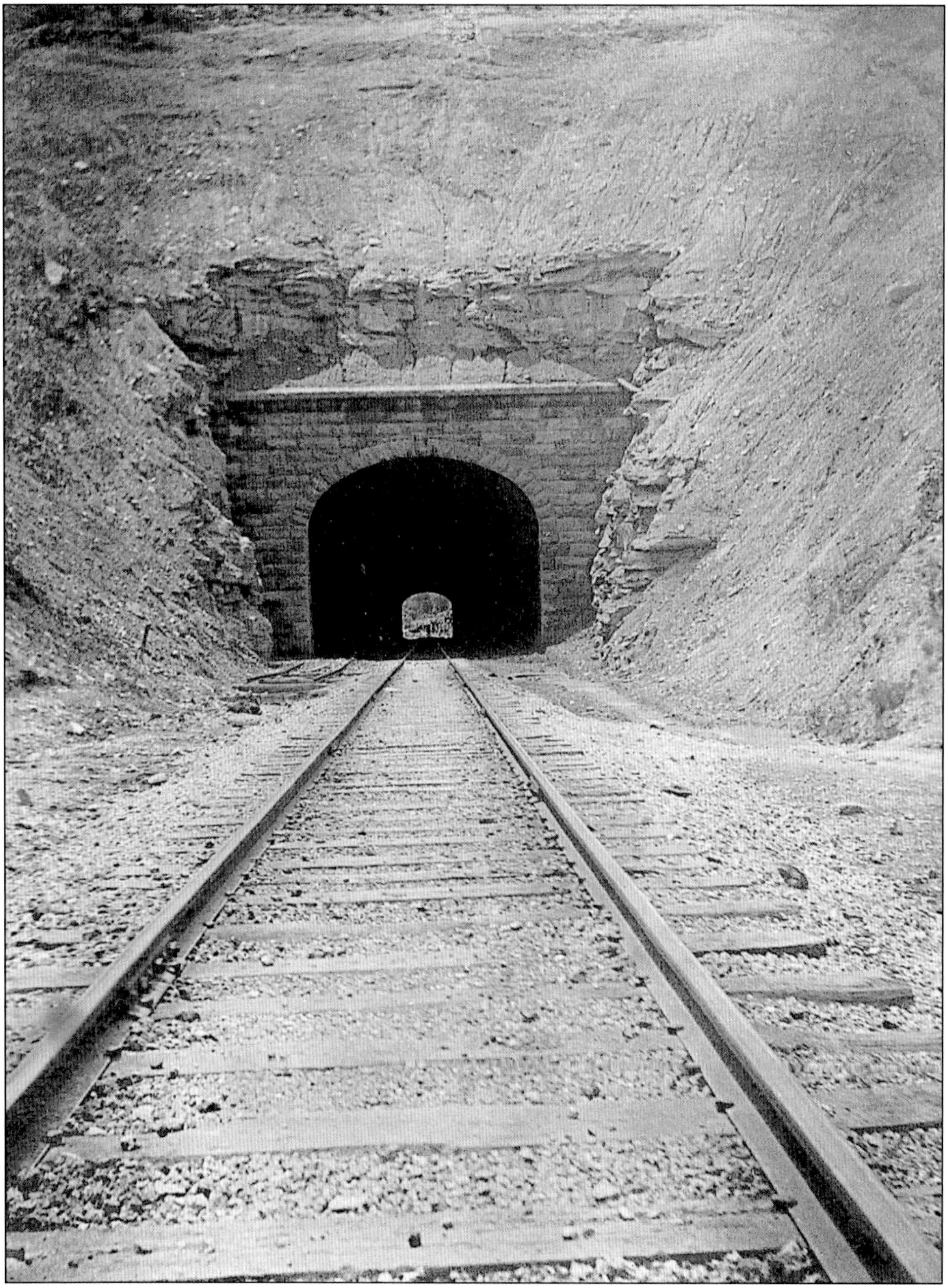

BREAKTHROUGH. One of the most dramatic events in the development of the southern West Virginia coalfields was the opening of the first tunnel through Coaldale Mountain in 1889 that connected the Mercer and McDowell County coalfields. While technological advancements would soon overshadow the engineering achievement, those early feats of construction made it easier for future generations to improve transportation construction methods. (Courtesy of Eve Cooper Murphy.)

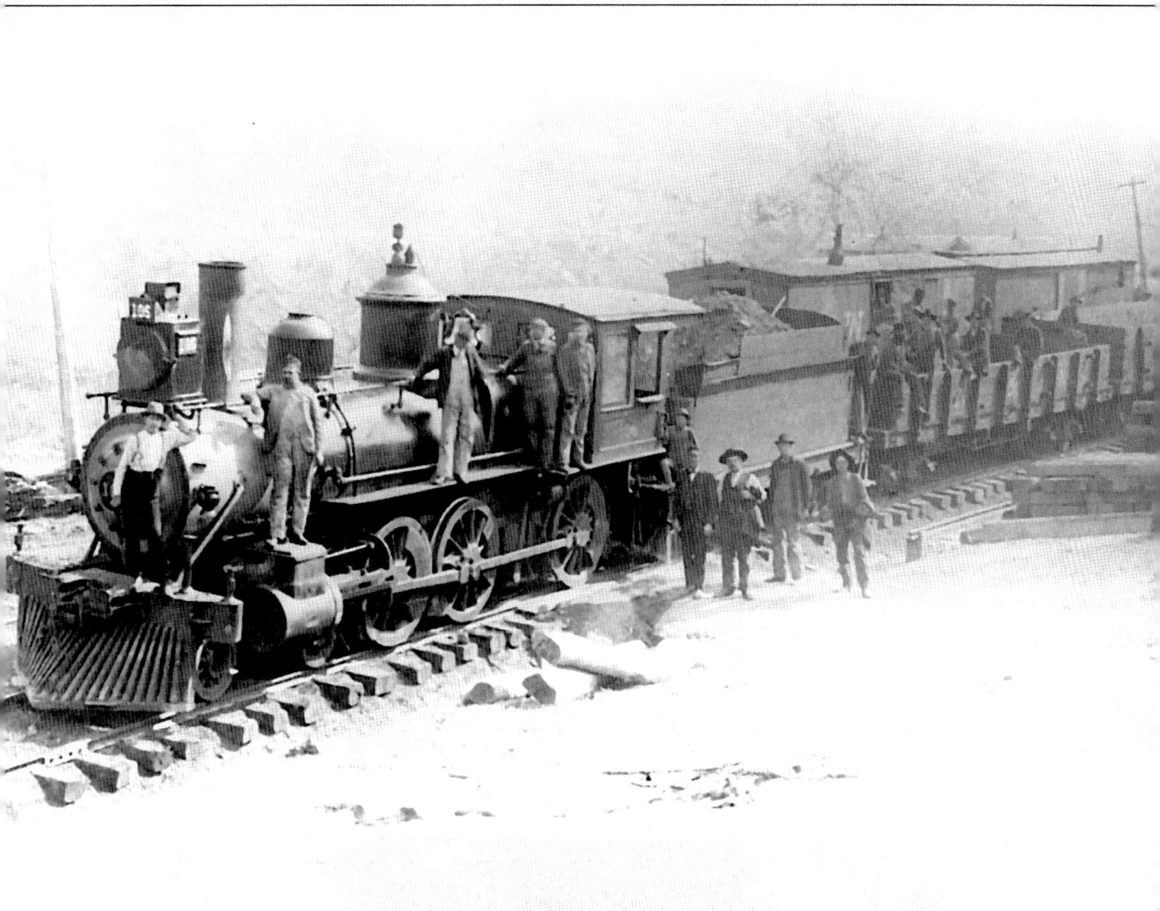

ANY TIME IS ON TIME. An unidentified group of railroaders is shown here posing for a photograph somewhere on the (then) Norfolk & Western mainline. Railroading in an unforgiving terrain is challenging, but Pocahontas Division employees have been consistently among the top in company safety programs. (Courtesy of Grubb Photo Service.)

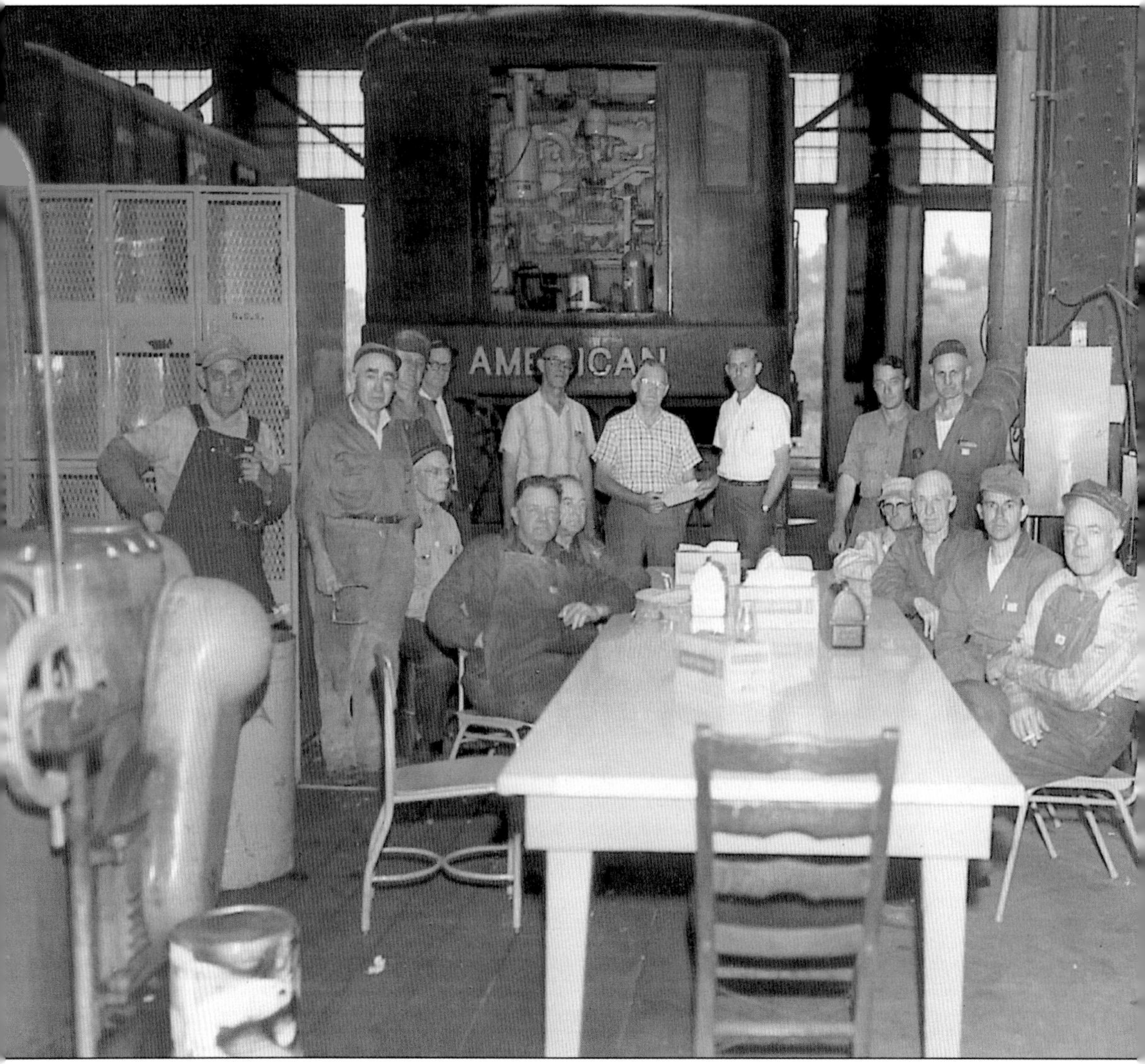

RETIREMENT PARTY. Otis Belcher was honored at a retirement party in 1967 at the old Virginian Car Shops in Princeton. Jess James said the shop primarily repaired large machinery. Shown in the picture are, from left to right, as follows: (seated) Johnny Walker, Charlie Oxley, Vaughan Smith, Sanford Jones, Johnny Dobbins, Pete Belcher, and Clarence Six; (standing) Bill Bates, Ray Bailey, Herb Shaffer, Milton Brookman, Bill Lovern, Otis Belcher, Jess James, Pete Vie, and Roy Dobbins. (Courtesy of Heber Stafford.)

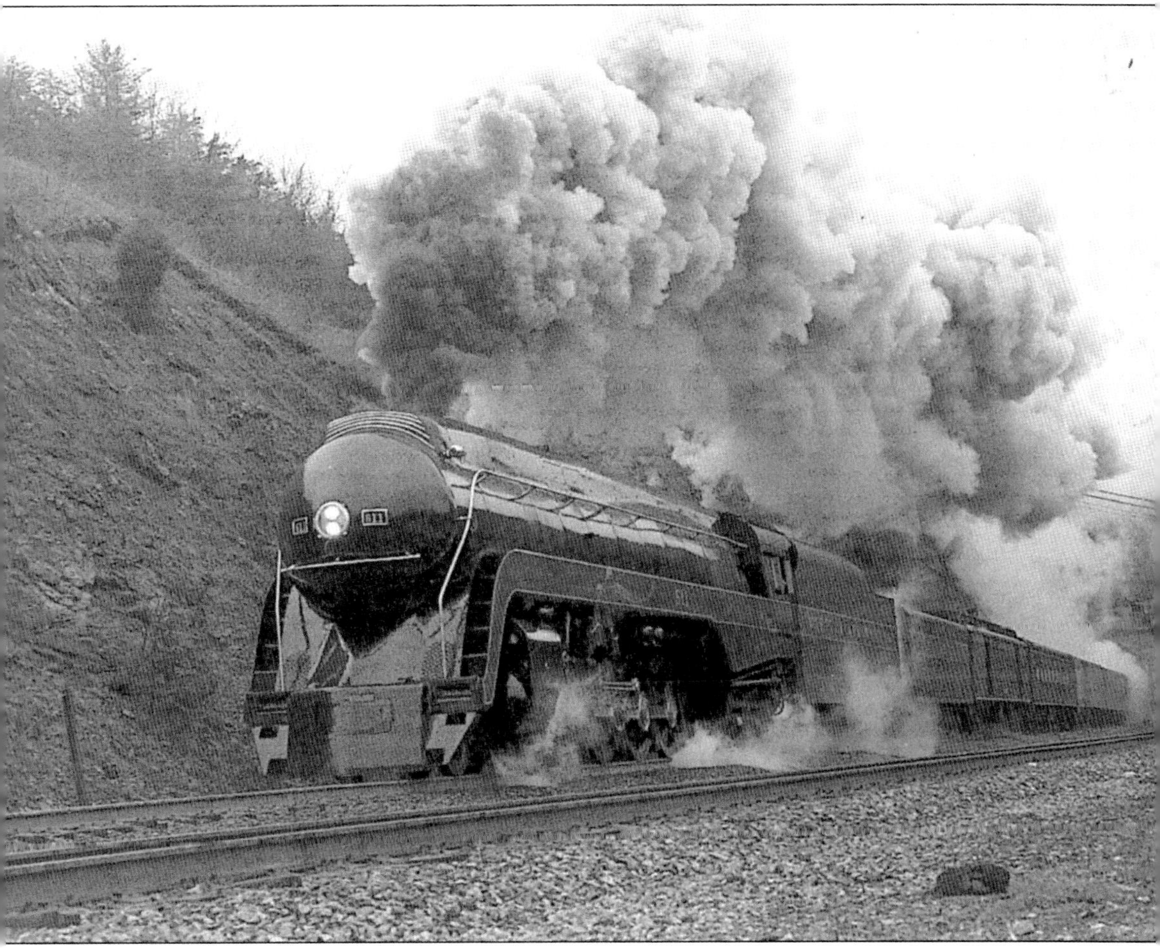

STEAMING THROUGH COALDALE. The mighty J-Class 611 locomotive is shown here steaming through the present-day Coaldale Mountain tunnel pulling the Bluefield Centennial Limited in 1989. Norfolk Southern discontinued the popular steam excursion trips due to the high cost of maintaining the old locomotives and other factors. (Courtesy of H. Edward "Eddie" Steele.)

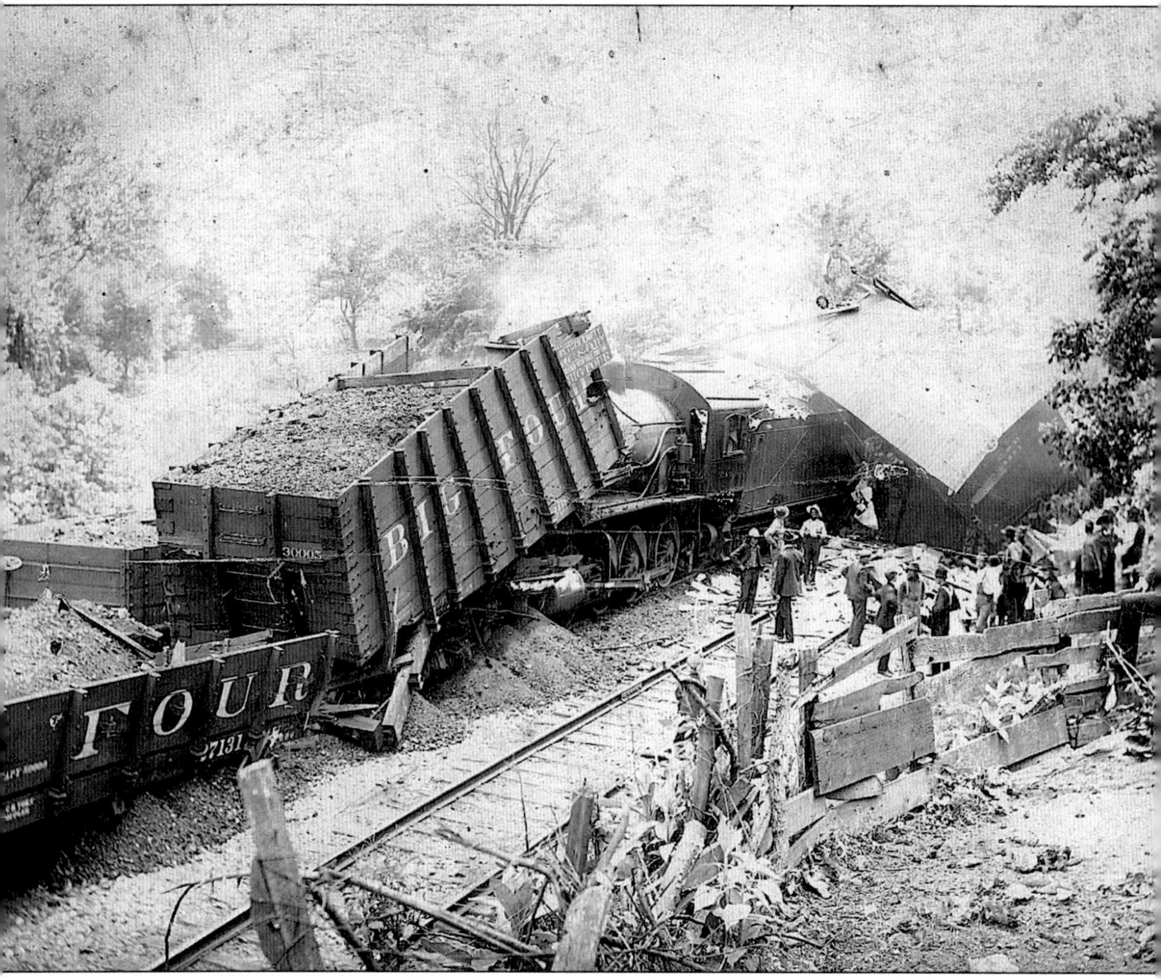

Between a Wreck and a Hard Place. L.F. Reed of Princeton is shown here in the far right of this photograph looking over the wreckage of a locomotive and cars at an unknown location, possibly Elgood, on June 7, 1919. Then, as now, train wrecks draw a lot of attention. (Courtesy of Rick and Jeanie Owens.)

Six

COMMUNITIES

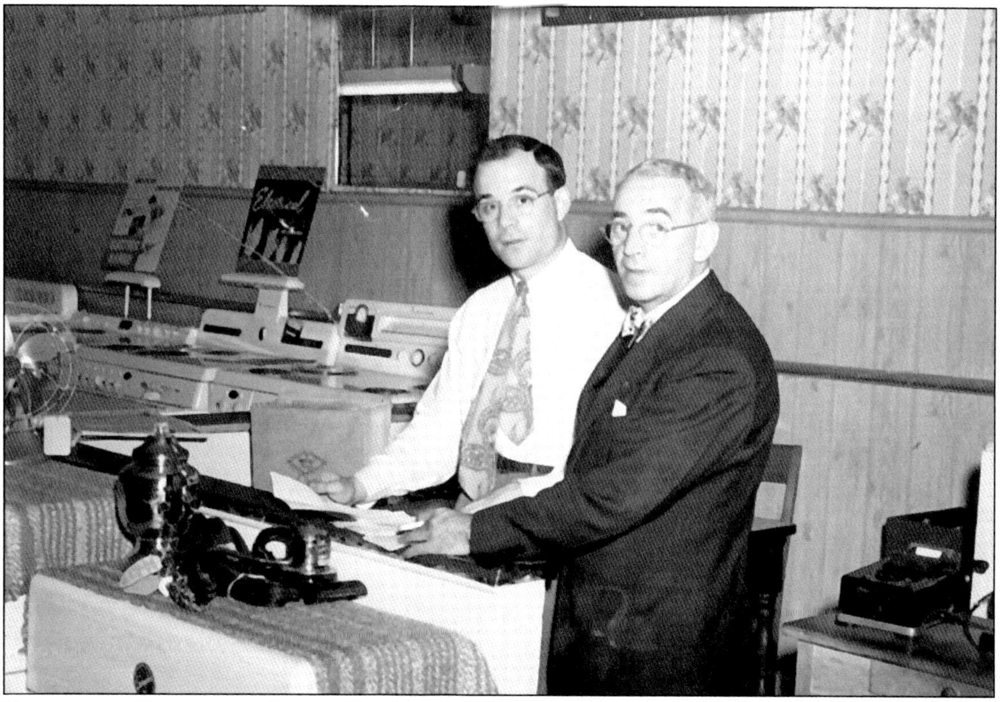

DREAMS OF THINGS TO COME. The Kammer Furniture Store in Bluefield has been a leader in spotting consumer trends and delivering the goods for decades. Established by Harry Kammer, right, who immigrated to the United States from Lithuania, the store is now operated by Max Kammer, left, and his son Harry. The Kammer family has a long-standing tradition of community service that extends through the generations. Max was recognized in 1999 as "Retailer of the Year" by the National Furniture Dealer's Association. The photo above was taken when the store was promoting electric ranges. (Courtesy of Max Kammer.)

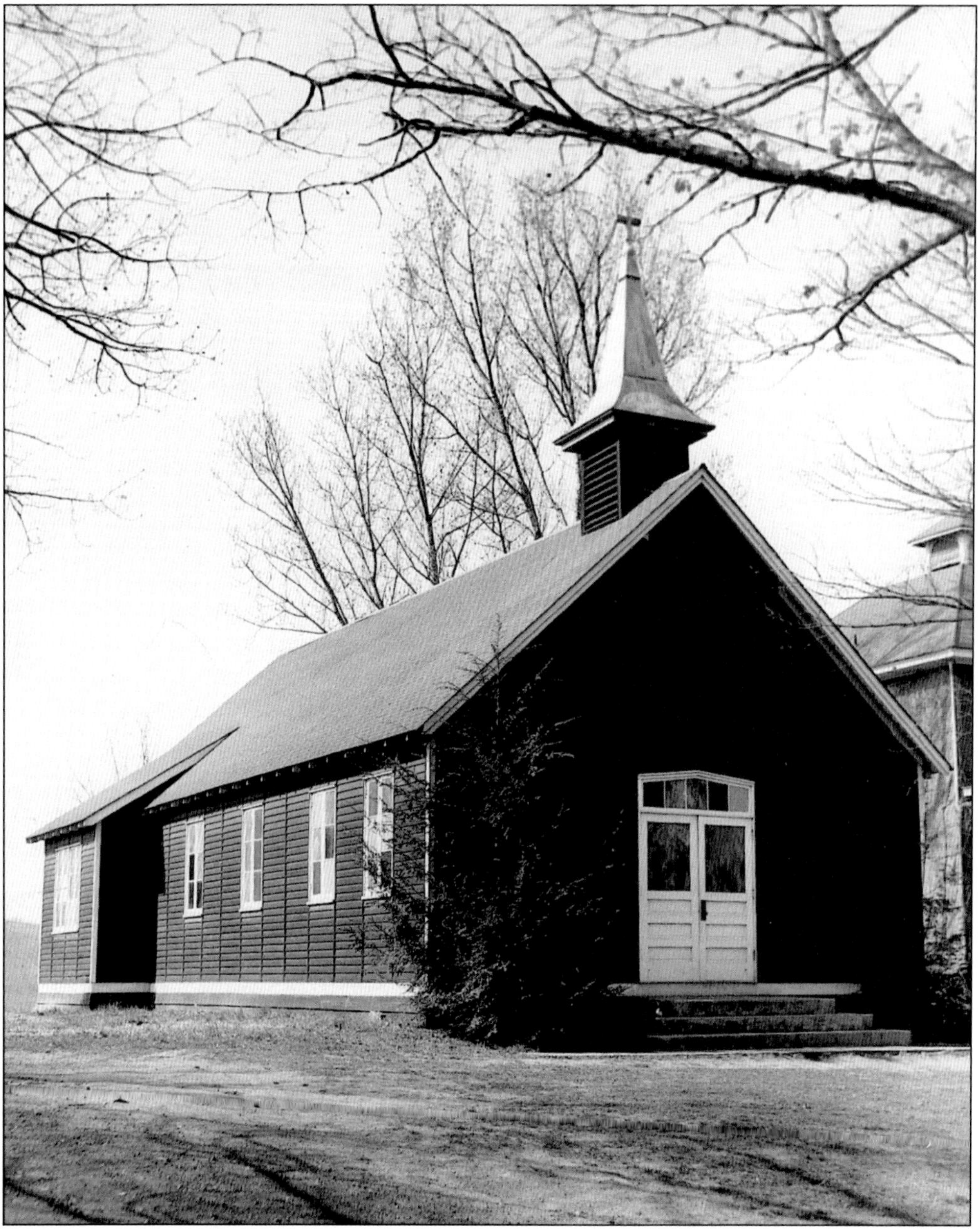

FAITH OF OUR FATHERS. The church shown in this 1950 photograph served the congregation of Princeton's Sacred Heart Catholic Church. Almost every faith and denomination is represented in Mercer County, from Islam to most Protestant faiths as well as a robust Jewish community. (Courtesy of Nick Buzzo.)

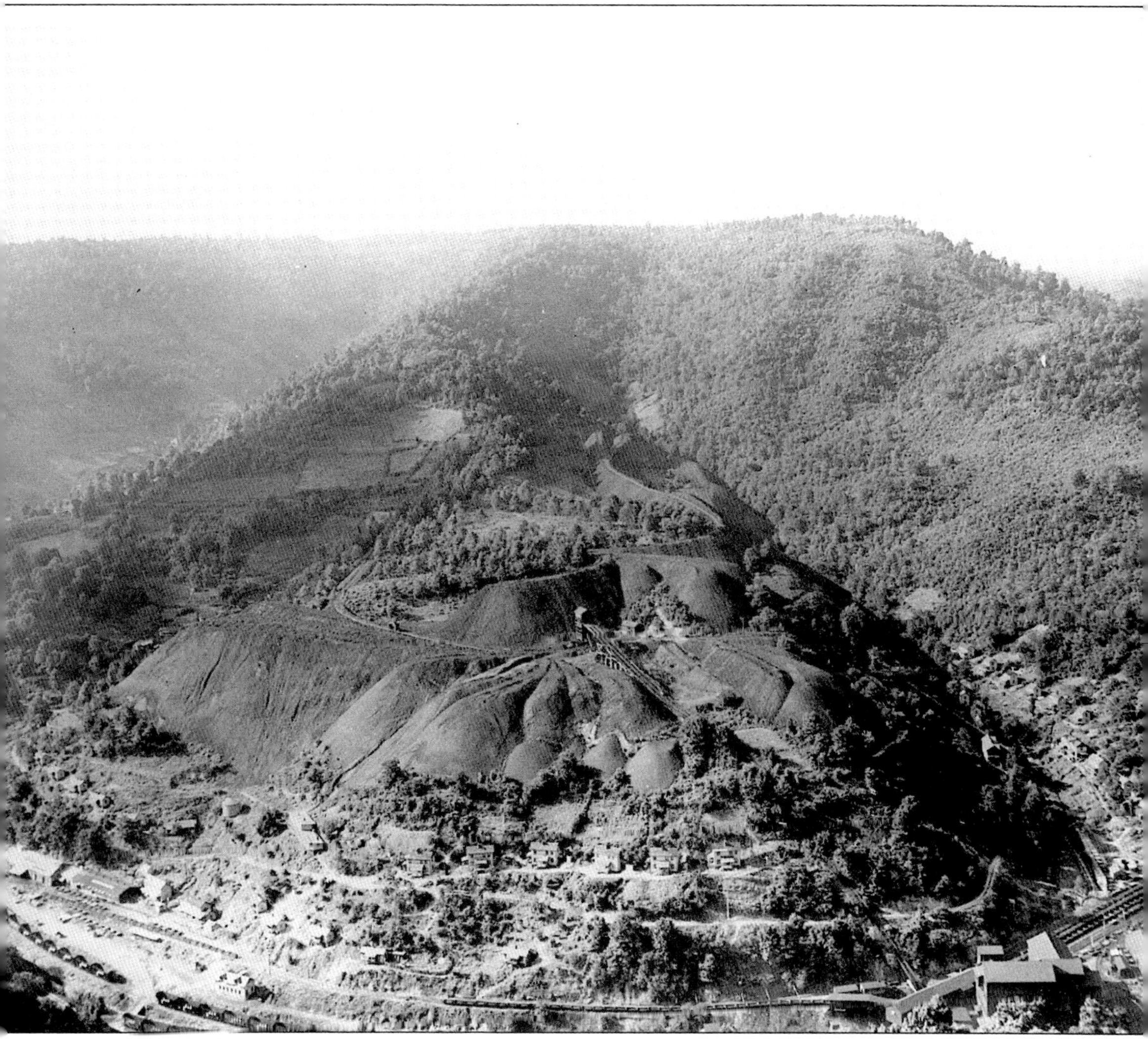

KING COAL. The Crane Creek Coal Mine in McComas was a massive operation as evidenced by this 1920s vintage aerial photograph. American Coal Company opened the Crane Creek Mine in 1902 and was producing coal through most of the 20th century. (Courtesy of Grubb Photo Service.)

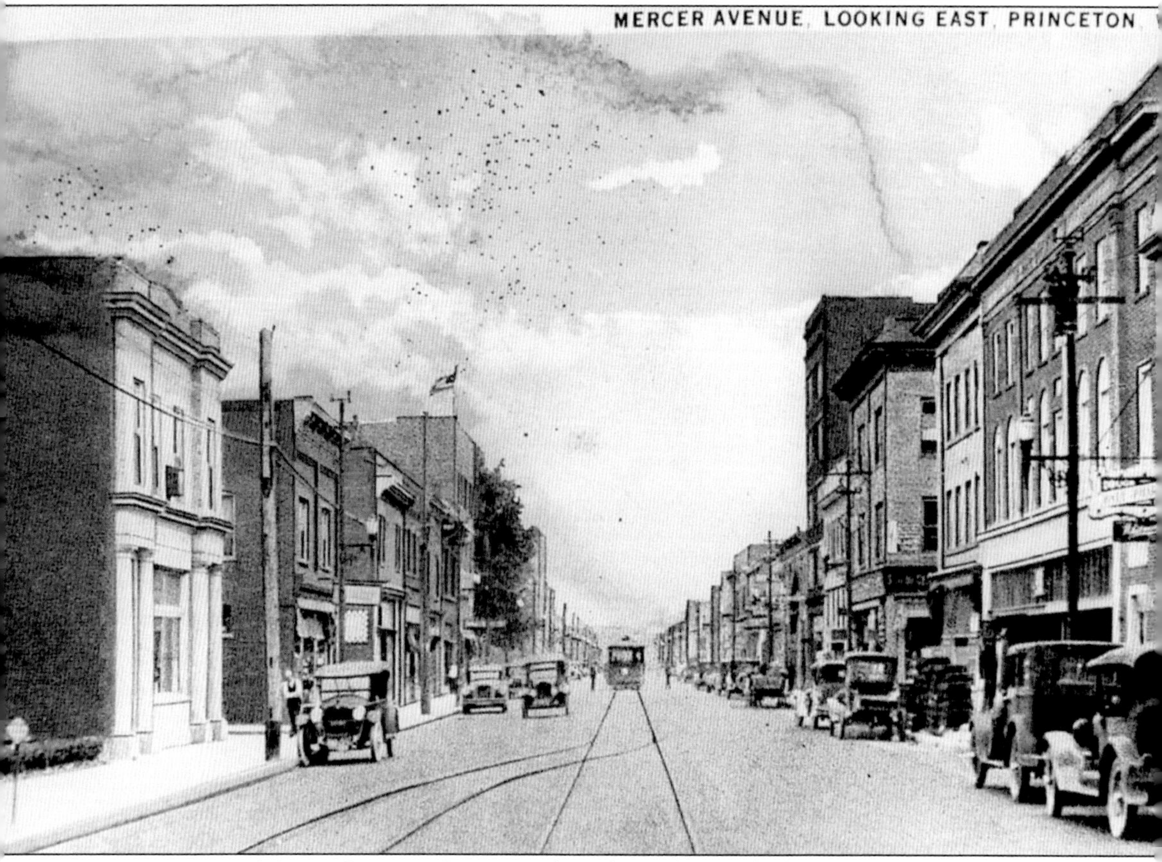

Downtown. Mercer Street in Princeton has always been a hub of activity and continues to serve the community with shopping, services, and entertainment. Tri-City Traction streetcars connected the cities of Princeton and Bluefield with Bluefield, Virginia and many points in between. (Courtesy of Grubb Photo Service.)

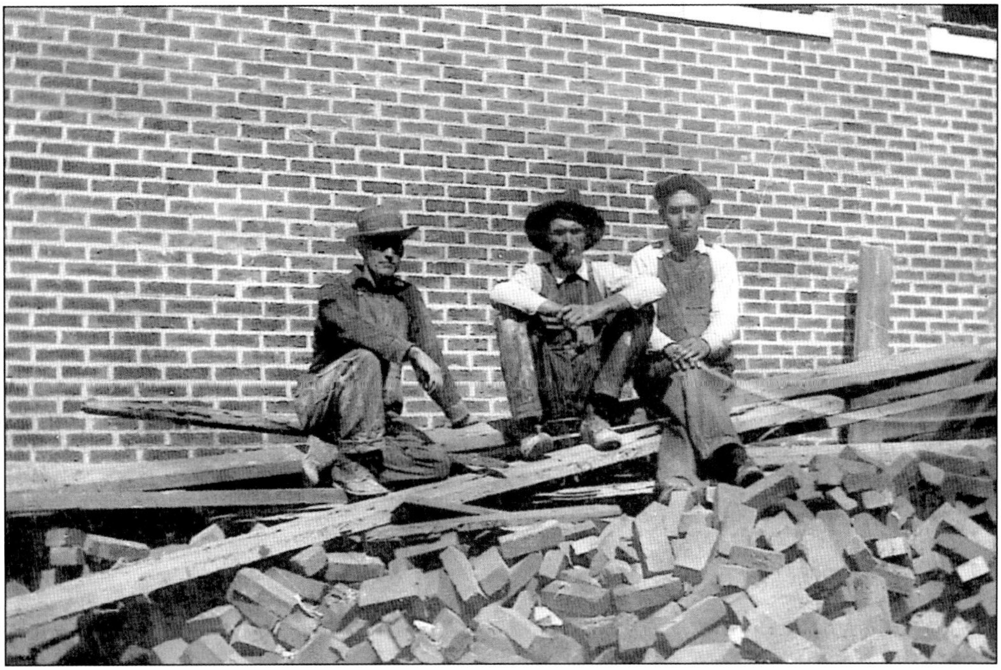

Like a Brick House. The crew that built the Mill Creek Coal & Coke company store in Coopers at the turn of the 20th century is shown here taking a much-deserved break. They are, from left to right, Mr. Martin, Dewey Young, and John D. Harman. (Courtesy of Betty Goins.)

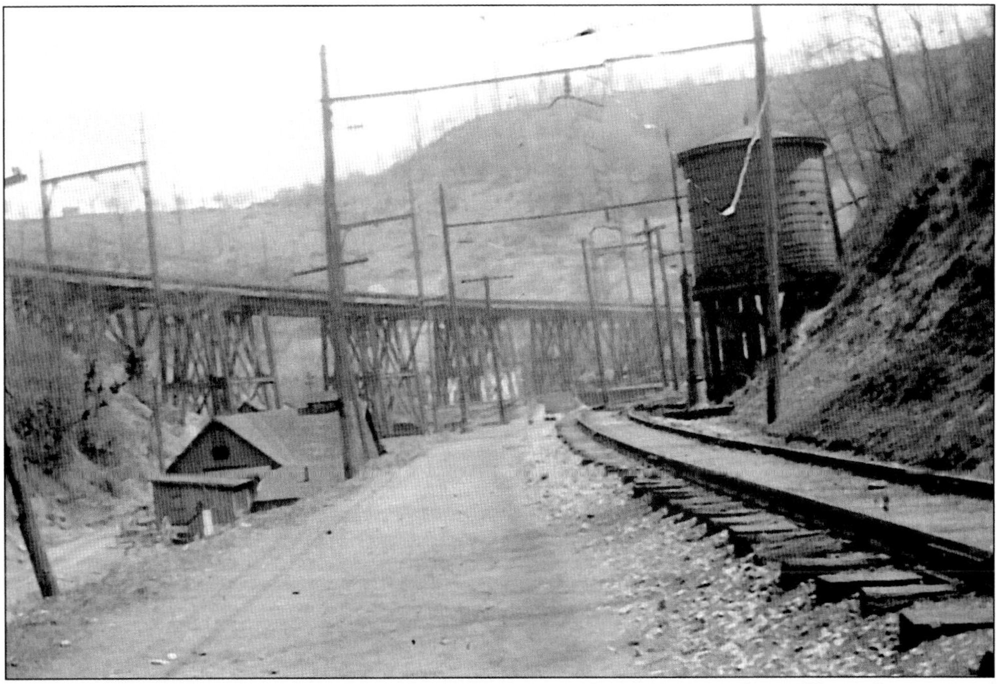

Making Tracks. The tracks in the right of the photo above went to the Mill Creek Mine and the upper set of tracks went to Pocahontas, Virginia. The row of houses following the contour of the tracks was called Ruth. (Courtesy of Betty Goins.)

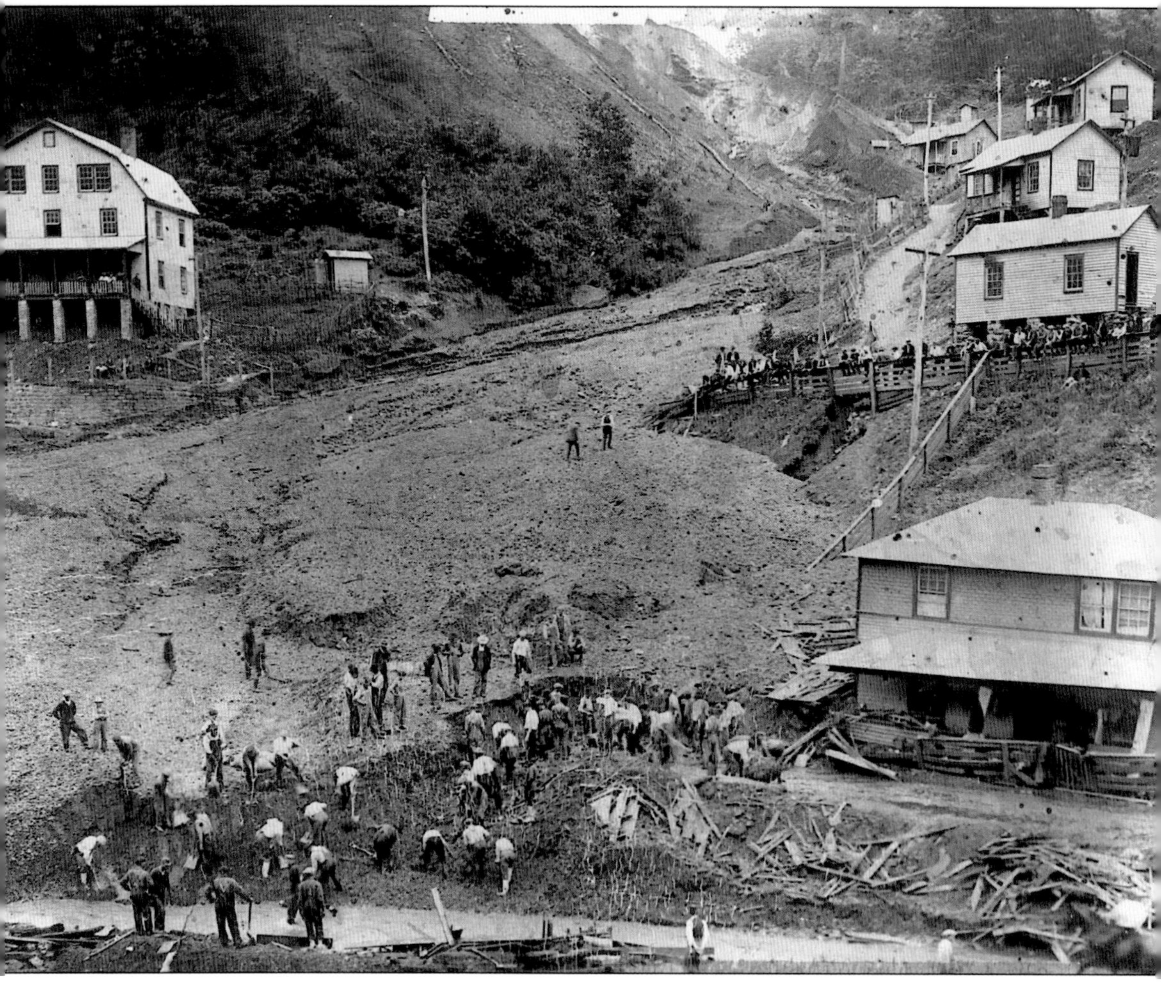

COALFIELD TRAGEDY. After several days of heavy rains, a massive gob pile of coal at American Coal Company's Crane Creek Mine gave way and collapsed on homes below, killing eight people including one rescuer caught in a successive slate dump slide. The tragedy occurred on June 9, 1924, and was described as "tragedy without parallel in the mining annals of southern West Virginia." (Courtesy of Grubb Photo Service.)

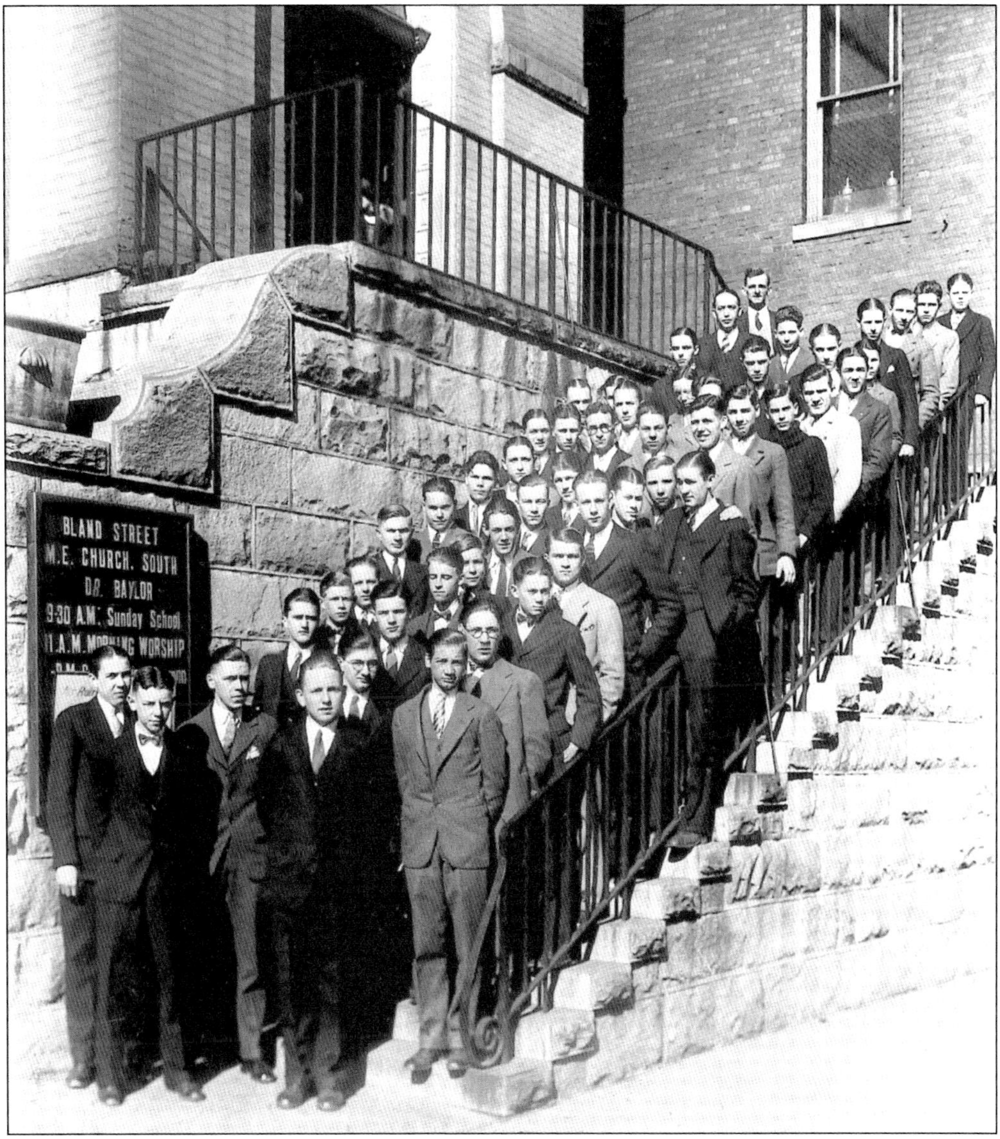

MEN OF THE CHURCH. The Wesleyan Bible Class of Bland Street Methodist Church in Bluefield gathered on the front steps of the church for this 1926 photograph. Included are the following: Sidney Bernard Jr., Sherwood Jones, Edgar Speidan, George Smoot, Charles Whitlock, Fred C. Goodall, Howard Barlow, David Watts, Ralph Eubanks, Robert Clifton, Jess Humphries, Raymond "Benny" Tilson, Carrol "Cac" Carpenter, Fred Alexander, Bennet Easley, Ralph "Goog" Millerand, W.C. Warlick, William Strader, James Wooldridge, Francis Peters, William Bailey, Kenneth Bruce, Marvin Helton, Carl Sheets, Alex Hufford, Clifton Mahon, Lonnie Rice, Tom Hawley, Millard Gilmore, Paul Daugherty, Edwin Johnson, Allen Pankey, Phil Harry Oliver, "Stonewall" Buddy Brooks, James McMullin Jr., Fred Francis, Houston Jackson, Harold Honaker, Edward Frazier, Wesley Cash, Ron Crabtree, Hamilton Hale, Elwood "Sleepy" Broyles, Mason Stewart, Ben Porterfield, Paul Barry, Hartsel Wassum, Claude Wade, Dennis Wickham, and Carl "Fats" Griffith. (Courtesy of Heber Stafford.)

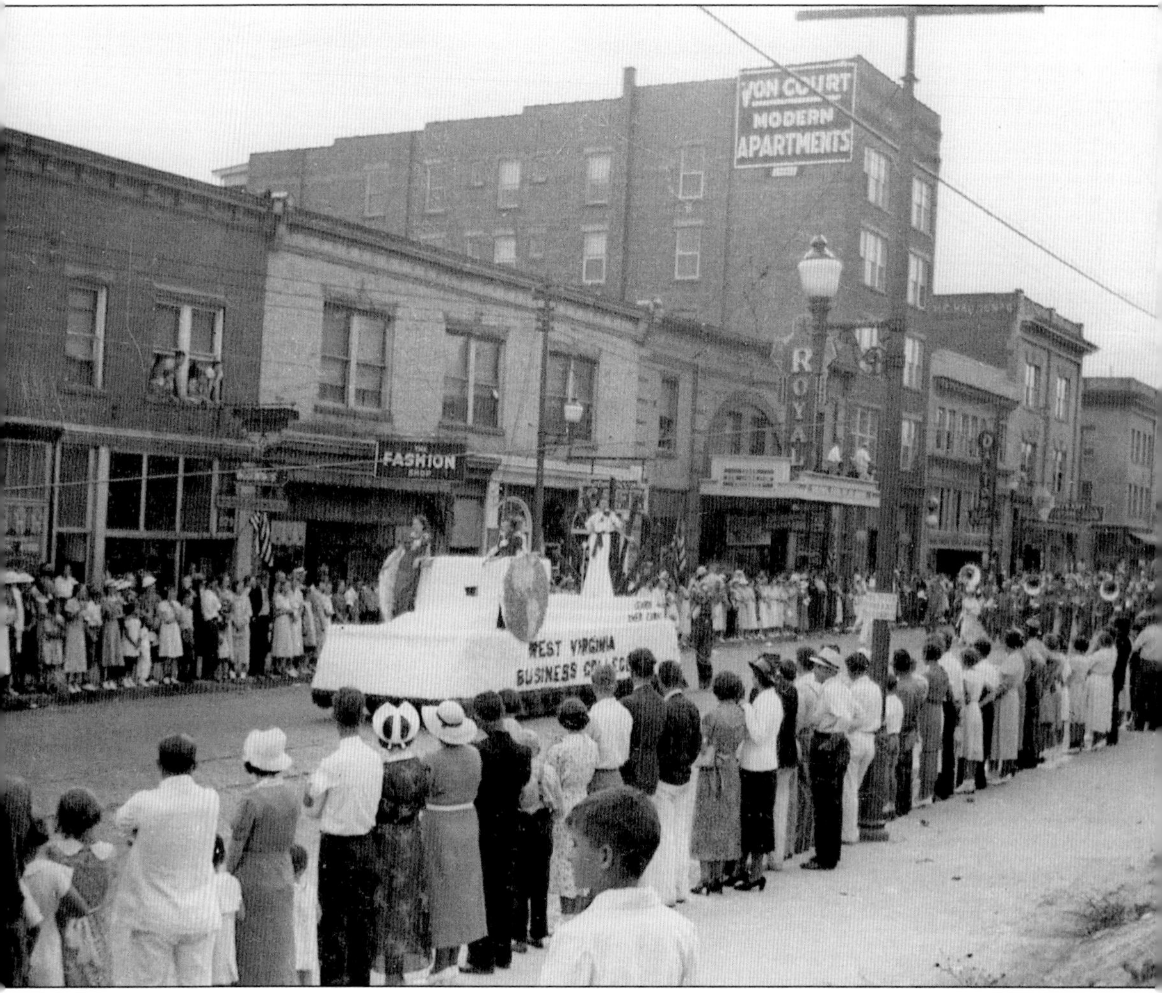

Love a Parade. Hundreds of people turned out for this vintage parade down Mercer Street in Princeton. The West Virginia Business College float is all decked out and a Red Skelton movie was playing at the Royal. Princeton parades still draw huge crowds into the downtown. (Courtesy of Nick Buzzo.)

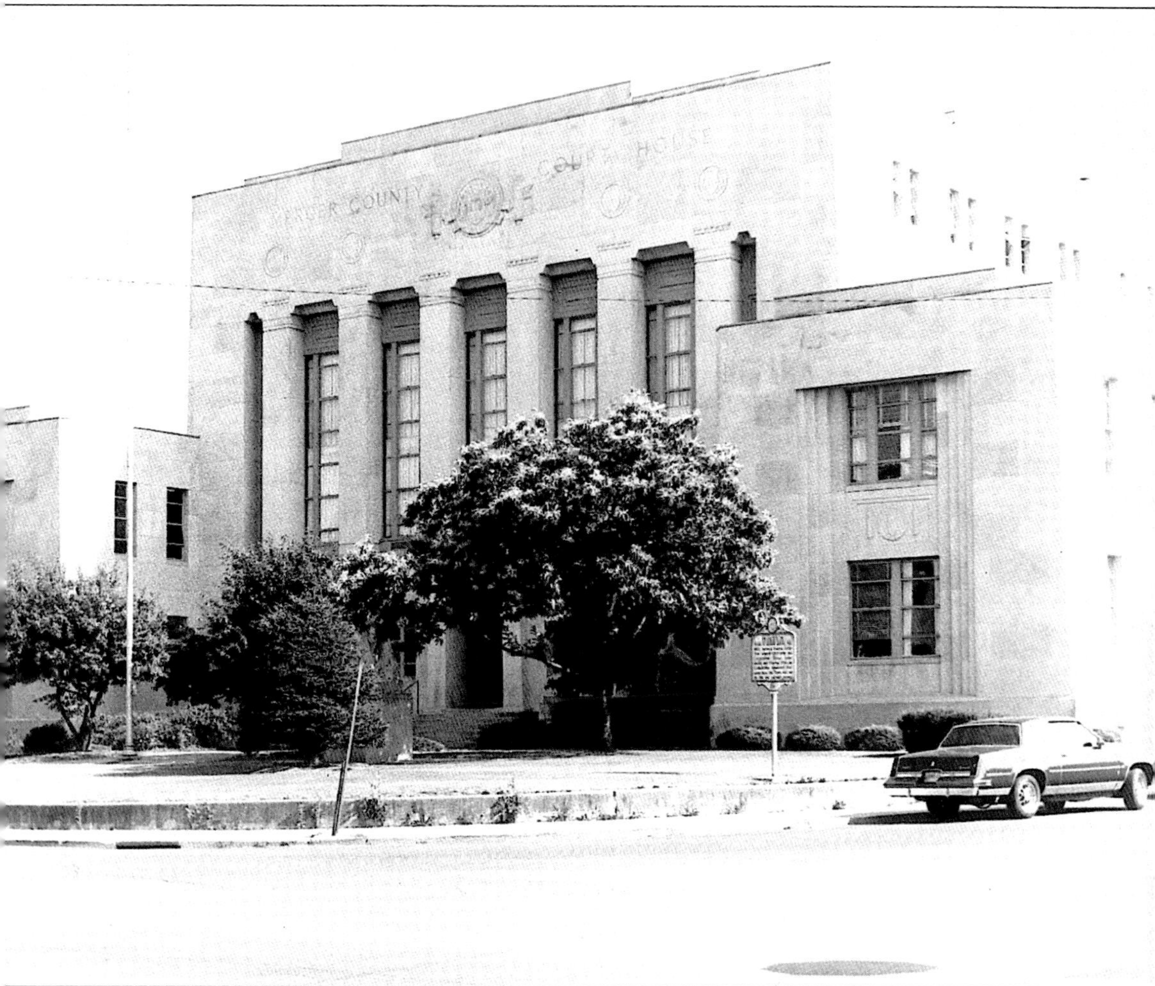

ROCK SOLID. Designed by Bluefield architect Alex B. Mahood and dedicated on August 8, 1931, the Mercer County Courthouse in Princeton has stood witness to a great many changes in its 70-year history. When the courthouse was dedicated, 61,323 people called Mercer County home. Although Mercer County lost population during the second half of the 20th century, that trend appears to have leveled off at the dawn of the 21st century. (Courtesy of Grubb Photo Service.)

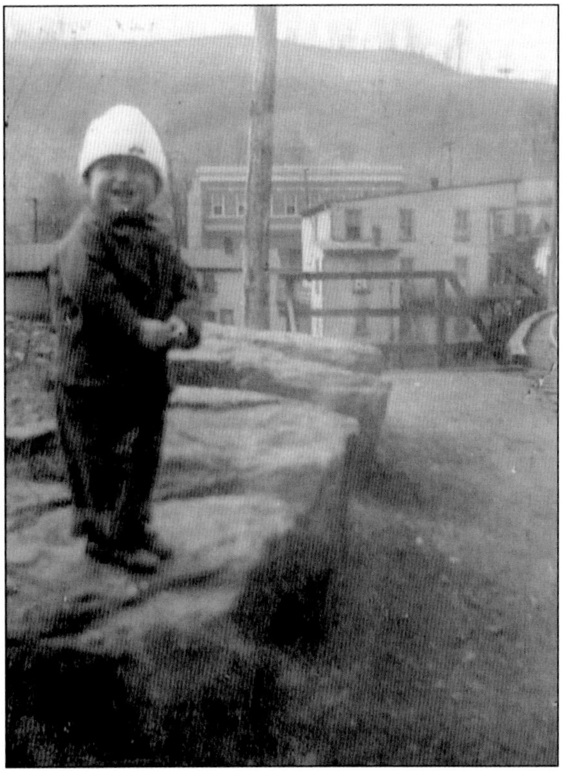

GOING TO TOWN. Thomas William Harman looks excited as he stands near the railroad track in Coopers. Note the Mill Creek Coal & Coke Company Store and the Coopers Hotel in this 1920s photo. (Courtesy of Betty Goins.)

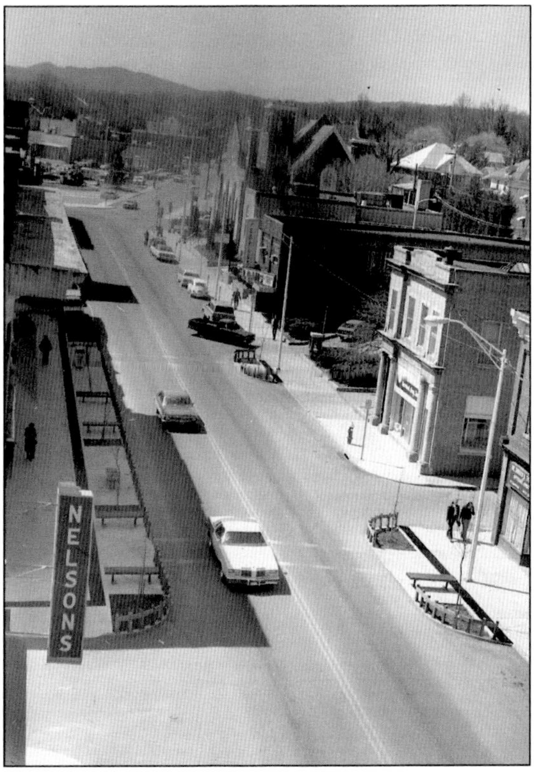

SHOP OF DISTINCTION. Nelsons Mens Store had been a mainstay in the Mercer Street business district for many years. (Courtesy of Nick Buzzo.)

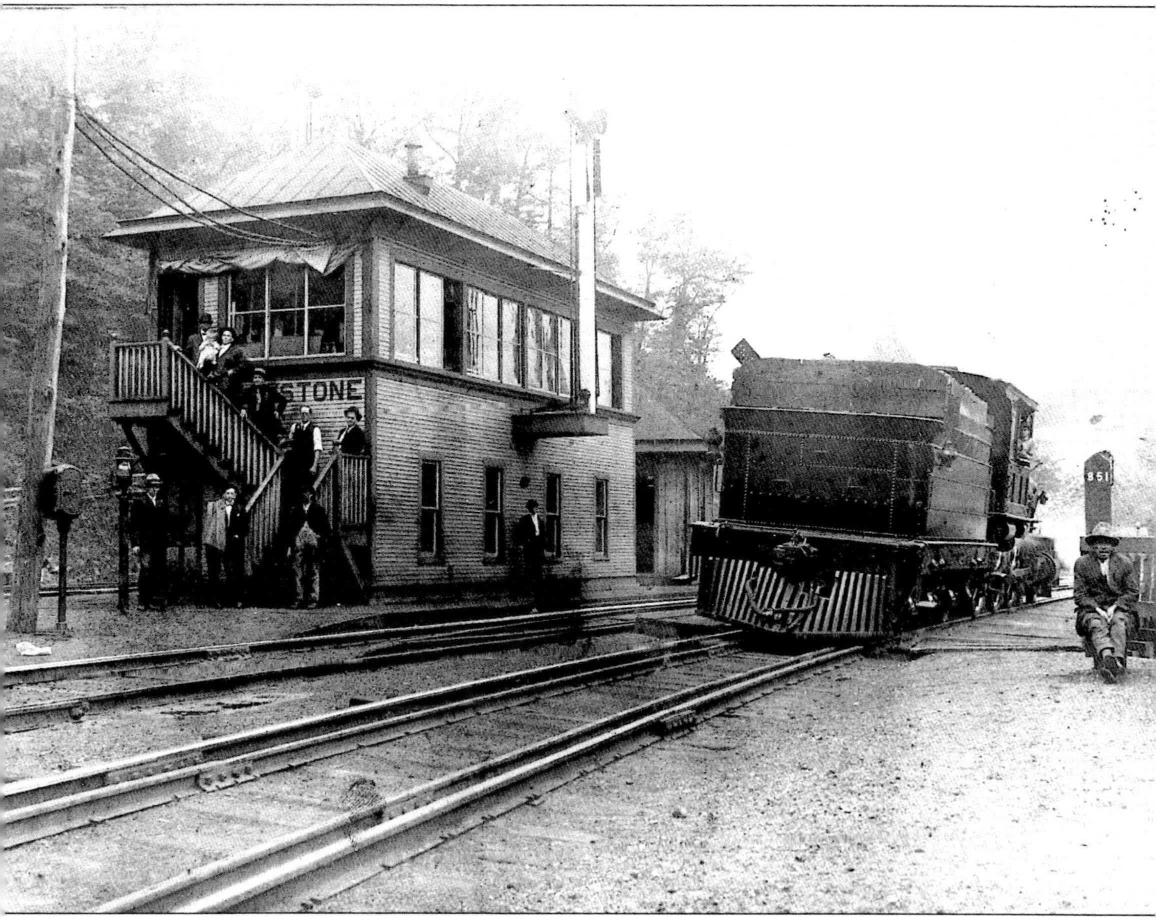

WHEN THE TRAIN LEAVES THE STATION. The train station at Bluestone Junction was an unlikely, but very important hub in the early days of the development of the Flat Top Coalfields. At Bluestone, trains could take one fork and head toward the Pocahontas, Virginia boomtown or travel the other fork into Coopers, Bramwell, and the budding McDowell County coalfield. Bluestone played a pivotal role in the area's development. (Courtesy of Grubb Photo Service.)

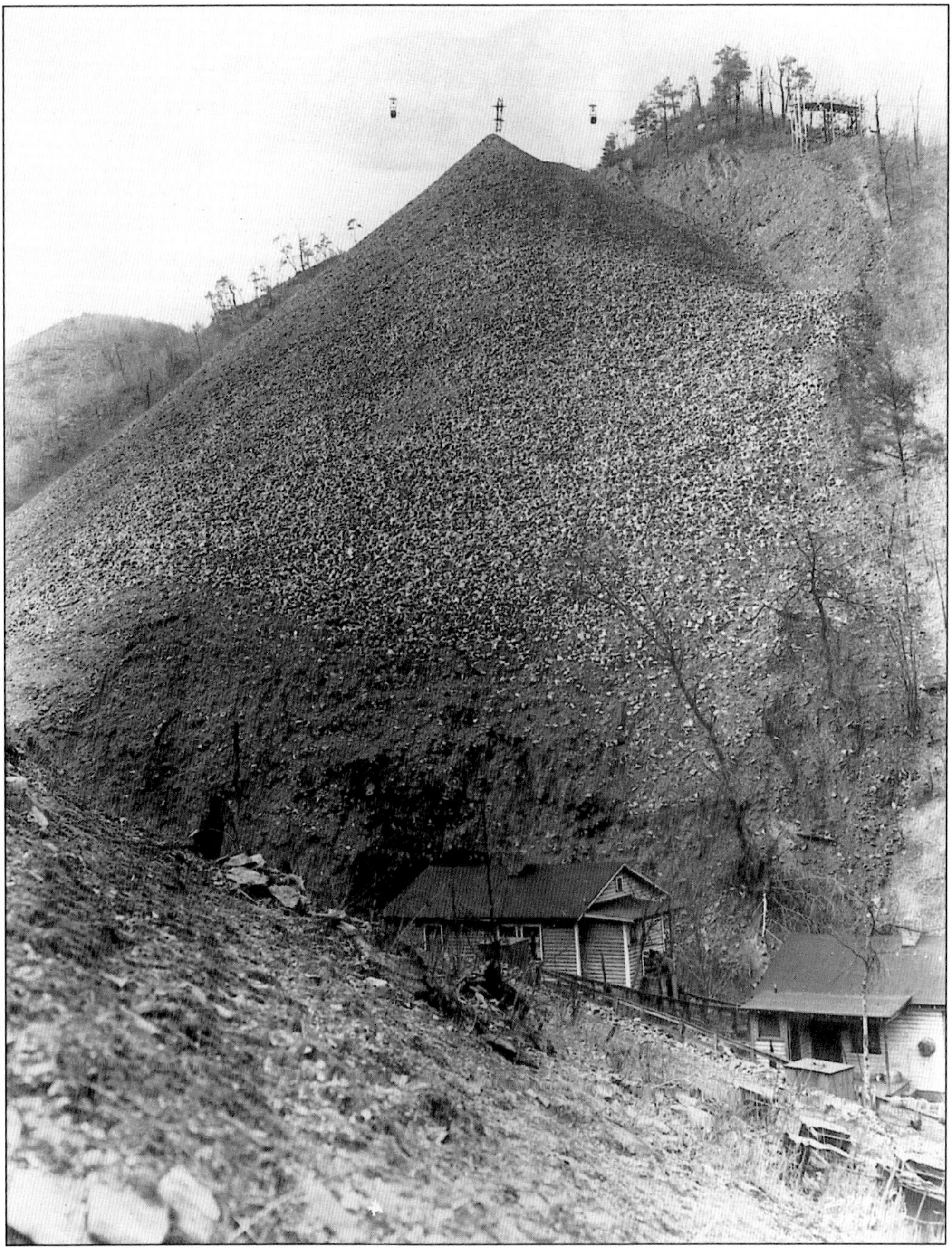

DANGER ZONE. These homes at McComas are situated beside a growing slag pile. In order to add value to their product, coal operators subjected the coal to a variety of preparation techniques. In the early days, coal miners called "bone pickers" cleaned impurities from the coal by hand, but various washing techniques are used today. The discarded refuse was often piled in unstable heaps that presented an almost constant threat to anyone living in their path. (Courtesy of Grubb Photo Service.)

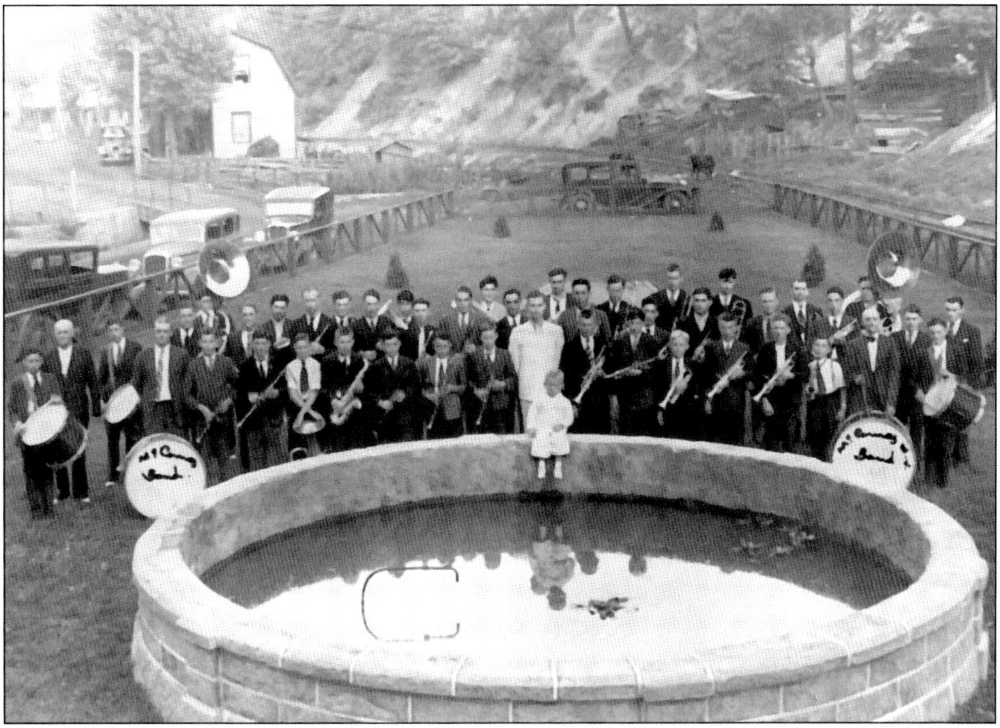

Seventy-six Trombones. Almost every coal camp had a variety of activities in which miners and their families could participate during their all-too-rare leisure time. Folks at McComas had their own coal camp band.

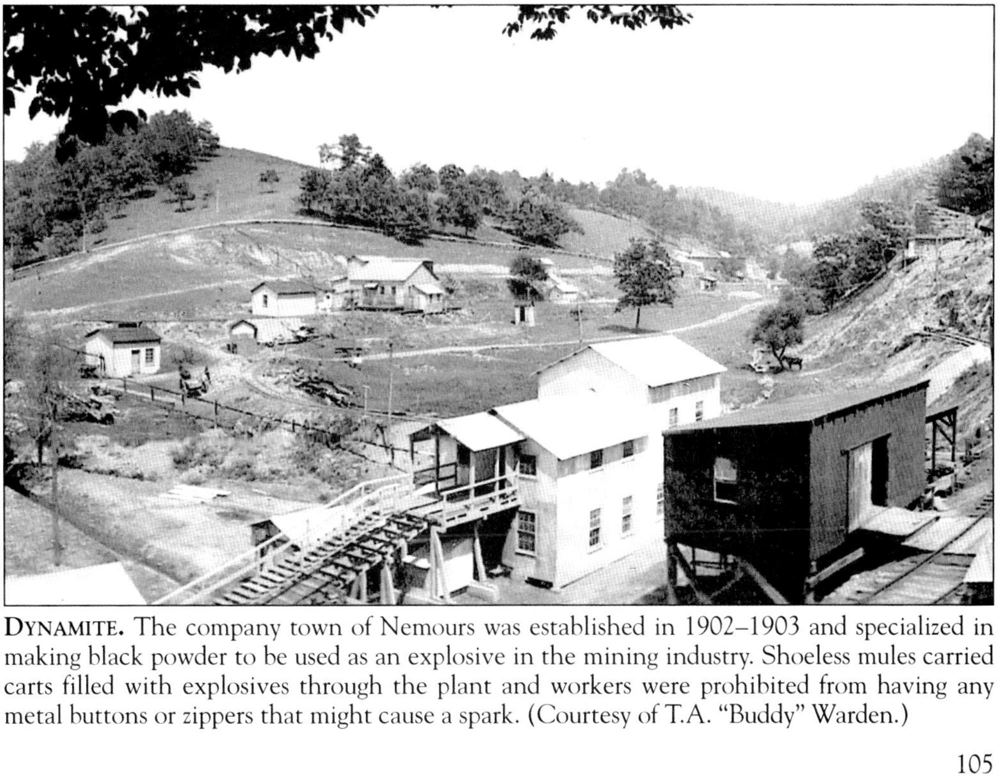

Dynamite. The company town of Nemours was established in 1902–1903 and specialized in making black powder to be used as an explosive in the mining industry. Shoeless mules carried carts filled with explosives through the plant and workers were prohibited from having any metal buttons or zippers that might cause a spark. (Courtesy of T.A. "Buddy" Warden.)

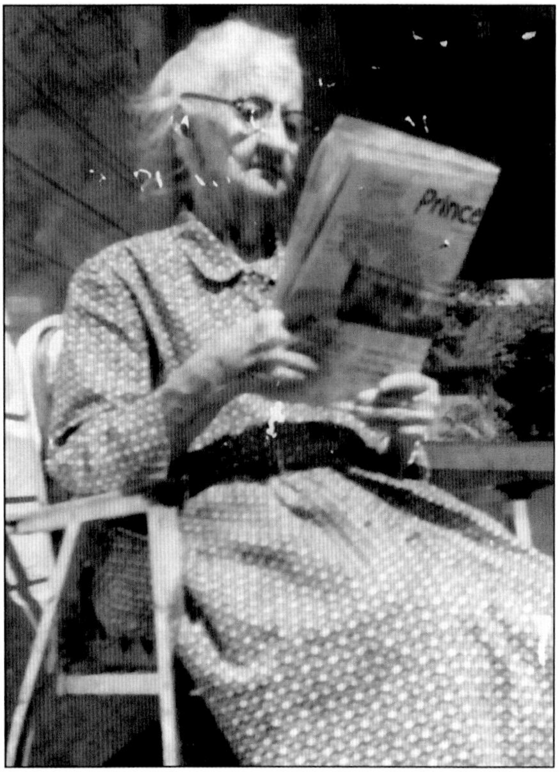

GOOD TIMES. Amanda Owens of Oliver Avenue in Princeton is shown here at age 94 reading an edition of the *Princeton Times* in 1965. The *Times* celebrated its 40th anniversary in 2001. The first edition was published on July 25, 1961. (Courtesy of Rick and Jeanie Owens.)

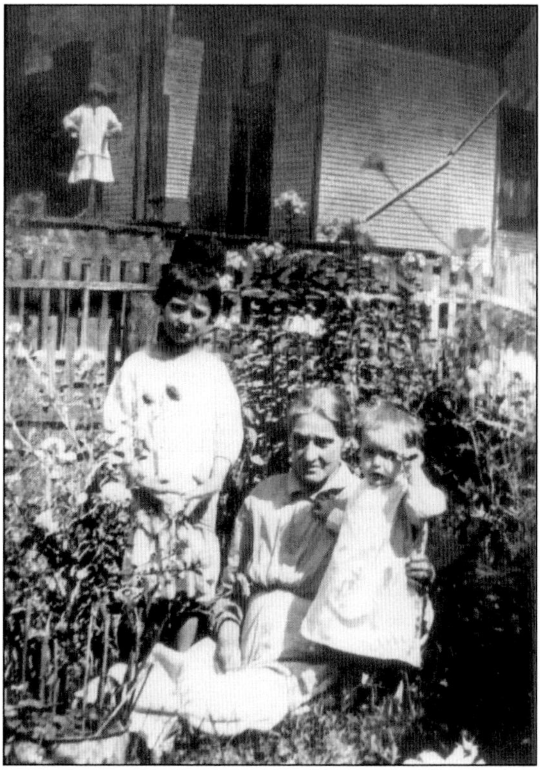

IN THE GARDEN. Maria Hurst, Margaret Hurst, Nancy Catherine "Granny Mack" McBride, and Dorothy Garrett are shown in this photograph taken at Granny Mack's Goodwill home, *c.* 1917. The building in the background is the Goodwill Community Center. (Courtesy of the Garrett family of Duhring; McBride's granddaughters, Dorothy Garrett and Vilda Gundisch.)

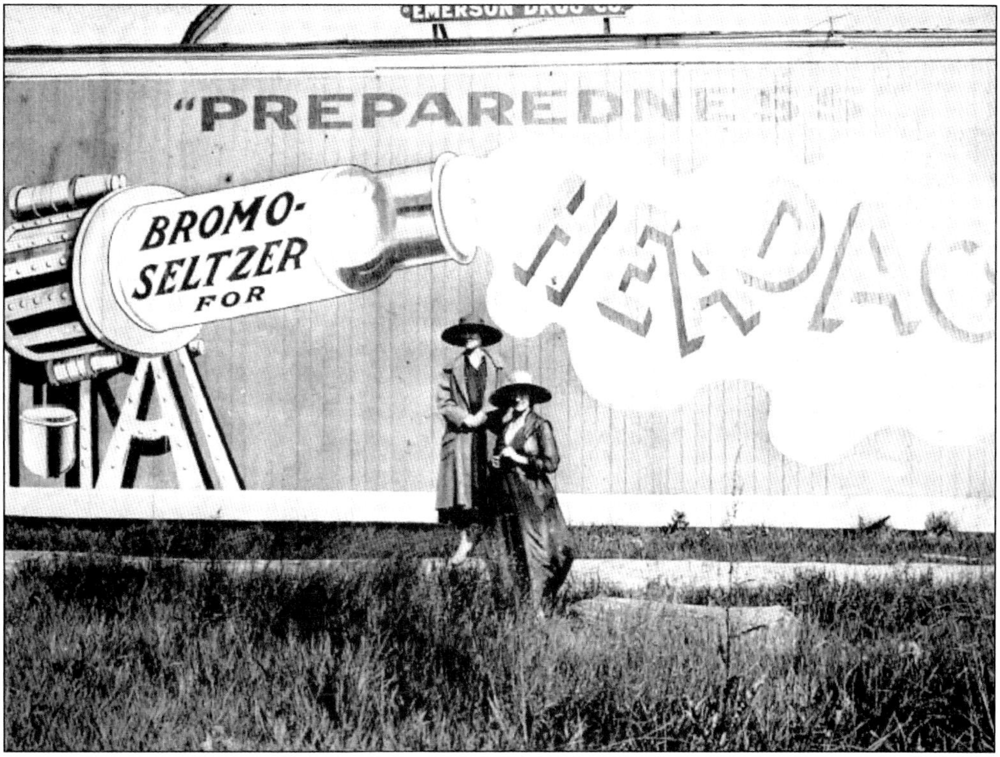

INSTANT RELIEF. Mildred Cooper and Glenna Pack are shown here standing in front of a billboard in Bramwell in this undated photograph. (Courtesy of Eve Cooper Murphy.)

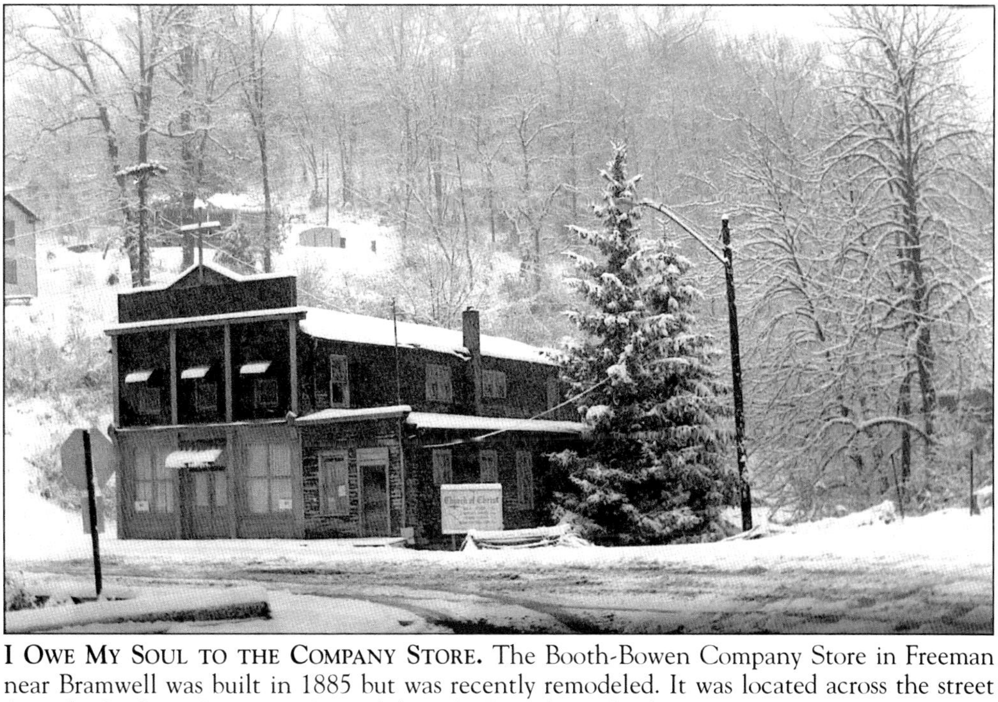

I OWE MY SOUL TO THE COMPANY STORE. The Booth-Bowen Company Store in Freeman near Bramwell was built in 1885 but was recently remodeled. It was located across the street from the Buckeye Company Store. (Photo by Evonda Archer.)

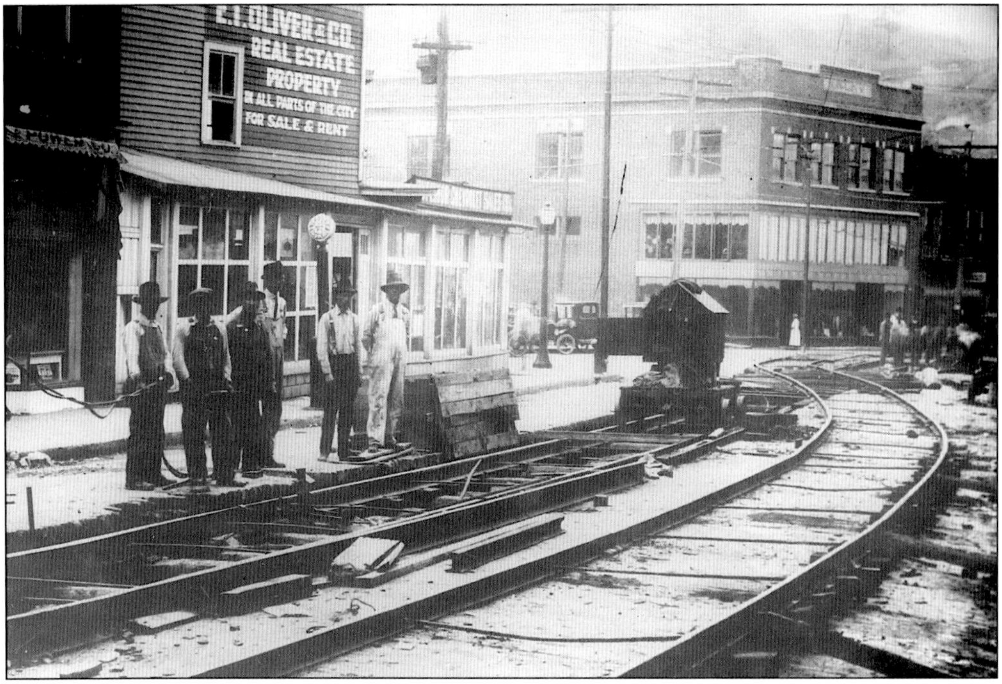

MAKING TRACKS. A work crew is shown here near the intersection of Bland and Federal Streets. The old Flat Iron Building in the background is now home to the Greater Bluefield Chamber of Commerce. (Courtesy of Nick Buzzo.)

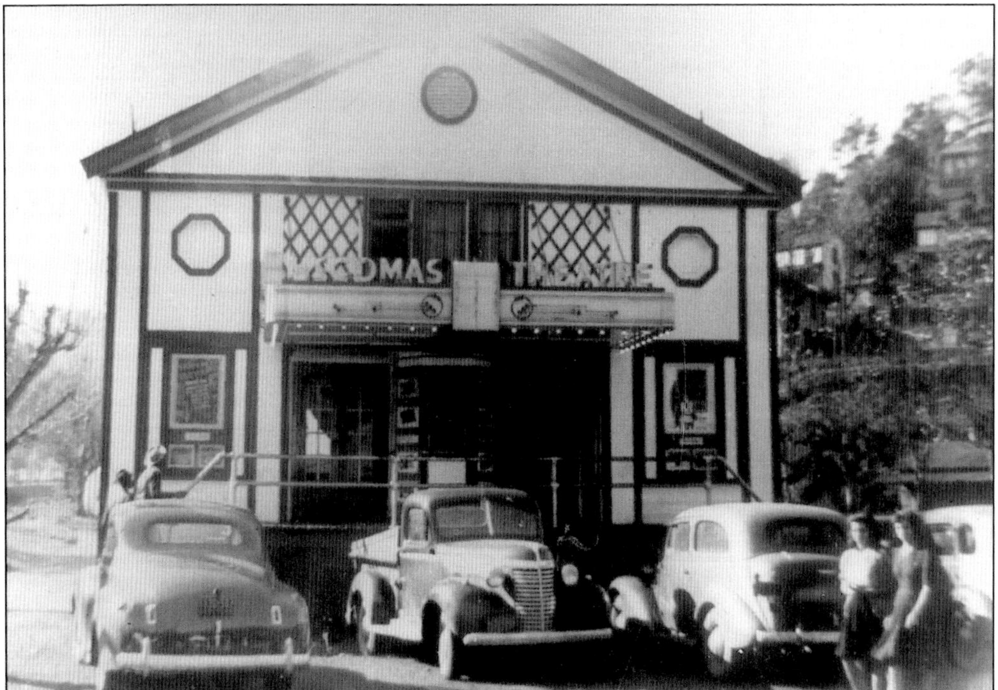

MAKE IT A DATE. Almost every coal camp had a movie theater, and several boasted of bowling alleys as well as other recreational facilities. (Courtesy of Grubb Photo Service.)

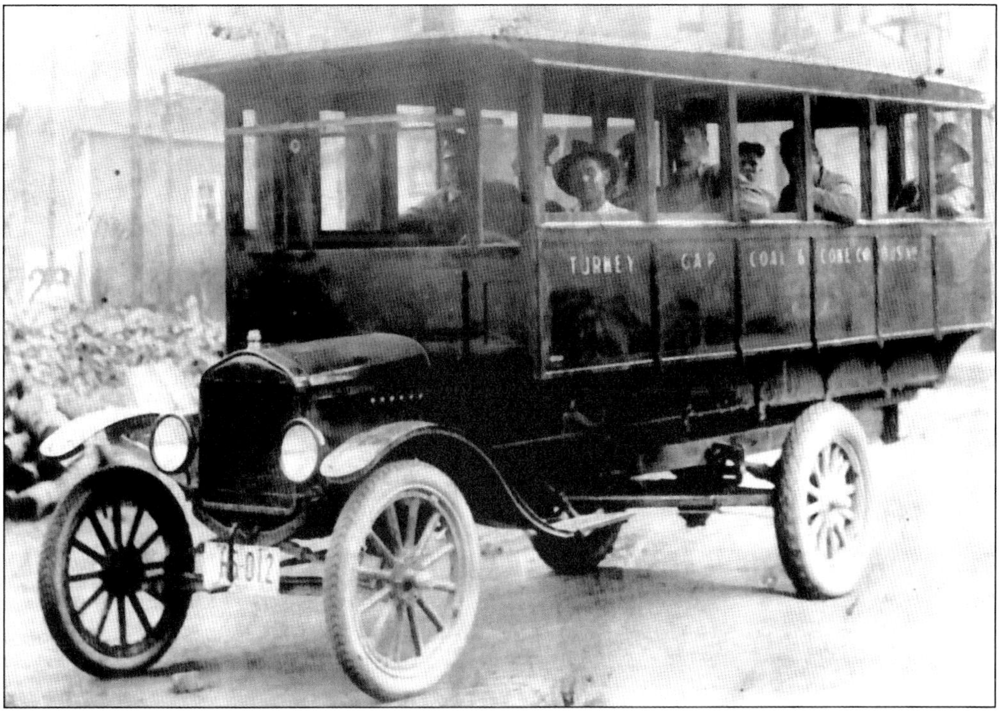

LEAVE THE DRIVING TO US. Harry Fagg is shown above preparing to transport coal miners from downtown Matoaka to the Turkey Gap Coal Mine. Turkey Gap is located in Dott and opened in 1904. Crozier Coal and Land acquired the mine in 1951 and later sold to Consol. (Courtesy of Grubb Photo Service.)

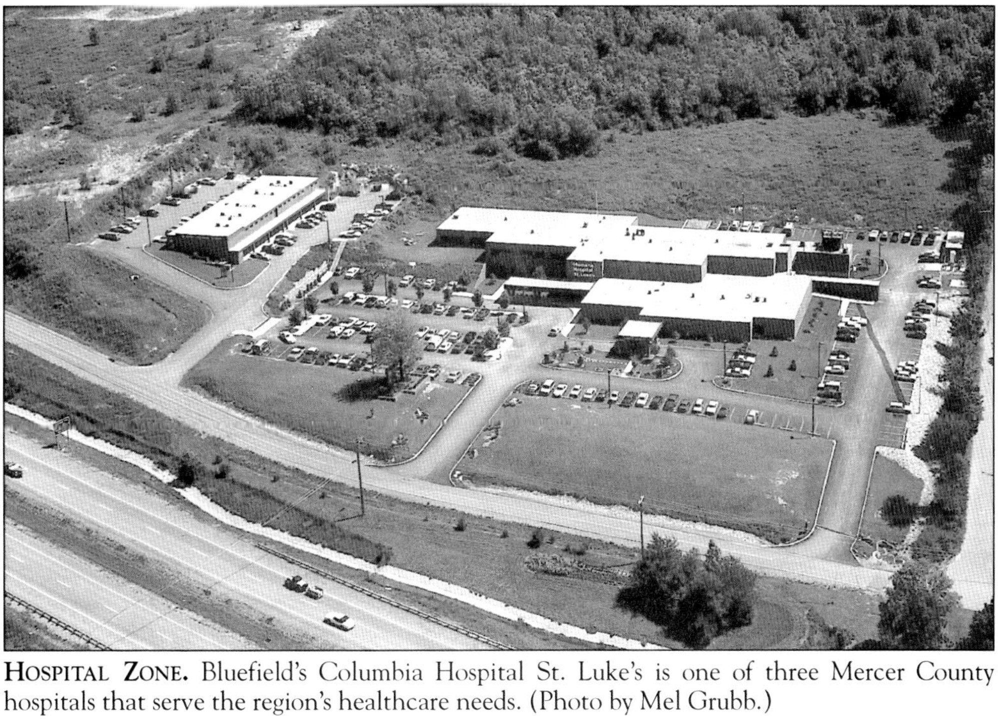

HOSPITAL ZONE. Bluefield's Columbia Hospital St. Luke's is one of three Mercer County hospitals that serve the region's healthcare needs. (Photo by Mel Grubb.)

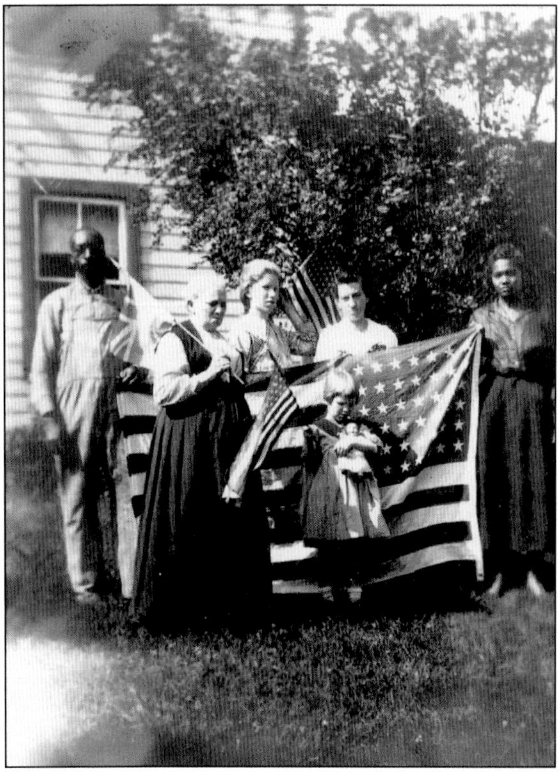

Wrapped in the Flag. Cooper family matriarch Maria Cooper and Jessamal Cooper are shown in front of the flag here while James Holt, Kate Cooper, Lara ?, and Mamie Holt stand holding the flag. The photo was taken at the Coopers' home in the town that bears their name, Coopers. (Courtesy of Eve Cooper Murphy.)

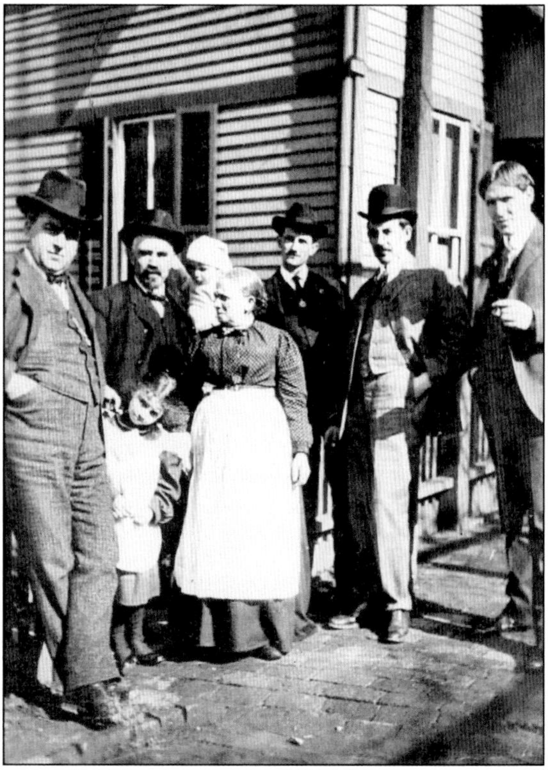

Streets of Bramwell. Maria Cooper with Katherine in the foreground of this photograph are flanked by Col. W.H. Thomas, Dave ? holding an unidentified infant, Tom Cooper, Mr. Shanklin, and Mr. Brophy. (Courtesy of Eve Cooper Murphy.)

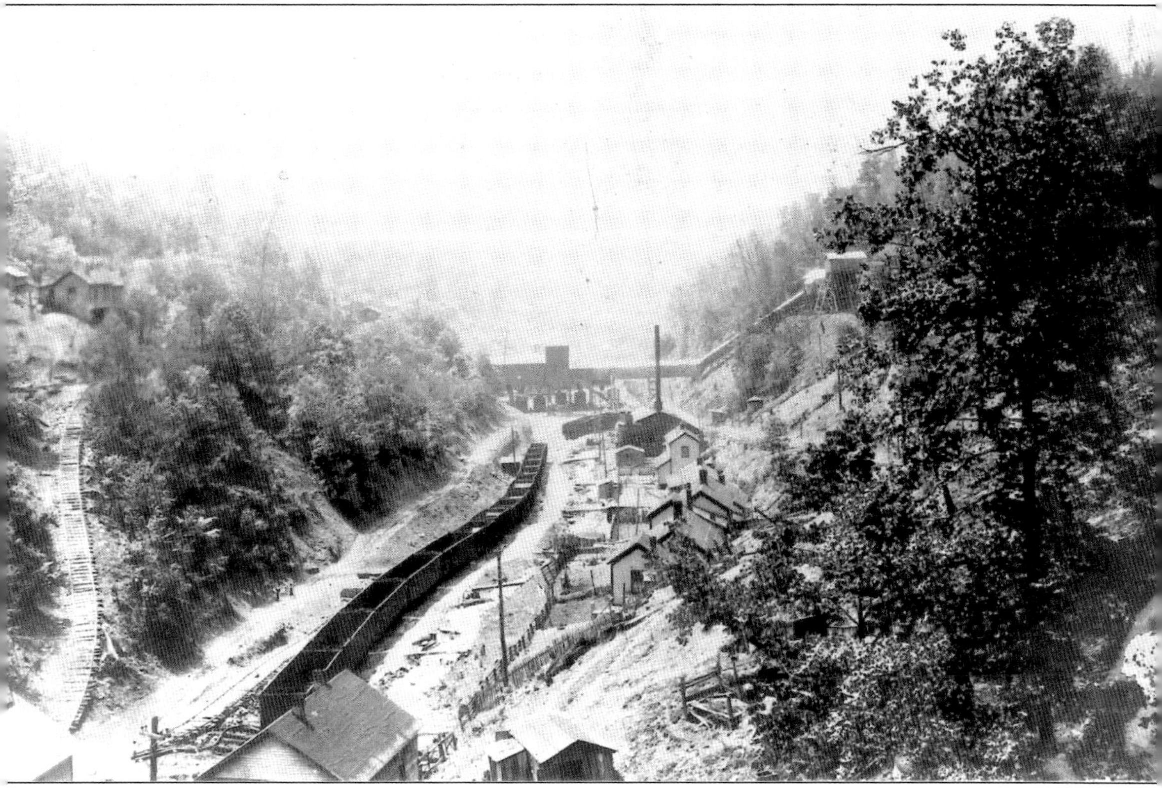

WENONAH COAL. The McQuail family interests developed the Wenonah Coal Company, shown here c. 1915. According to Theodore Bones, who was born there in 1922 and grew up in the coal camp, the mine was later sold and renamed Turkey Gap. The plank track on the left was the motor road to the No. 1 Mine and the tipple chute and water pump house are on the right. Coal camp homes shown to the right of the railroad tracks housed African-American miners. There was no electricity in the camp at the time. (Courtesy of Grubb Photo Service.)

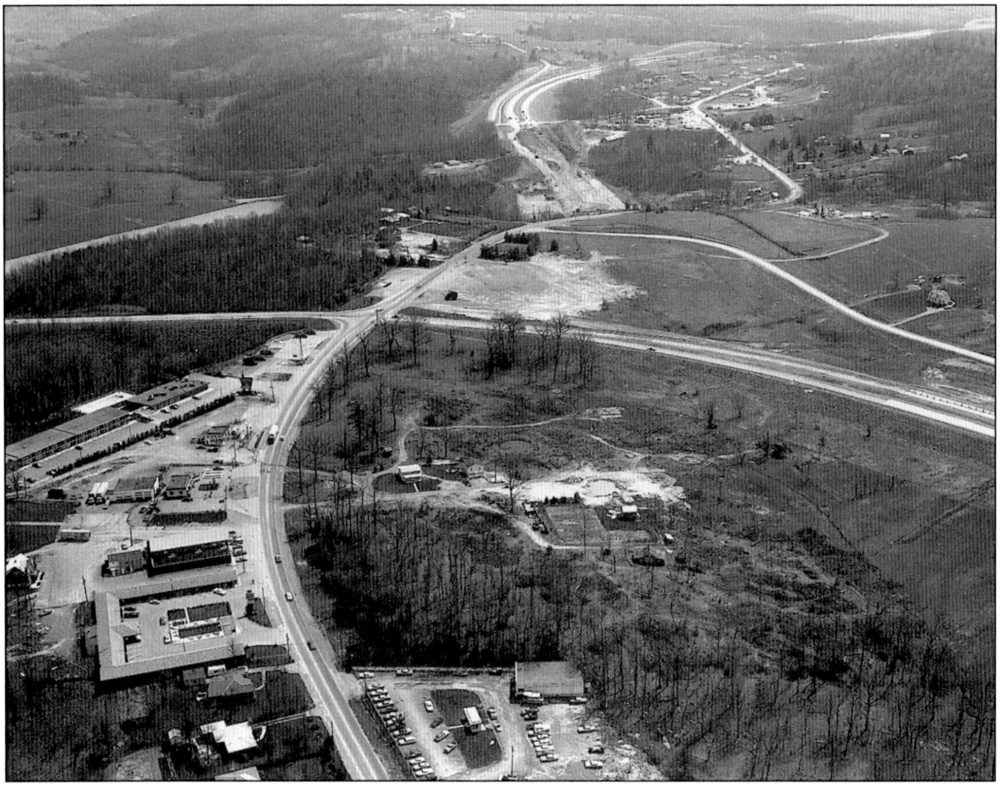

HIGHWAY AHEAD. When I-77 arrived in Princeton, it brought a business boom where it intersects with U.S. Route 460. However, the area was primarily farmland before the coming of the new highway. (Photo by Mel Grubb.)

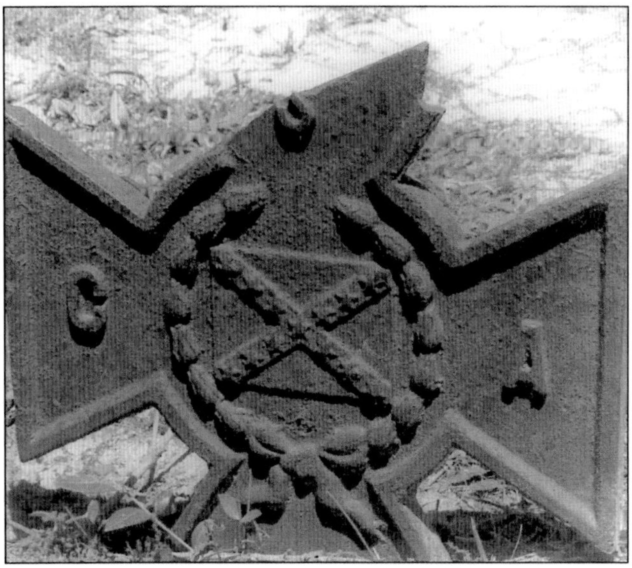

SON OF THE SOUTH. Although Mercer County was included in the counties that would create the only state formed during the American Civil War—West Virginia, most county residents supported the Confederacy. This marker at a Princeton cemetery marks the resting place of a Confederate soldier. The area's largest engagement was the on May 16–17, 1862, and was called the Battle of Pigeon Roost. Twenty-three Union Army soldiers died and three Confederate soldiers were killed in action. (Photo by Evonda Archer.)

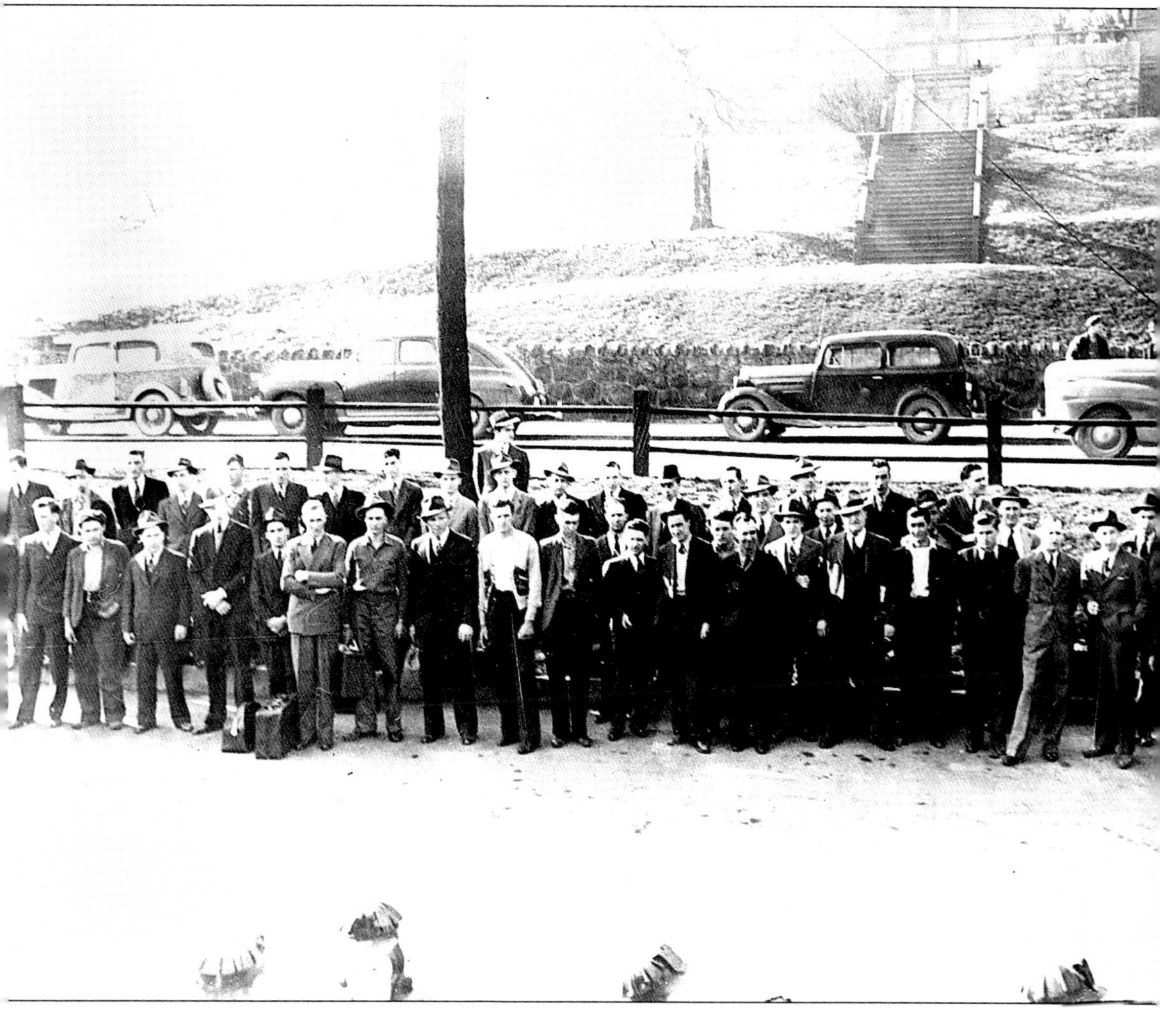

READY TO SHIP OUT. The original group of pre–World War II draftees shown here is preparing to leave from the Bluefield passenger station on Princeton Avenue on April 12, 1941. Pictured from left to right are (front row) Millard "Mit" Gilmore, Odell O. Reynolds, unidentified, Estil "Bev" Hoops, John H. Childress, William H. "Bill" Gilpin, unidentified, Olaf N. Hanger, Giles P. Butt, Mark H. Riley, James E. Williams, John A. Hypes, unidentified, Everett Douglas, unidentified, William "Bill" O'Keefe, Clarence Doyle, Hobert Wyrick, David L. Hypes, Henry Call, George A. "Bob" Parks, and Draft Board Clerk Robert "Bob" Lampton; (second row) James P. Waters, Willis "Buck" Cowling, Frank T. Hancock, George A. Birkelbach, unidentified, Carle "Dopey" Compton, Douglas L. French, Baron H. Cornett, Frank Gilpin, Harold Shupe, Thomas R. Thornton, unidentified, C.W. Howell, Albert F. Stafford Jr., Woodrow W. Wilson, Robert R. Austin, James L. Dean, Otwell W. Thompson, Blain H. "Bus" Linkous, Fred L. Honaker, Alvis Coleman, James E. Pritchett, unidentified, and Rufus A. Williamson. Robert Austin is standing in the back. (Courtesy of Heber Stafford.)

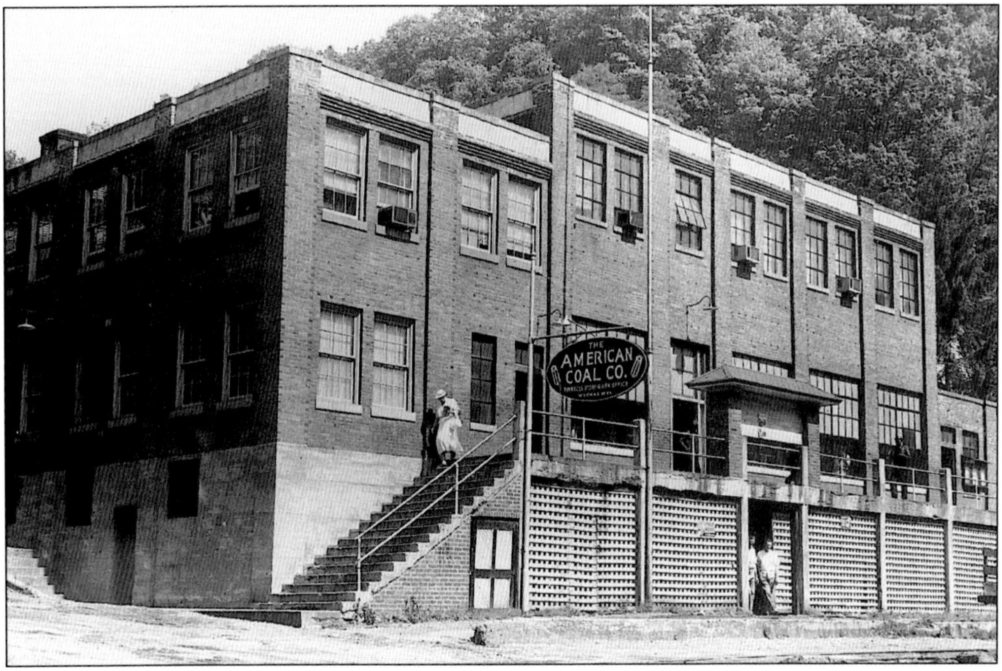

SHOP 'TIL YOU DROP. Company stores, like the one owned by the American Coal Company, provided for just about every need of coal miners and their families. (Courtesy of Grubb Photo Service.)

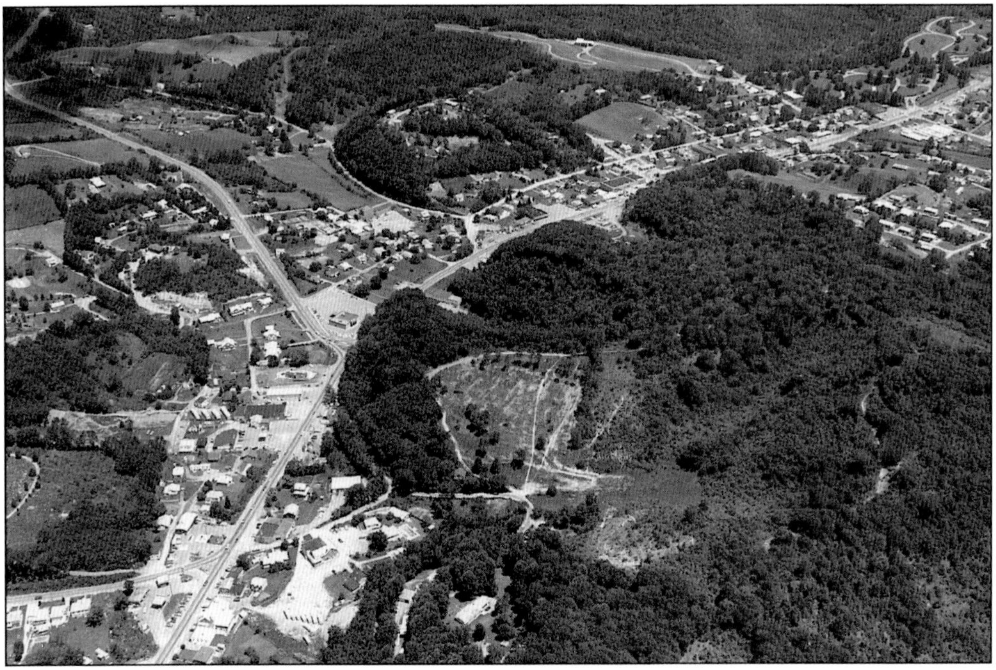

IN THE MIDDLE. The community of Bluewell is an important crossroads in Mercer County. The lowest fork shown enters from Montcalm and Bramwell and the fork in the middle goes to Princeton (left) through Glenwood. Brushfork and Bluefield are to the right. (Photo by Mel Grubb.)

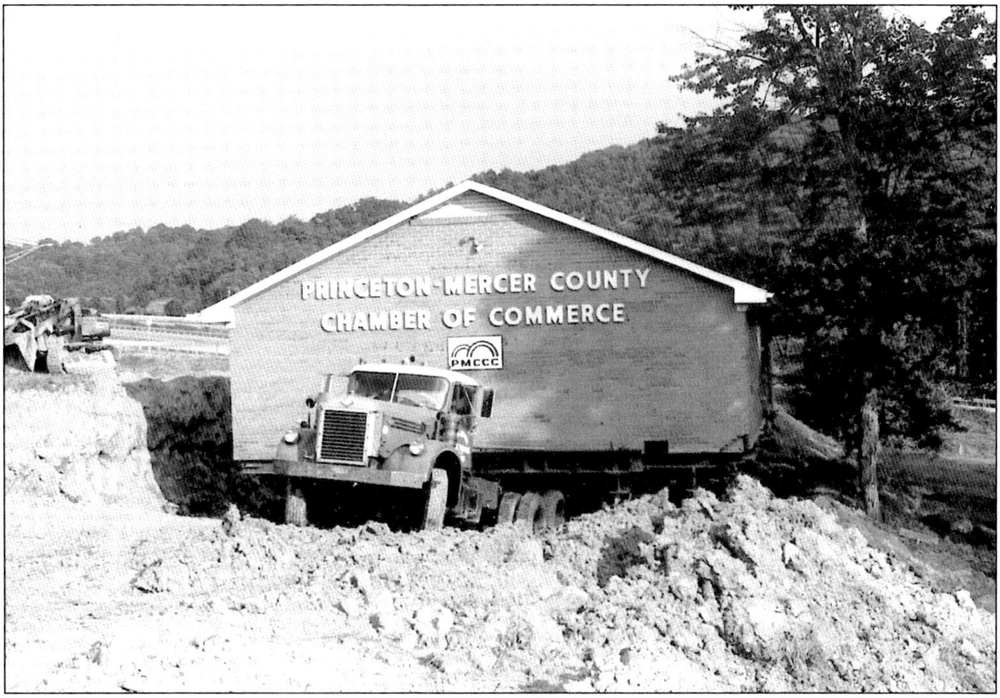

SOLID FOUNDATION. The Princeton/Mercer County Chamber of Commerce was literally moved to a new location near the I-77–U.S. Route 460 intersection in the late 1980s. (Courtesy of George Santon.)

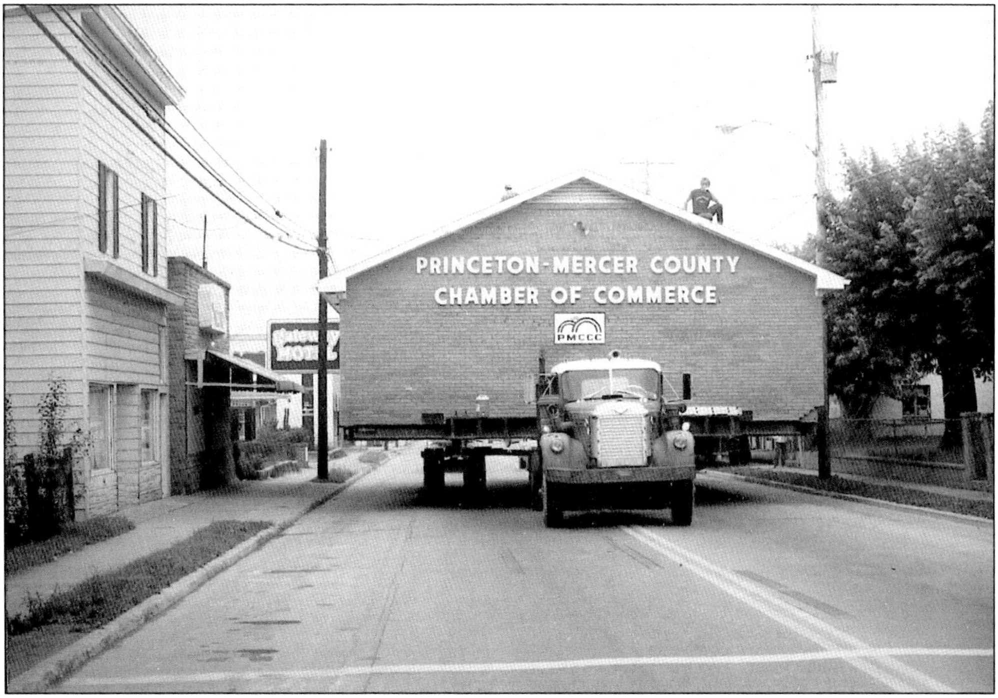

UNUSUAL DEVELOPMENT. When the Chamber rolled through the city, it caused as much commotion as a typical Princeton parade. (Courtesy of George Santon.)

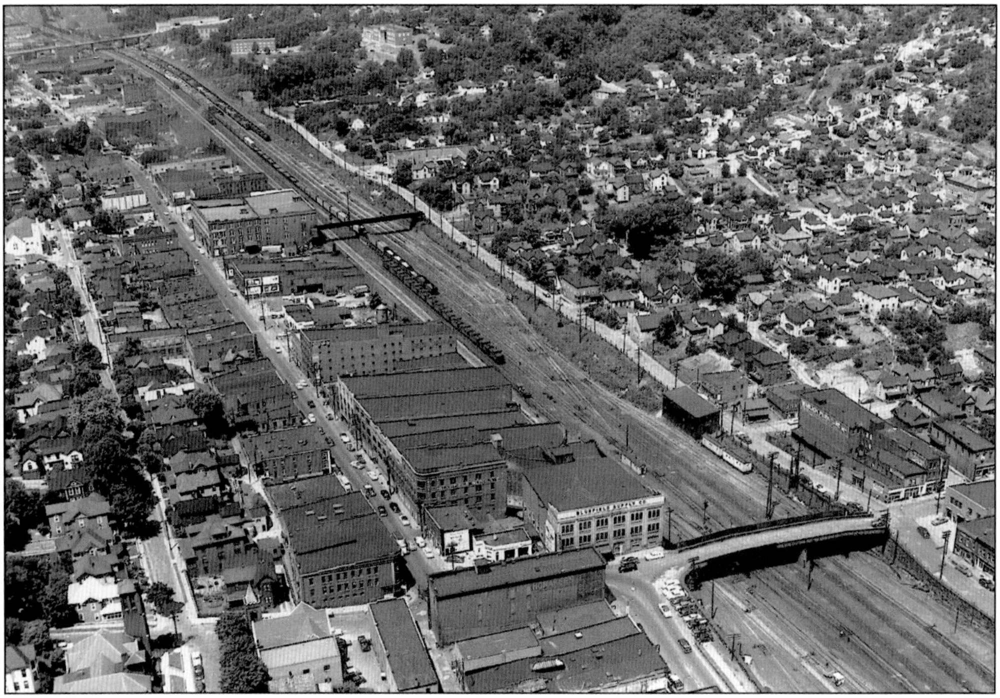

AS SEEN FROM THE SKY. This dramatic 1950s vintage photograph shows Bluefield Avenue in its heyday. Many of the buildings shown here fell to the wrecking ball during a massive urban renewal project of the 1960s. (Photo by Mel Grubb.)

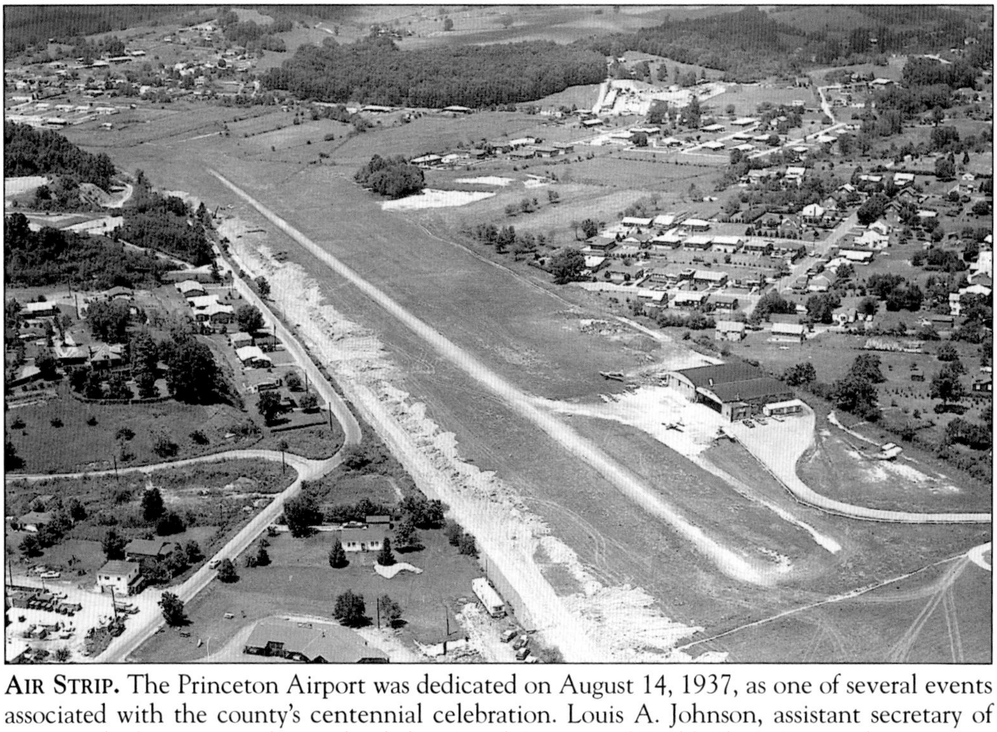

AIR STRIP. The Princeton Airport was dedicated on August 14, 1937, as one of several events associated with the county's centennial celebration. Louis A. Johnson, assistant secretary of war, was the keynote speaker at the dedication. (Courtesy of Grubb Photo Service.)

CHURCH ON THE HILL. Mill Creek Baptist Church in Coopers was one of the first churches in the Flat Top Missionary Baptist District. The church was built to serve the spiritual needs of the African-American miners of Coopers and has served its congregation continuously since 1884. (Courtesy of Eve Cooper Murphy.)

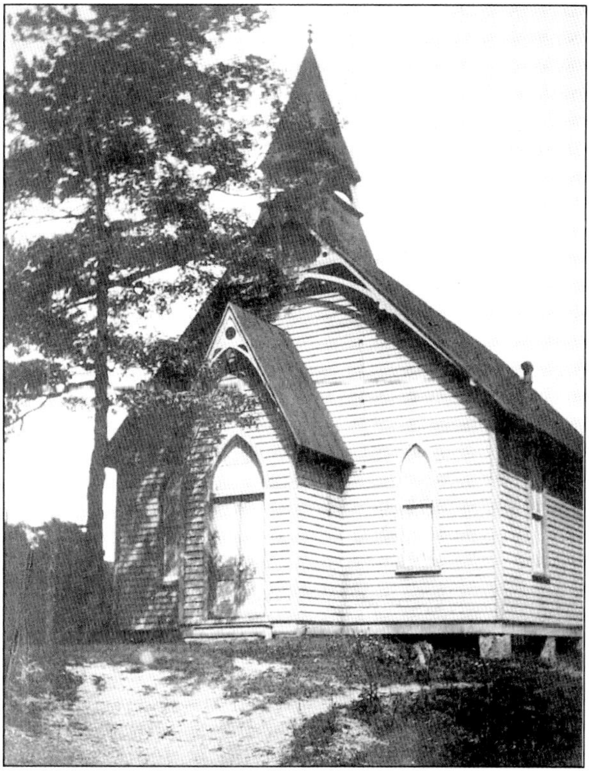

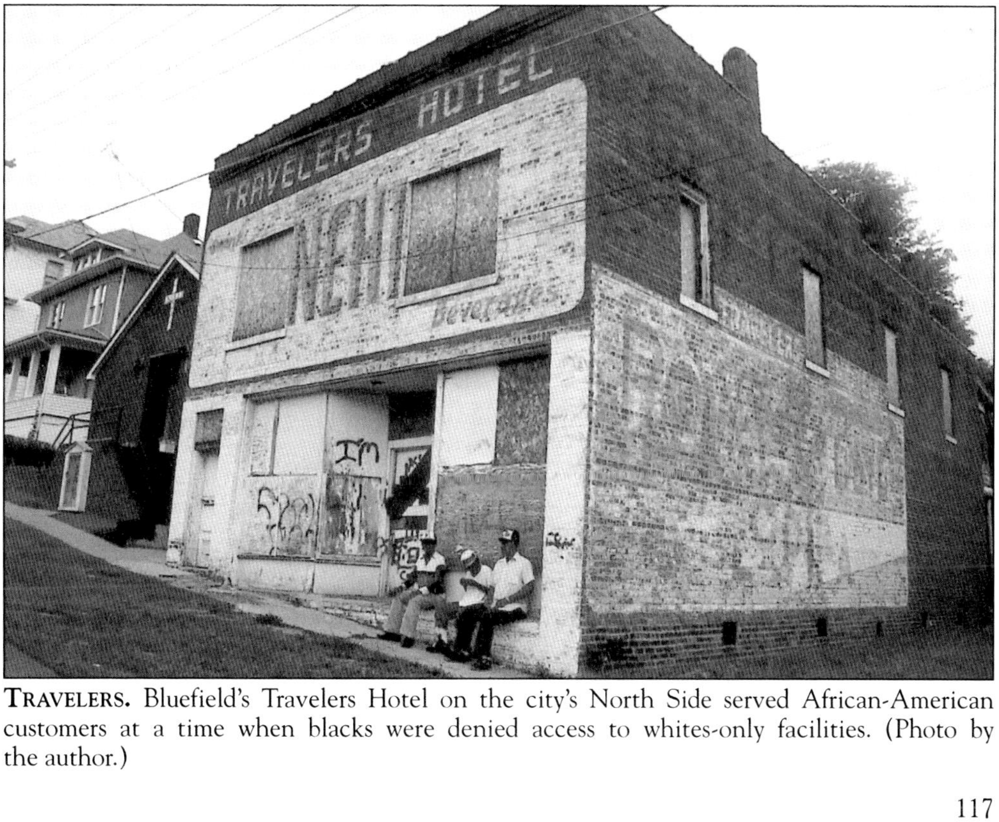

TRAVELERS. Bluefield's Travelers Hotel on the city's North Side served African-American customers at a time when blacks were denied access to whites-only facilities. (Photo by the author.)

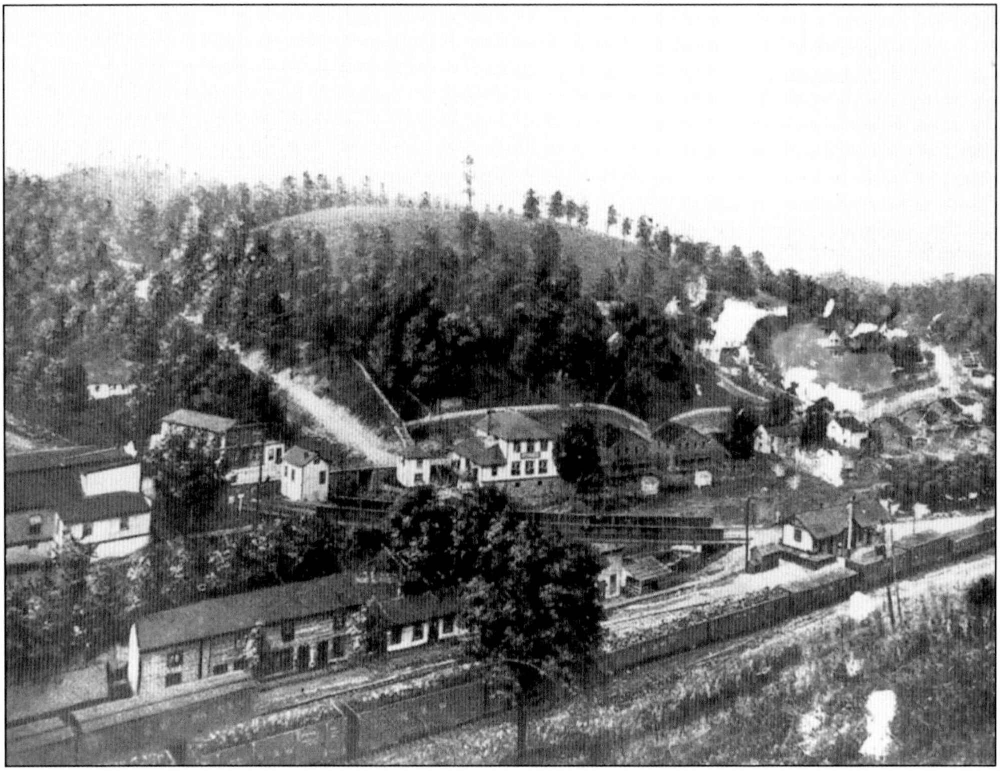

BIRTH OF AN INDUSTRY. The community of Simmons grew up in the shadow of Bramwell and Coopers but provided goods, services, and housing for coal miners working at mines in the area and their families. (Courtesy of Grubb Photo Service.)

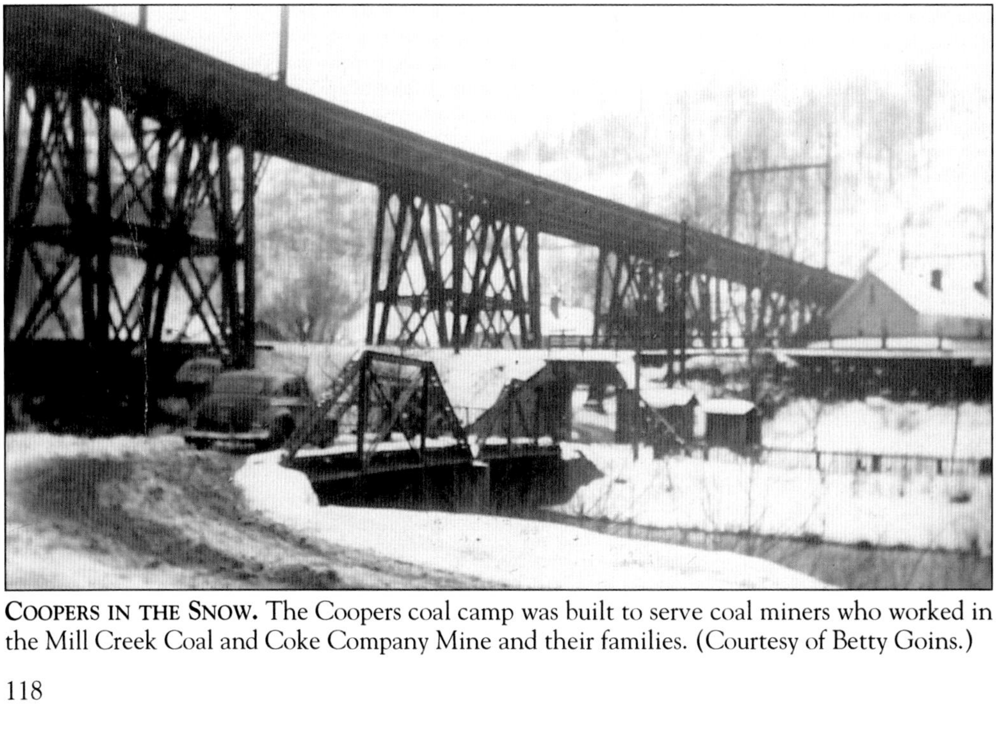

COOPERS IN THE SNOW. The Coopers coal camp was built to serve coal miners who worked in the Mill Creek Coal and Coke Company Mine and their families. (Courtesy of Betty Goins.)

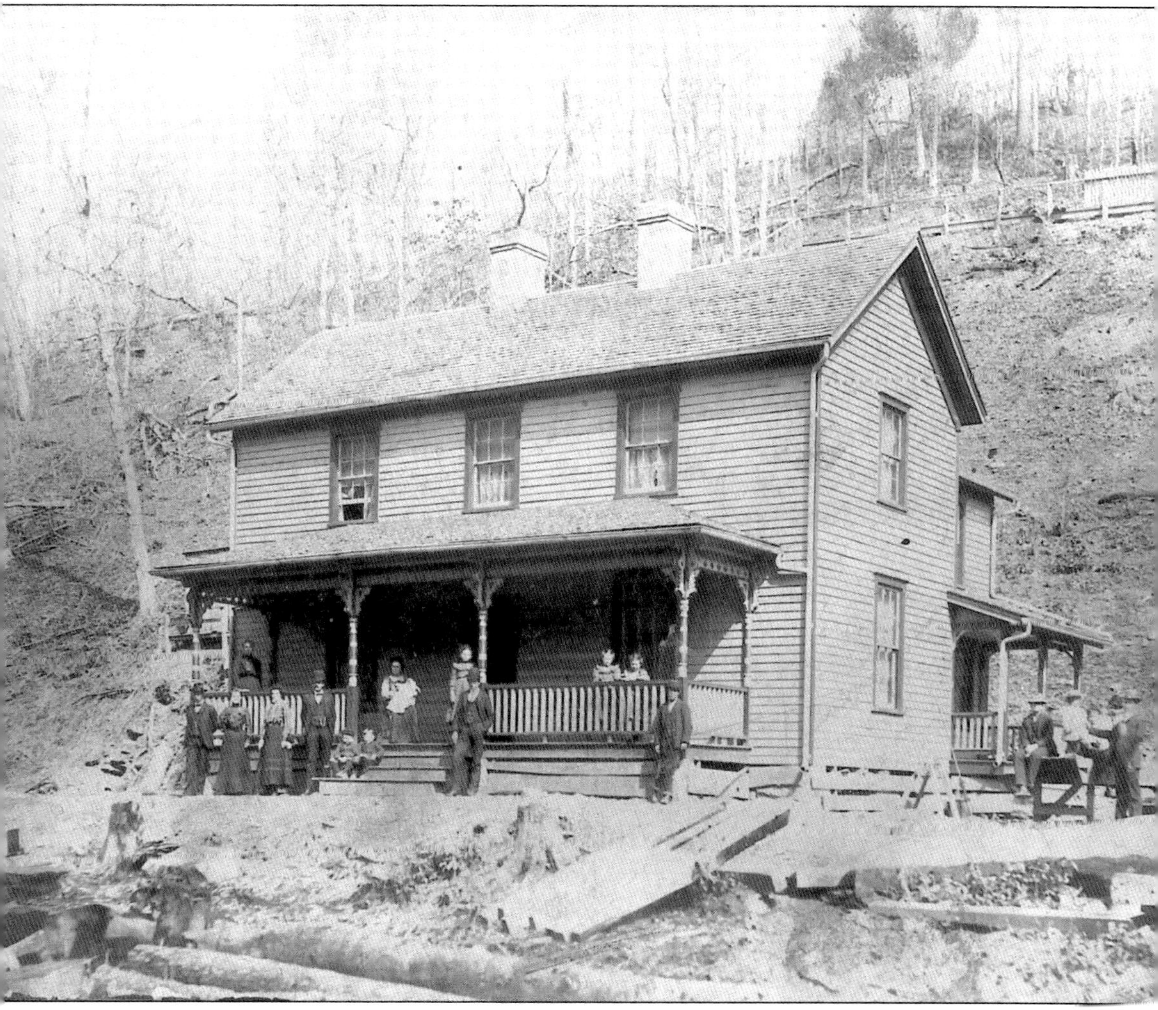

HOME SWEET HOME. E.T. Brooks built this home in Crane Creek in 1902. Company houses were a must for coal operators who had to import a workforce into a region that was scarcely populated. While many of the early company houses looked good on the outside, most people who lived in them routinely attest to the fact that they were poorly insulated. One woman who spent her early years in a coal camp company house observed that she learned newspapers were for more than just reading. They were stuffed in the cracks of the walls. (Courtesy of Grubb Photo Service.)

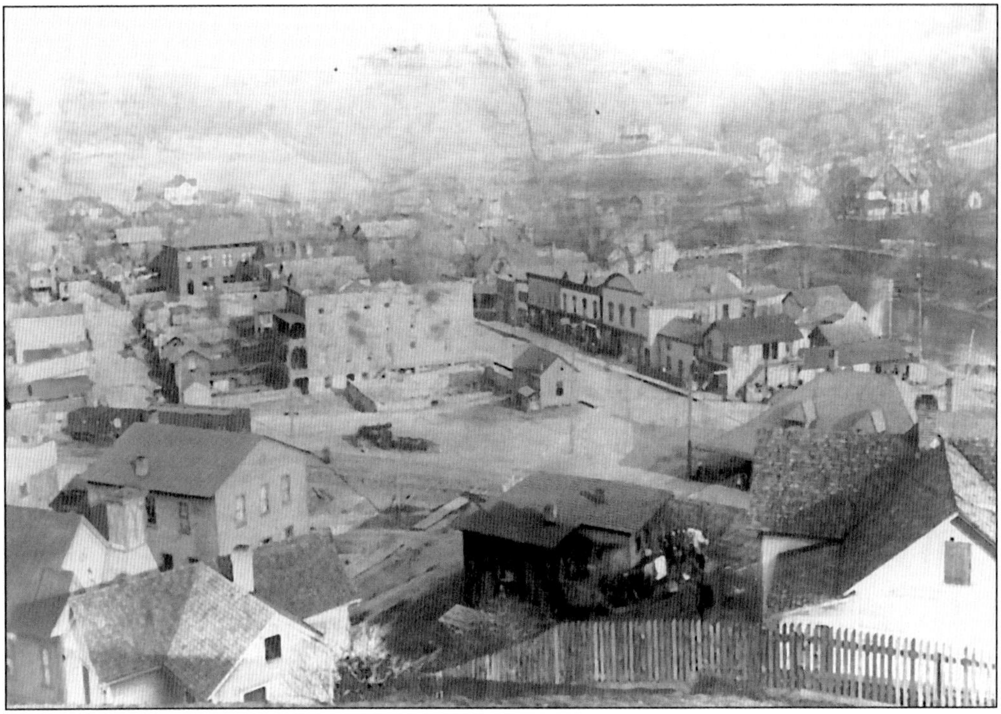

HOME OF THE MILLIONAIRES. Bramwell was a bustling community as shown in this early 1900s photograph. It was largely considered a "bedroom community" for the millionaire coal barons of the Flat Top coalfields. (Courtesy of Grubb Photo Service.)

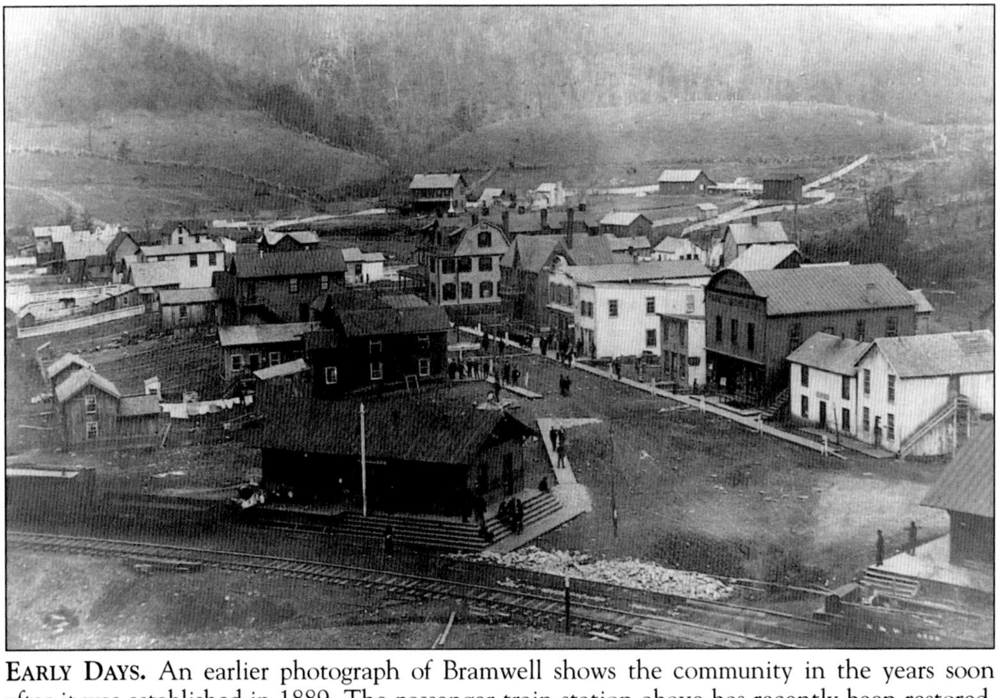

EARLY DAYS. An earlier photograph of Bramwell shows the community in the years soon after it was established in 1889. The passenger train station above has recently been restored. (Courtesy of Grubb Photo Service.)

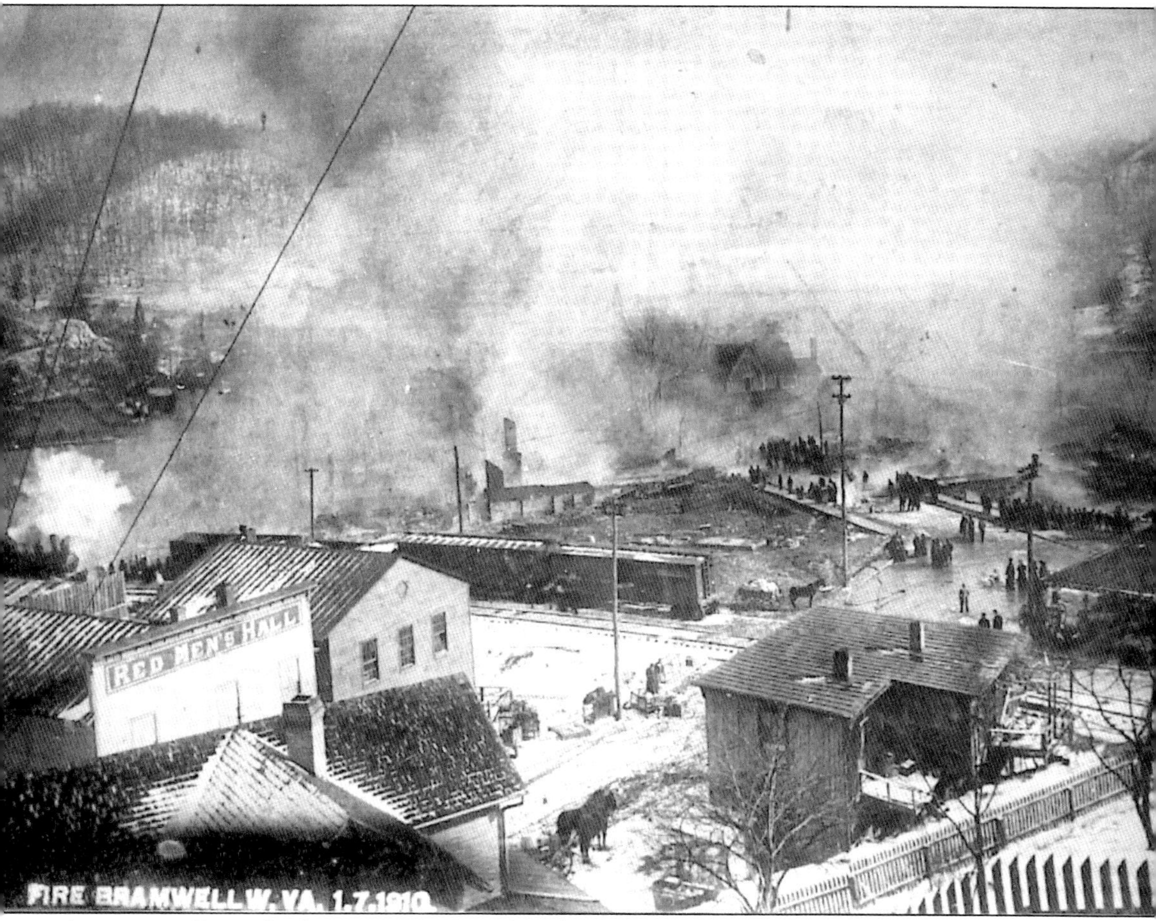

AFTER THE FIRE. On January 7, 1910, a fire that started in a pool hall in Bramwell quickly swept through the community destroying almost all of the homes and businesses in the downtown. Frigid temperatures hampered firefighting efforts. However, a remarkable thing happened after the fire; people from neighboring communities all came to Bramwell to pitch in and restore housing for the homeless and help businesses get back on their feet. (Courtesy of Eve Cooper Murphy.)

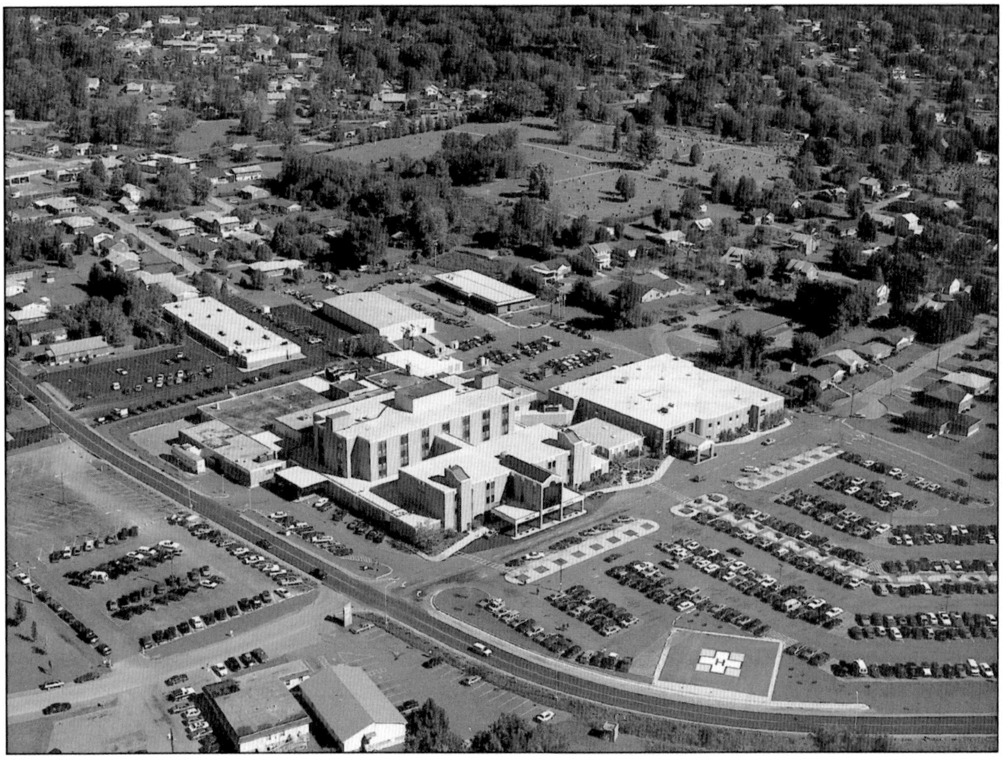

HOSPITAL ZONE. Princeton Community Hospital is one of three hospitals located in Mercer County. (Photo by Mel Grubb.)

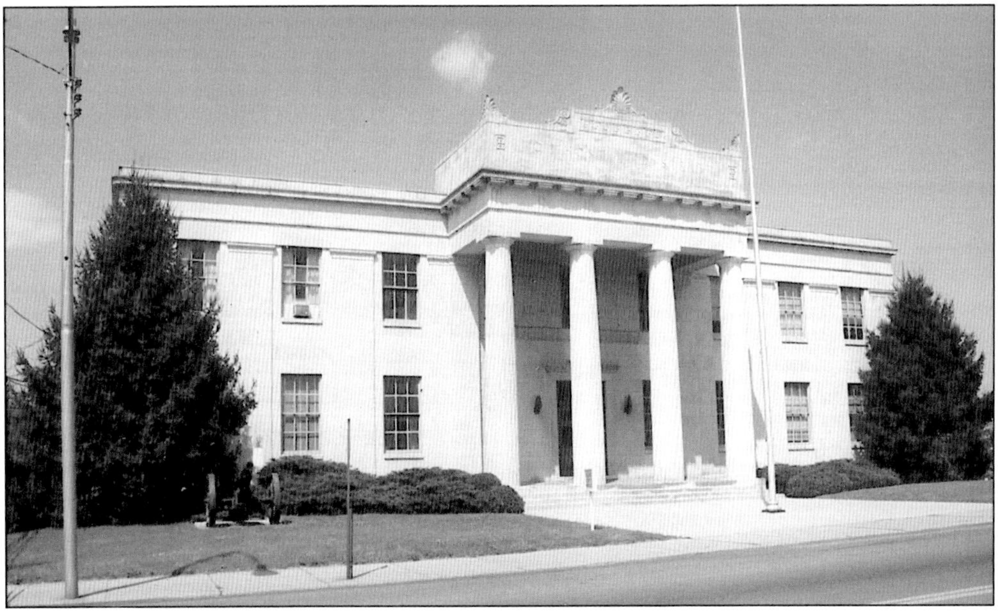

WAR MEMORIAL. The Mercer County Soldiers' and Sailors' Building was erected in 1930 and dedicated in November of 1931. After construction, it served as headquarters for the local American Legion, the Red Cross, and Civic Welfare Societies and had been the proposed site of a county library. (Photo by the author.)

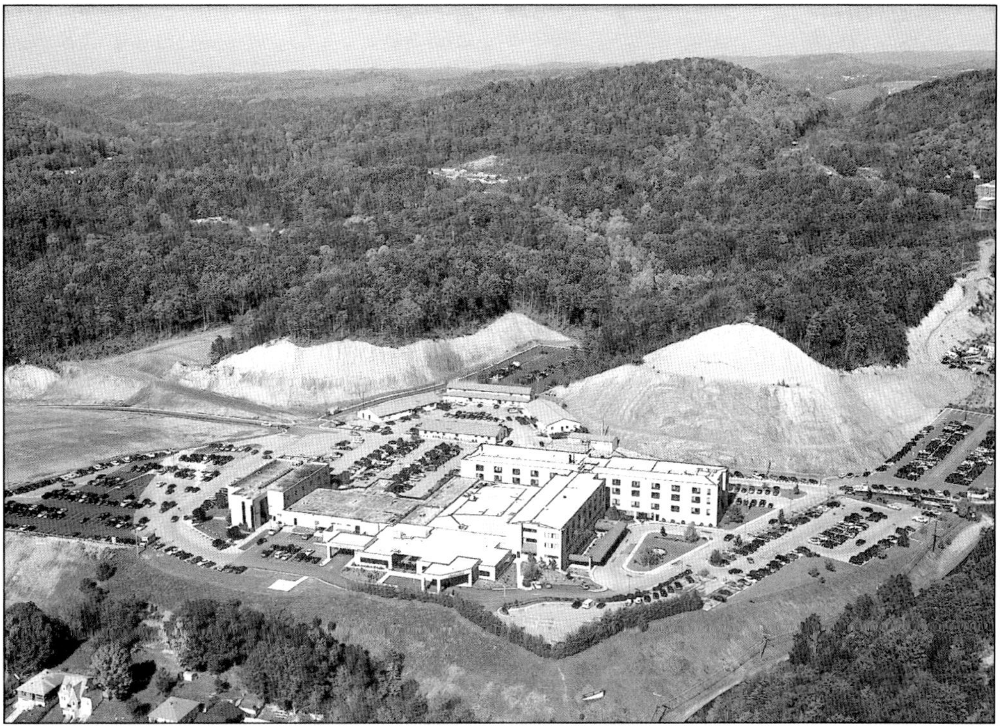

HOSPITAL ZONE. Bluefield Regional Medical Center is one of three hospitals located in Mercer County. (Photo by Mel Grubb.)

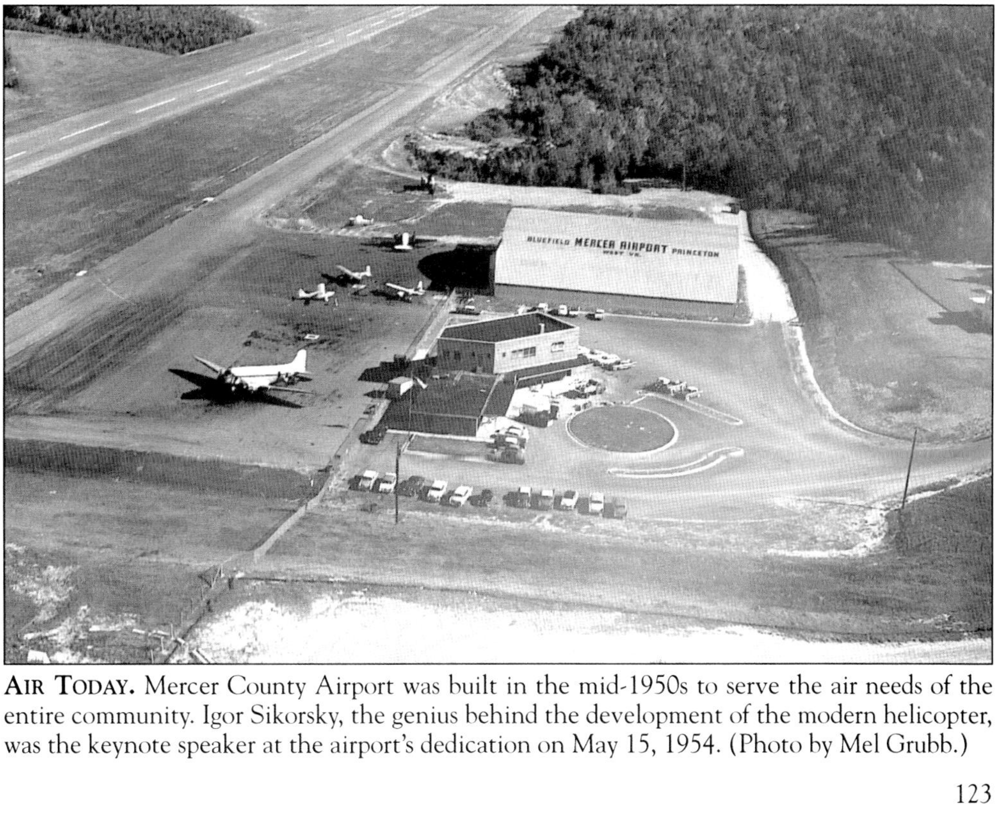

AIR TODAY. Mercer County Airport was built in the mid-1950s to serve the air needs of the entire community. Igor Sikorsky, the genius behind the development of the modern helicopter, was the keynote speaker at the airport's dedication on May 15, 1954. (Photo by Mel Grubb.)

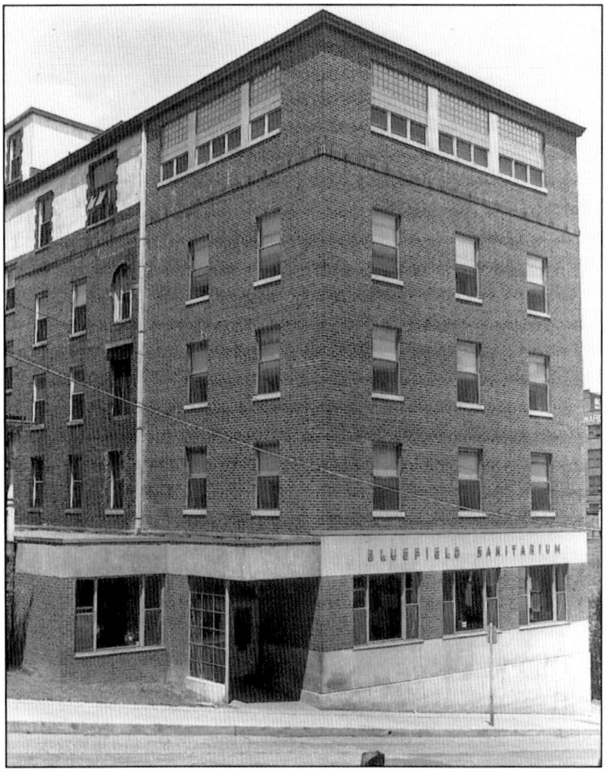

OLD FACILITY. The Bluefield Sanitarium was established in the early part of the 20th century and provided a "list practice" for subscribing coal company workers similar to the Health Maintenance Organizations of the modern era. (Courtesy of Grubb Photo Service.)

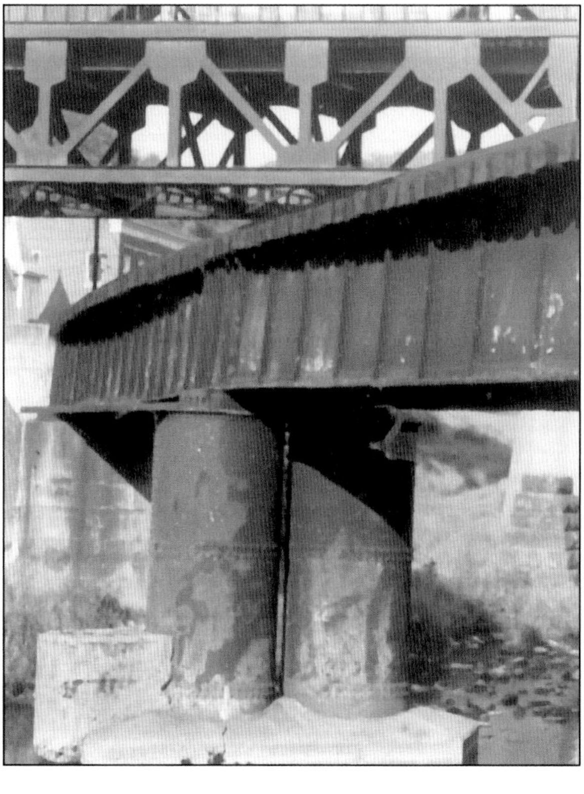

CONNECTIONS. The railway bridges in the heart of Coopers still offer a dramatic view of how the region was tamed. (Photo by Evonda Archer.)

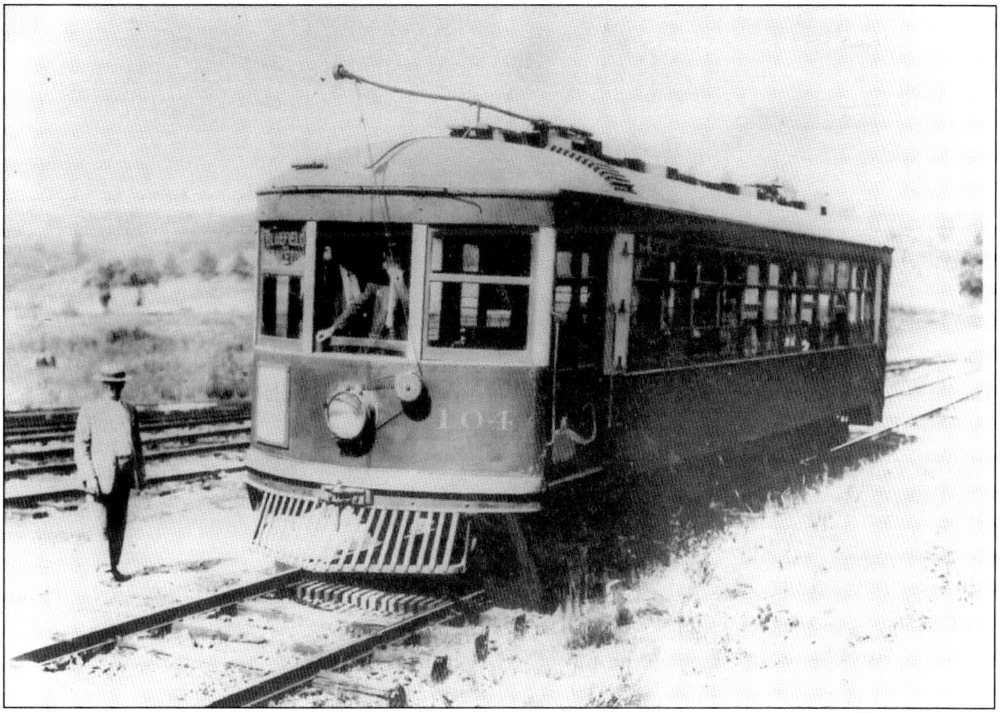

In Green Valley. Tri-City Traction maintained a "car barn" in Green Valley to service the streetcars that used to serve the two Bluefields and Princeton. (Courtesy of Nick Buzzo.)

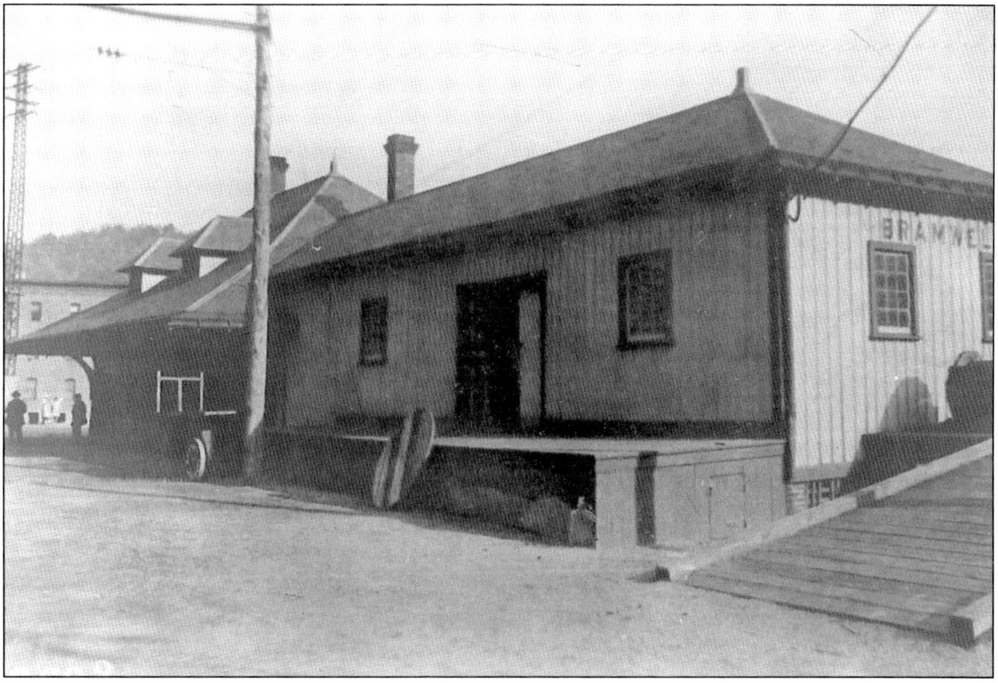

Back Side of Bramwell Station. The ramp of the Bramwell Passenger Station was an ideal place for young people to try out roller skates and bicycles in the early days. (Courtesy of Eve Cooper Murphy.)

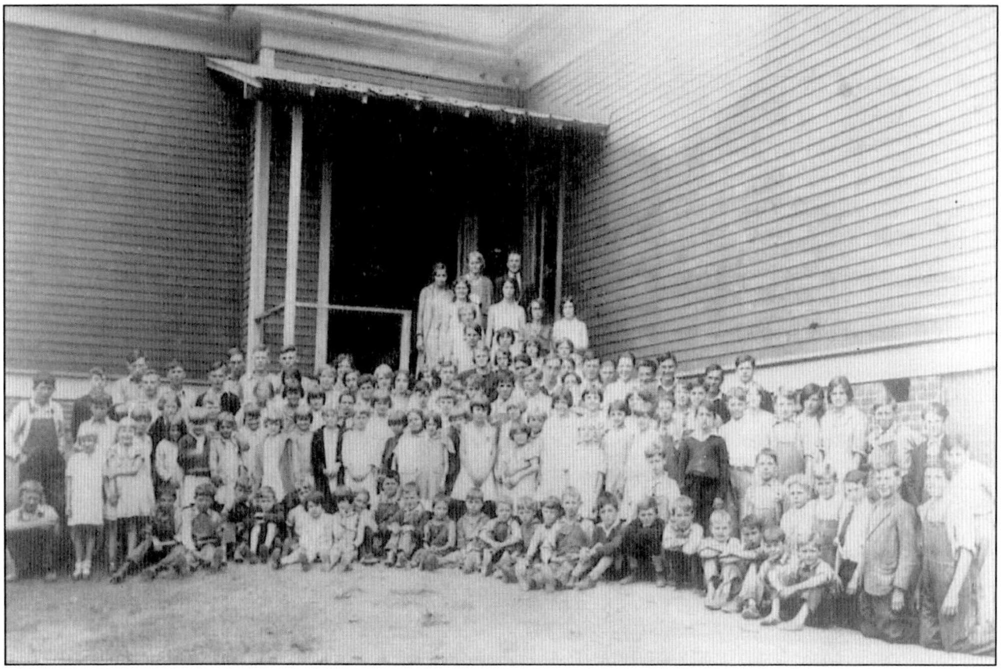

NEMOURS SCHOOL. Joe Davidson attended school at the Nemours Two-Year High School and is shown here standing in the dark suit in the second row. Madock McKenzie was principal at the time. (Courtesy of Joe Davidson.)

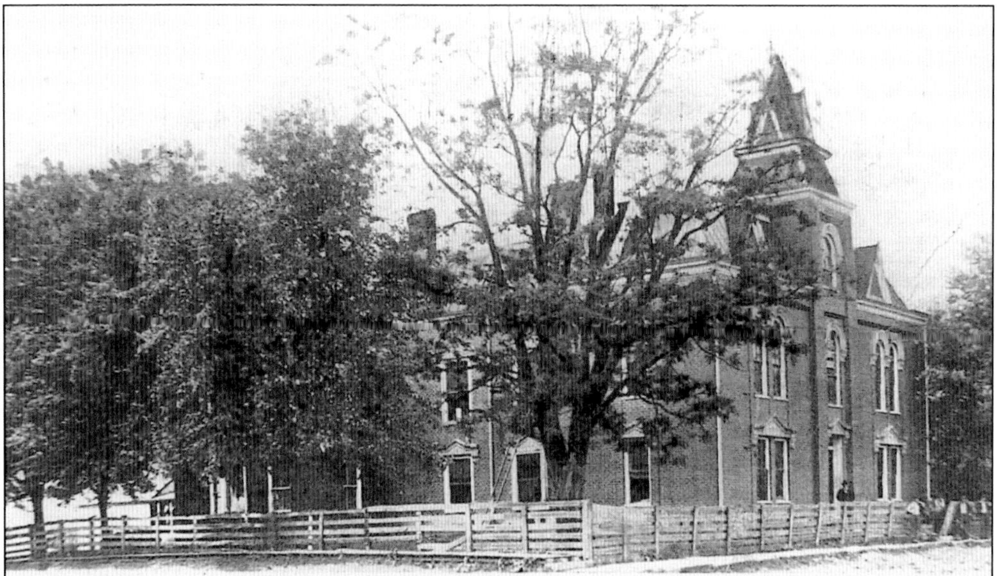

OLD COURTHOUSE. The first Mercer County Courthouse was erected in 1839, but the construction was said to be so bad that it was torn down and rebuilt the following year. In 1871, after nine years "on wheels," Judge Harrison tried to move the courthouse to Concord Church (Athens), at least partly because of the Confederate leanings of the people in the heart of the county. The building shown here was erected in 1909. (Courtesy of Grubb Photo Service.)

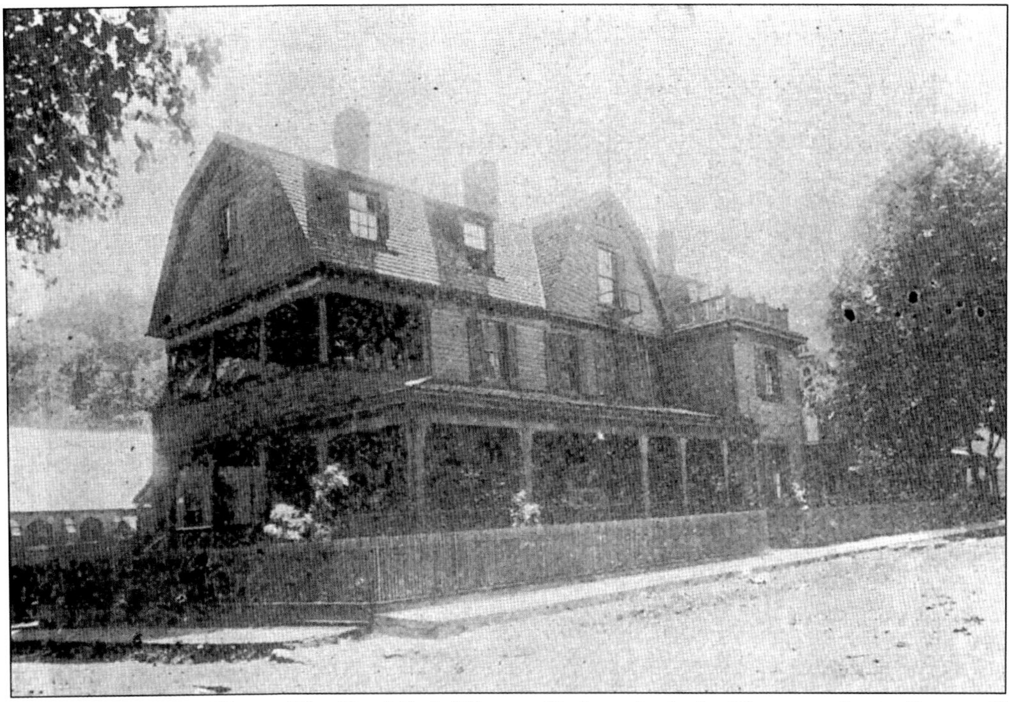

Home Away from Home. The Norfolk & Western Railway built the Bluestone Inn in Bramwell to provide lodging for workers and railroad offices. (Courtesy of Eve Cooper Murphy.)

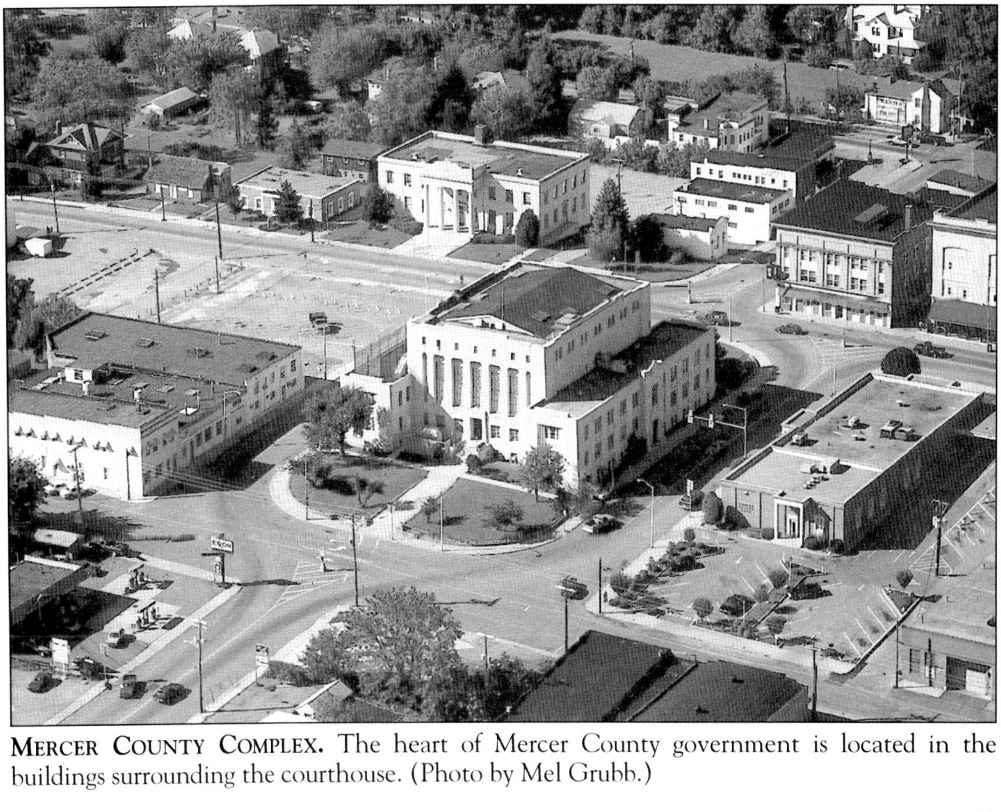

Mercer County Complex. The heart of Mercer County government is located in the buildings surrounding the courthouse. (Photo by Mel Grubb.)

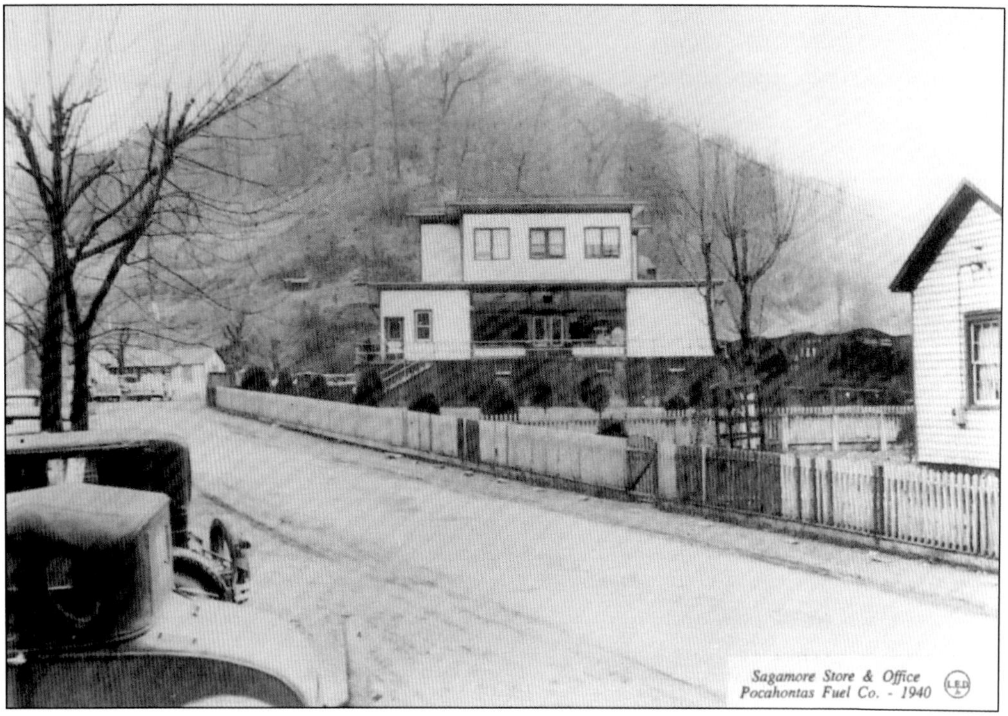

DAYS GONE BY. The Sagamore Coal Company store and office shown in this 1940 photograph harken back to an older, simpler time in Mercer County history. (Courtesy of Grubb Photo Service.)

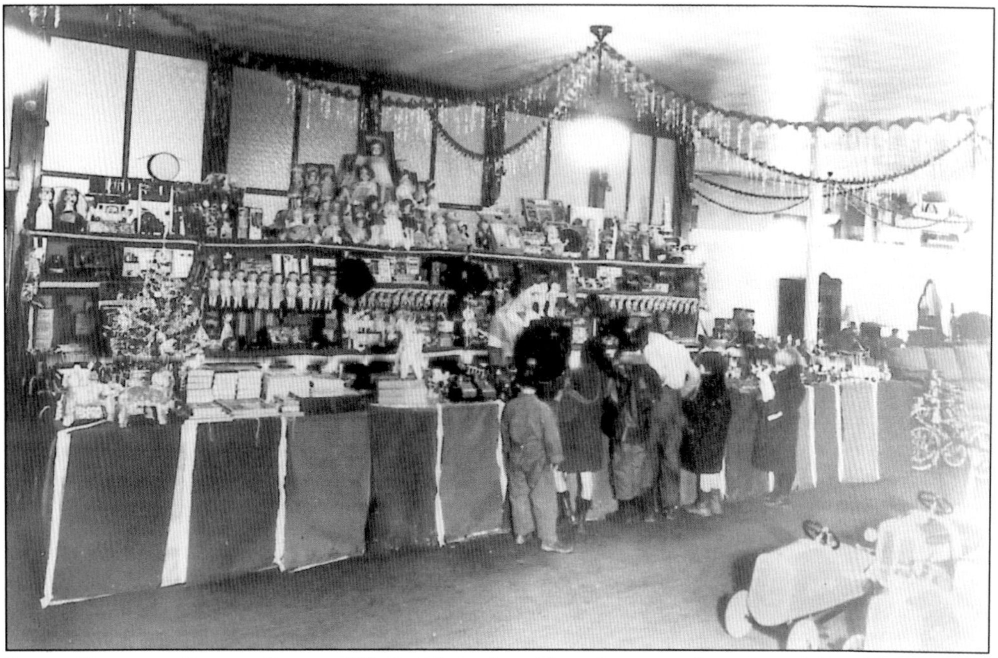

LIKE A KID IN A CANDY STORE. While life in the old coal camps of southern West Virginia was hard, there were always special moments that live forever like this scene of kids buying candy at the Sagamore Company Store. (Courtesy of Grubb Photo Service.)